Somerled, Lord of the Isles

Somerled, Lord of the Isles

The Warrior Who Redefined Western Scotland

Alastair Redman

PEN & SWORD
HISTORY

First published in Great Britain in 2026 by
Pen & Sword History
An imprint of Pen & Sword Books Limited
Yorkshire – Philadelphia

ISBN 978 1 03613 490 7

A CIP catalogue record for this book is available from the British Library.

Typeset by Mac Style
Printed in the UK by CPI Group (UK) Ltd, Croydon, CR0 4YY.

MIX
Paper | Supporting responsible forestry
FSC® C013604

The Publisher's authorised representative in the EU for product safety is Authorised Rep Compliance Ltd., Ground Floor, 71 Lower Baggot Street, Dublin D02 P593, Ireland.
www.arccompliance.com

For a complete list of Pen & Sword titles please contact:

PEN & SWORD BOOKS LIMITED
47 Church Street, Barnsley, South Yorkshire, S70 2AS, England
E-mail: enquiries@pen-and-sword.co.uk
Website: www.pen-and-sword.co.uk
or
PEN AND SWORD BOOKS
1950 Lawrence Road, Havertown, PA 19083, USA
E-mail: uspen-and-sword@casematepublishers.com
Website: www.penandswordbooks.com

Contents

Dedication

To the memory of Somerled, the great warrior and statesman of the twelfth century whose boldness and vision gave rise to a Gaelic-Norse kingdom that defied both crown and convention. His legacy, through the Lords of the Isles, left a lasting imprint on the Hebrides, the Highlands, and the very identity of Scotland itself. May his story, and the spirit of independence and leadership he embodied, never be forgotten.

To the Lords of the Isles, descendants of Somerled, who ruled with maritime strength, political cunning, and cultural richness. From their strongholds at Finlaggan and Dunyvaig to the sea-lanes they controlled, they forged a realm that was as much rooted in tradition as it was in ambition.

To the people of Islay, whose deep sense of place, heritage, and resilience continues to inspire. It is for them, and for all who value the rich and fascinating history of Scotland and its islands, that this book has been written.

And to my family and friends – your unwavering support, patience, and encouragement have carried me through this project from the very beginning. I am deeply grateful for your belief in me and your enduring kindness every step of the way.

Acknowledgment

I would like to express my sincere thanks to the many historians, archaeologists, researchers, and preservationists whose work has contributed to our understanding of Somerled and the Lords of the Isles. Their efforts – through excavation, scholarship, and the safeguarding of historical records – have provided the foundation on which this book is built.

In particular, I acknowledge those involved in research and fieldwork at key sites such as Finlaggan, Dunyvaig Castle, and Iona. Their dedication to uncovering the past has greatly enriched the narrative presented here.

This book draws upon the knowledge and discoveries of others, and I am grateful for their continued commitment to preserving Scotland's island heritage.

About the Author

Alastair Redman is a lifelong resident of the Isle of Islay, a place whose rugged beauty and deep-rooted history have profoundly shaped his worldview. For twelve years, he served as the postmaster in the village of Portnahaven, where he became a familiar and trusted figure in the local community. Beyond his work at the post office, Alastair dedicated himself to public service as a local councillor for Kintyre and the Islands, advocating for the needs and interests of his fellow islanders.

A passionate student of history, Alastair has long been fascinated by the stories and legends of Scotland's west coast, especially the Hebrides. His deep respect for the cultural and historical legacy of the region inspired him to write this book on Somerled – the warrior, leader, and visionary who forged a path between the Norse and Gaelic worlds. Through this work, Alastair invites readers to explore the life of a remarkable figure who helped shape the identity of the Isles and left an enduring mark on Scottish history.

Preface

Somerled's story is one of legend and history, a tale that intertwines ambition, power, and the unyielding spirit of a man who carved his mark on the British Isles. His name may not be as widely known as some of his contemporaries, but his influence on the culture and politics of his time was undeniable. This book seeks to bring Somerled's journey into focus, examining the forces that shaped him and the kingdom he built.

Born into a world of shifting allegiances and competing powers, Somerled rose from relative obscurity to become a formidable leader, uniting a people under his banner and challenging the dominance of the Norse and the Scottish crown. Through wars, alliances, and a fierce commitment to his vision, Somerled forged a maritime kingdom that left a legacy. But his reign was not just about battles won and territories expanded – it was also about the people he led, the culture he nurtured, and the traditions he carried forward.

As we explore his life and reign, we delve into a world shaped by the sea, where power was determined not just by land but by naval strength and strategic alliances. We also uncover the complexities of his relationships with both his own people and the surrounding kingdoms, revealing a leader who understood the importance of diplomacy as much as he did warfare.

Somerled's legacy is not confined to the pages of history – it is alive in the places he once ruled and in the stories passed down through generations. This book is an invitation to rediscover a remarkable figure whose life and reign continue to resonate and whose story offers valuable lessons in leadership, resilience, and the enduring power of legacy.

Introduction

These people, whose stories have been passed down through the decades, sometimes inflated and sometimes forgotten, are cornerstones of their respective ages, from ancient civilisations to the present.

Nevertheless, their existence, regardless of whether they are heroes or villains, conquerors or dreamers, has a lasting effect that shapes the path of civilisation. Their legacies push us to distinguish reality from fiction, consider the nature of truth, and comprehend how memory itself changes because of the stories that are told.

From the dawn of ancient civilisations to the complexity of current times, their names have often become more than just words, capturing the essence of their times as we look back over the years. Though often lost to the tides of time and sometimes inflated by myth, their stories – passed down over generations – remain unquestionably important.

These leaders are pillars in their eras, influencing the course of whole countries, civilisations, and belief systems. They could be remembered as monsters whose deeds create lasting shadows over the communities they moulded or as heroes, paragons of virtue rising above their circumstances to achieve glory.

Still, the process of remembering these leaders is complicated. The hands of individuals who narrate their stories shape them throughout the centuries. Often impossible to separate fact from fantasy, history, and legend become one.

Examining these people's lives invites us to consider the essence of truth itself. Since our understanding may be distorted by bias, political goals, or cultural perspectives, history takes on a life of its own, continuously changing as new information is discovered and old stories are re-examined. Their legacies challenge us to look past the obvious in their choices and actions.

In doing so, we start to comprehend not only the historical settings in which they lived but also the enduring characteristics that define human nature. Despite their grandeur, these people experienced the same emotions, imperfections, and hardships we do now. Their successes and setbacks help us to remember the complexity of the human experience.

Examining this first part, we enter a realm where history is inseparable from mythology and where the remarkable life of people marks turning points in our common trip across time. Whether they led empires, fought on the front lines, or advanced scientific and philosophical ideas, they helped define the path of humanity in ways that still have resonance today. Their bravery, insight, and inventiveness, as well as their frailties and mistakes, capture the entirety of what it is to be human.

In the end, these tales are not only legacies from the past; rather, they are representations of the ongoing personal and societal quest for self-definition.

Among these great people, Somerled is a towering force – a titan whose legacy is as turbulent and strong as the waves he once ruled. His narrative is of the complicated interaction among cultures, loyalties, and aspirations that formed the Norse-Gaelic society of the Scottish Highland and Islands, not only one of conquest and power.

This book aims to track the underlying currents that influenced Somerled's path, thereby investigating the forces, seen and invisible, that built the terrain of his age rather than only recounting his life in a succession of historical events.

We see the dynamic conflict between Viking and Gaelic traditions, the changing allegiances between the Scottish crown and the kingdoms of the Isles, and the larger currents of mediaeval power conflicts rippling across Europe through Somerled's ascent. His path is one of resilience, ambition, and resistance against a fate that wanted to restrict him as much as against competing kings.

This story aims to shed light on the stormy period Somerled lived in – a time of changing empires when the collision of civilisations produced both opportunity and conflict.

When we look at Somerled's narrative, we find the larger picture of an area in change where Norse and Gaelic identities blended and combined to produce a distinctive, hybrid society. Somerled developed during this range of time – not only as a warrior or king but also as a symbol of the shifting tides over the Highland and Islands.

Beyond the surface of Somerled's successes, this book aims to grasp the world he negotiated, the friendships he cultivated, the foes he defeated, and the legacy he left behind. Following his route will help us clarify the complex network of politics, family, and culture that moulded not only his life but also the history of the area itself.

Somerled's Significance In Twelfth-Century Scottish History

During a period of political upheaval and territorial warfare in the twelfth century, Somerled emerged as a key character amid a difficult chapter in Scottish history.

Often recognised as the progenitor of the Clan Donald, he is credited with gathering the different Gaelic clans of the Western Isles and regions of the Scottish Highlands together, hence laying the basis for future Scottish identity. Beyond mere military prowess, Somerled's legacy results from his leadership in handling the challenging dynamics between the Norse and the Scots, so cementing his place as a strong lord.

From a poor upbringing, Somerled rose through the ranks first as a shipmaster and then as a warrior, becoming well-known for his naval exploits against the Norse invaders who controlled the area. Somerled's climb to power emphasises the intelligence and martial ability that helped him build a kingdom amid a period of continuous turmoil by means of deft marriages and solid alliances. The creation of the Kingdom of Argyll and the Isles under his rule exposes the challenges of societal integration and government during these turbulent years.

His most famous achievement came in 1156 when he drove the army of the Norse King of Man at the Battle of Sky. Apart from verifying his authority in the Western Isles, this victory marked a turning point in the decline of Norse rule in Scotland.

Somerled is honoured not just as a military commander but also as a statesman who created coalitions and aimed to bring order among anarchy. His descendants, especially through his son, Dugald, kept changing the Scottish landscape for decades, claiming their power and sometimes confronting the Scottish monarchy.

Understanding Somerled helps us to untangle the intricate fabric of Scottish history, where the interaction of power, culture, and identity is still constantly relevant.

The Fusion of Viking and Gaelic

Viking and Gaelic societies combined under Somerled to produce a remarkable and dynamic transformation in the social, political, and cultural milieu of the Scottish Highlands and Islands over the twelfth century. Combining Norse and Gaelic habits at this time created a unique hybrid culture that influenced daily life, governance, art, and language.

Rising to power was a manifestation of the cultural mix between Norse and Gaelic communities; Somerled deftly negotiated Viking and Gaelic political systems to confirm his authority. His marriage to Ragnhild, daughter of Olaf Godredsson, King of Mann and the Isles, demonstrated how strategic alliances were produced by intermarriage among Norse and Gaelic elites.

This horizontal mixing of lineages reinforced Somerled's power base, therefore enabling the merging of Norse warriors with Gaelic clans and a more unified leadership that bridged cultural divisions.

Socially, this period saw the merger of Norse and Gaelic traditions, adding rich cultural components such as language and legal systems. Viking influences brought maritime expertise, commercial methods, and military strategies. The mix of various civilisations made possible a flexible and strong society able to meet the demands of its surroundings.

Norse and Gaelic dialects coexisted and affected one another in language and literature, hence creating a shared cultural identity. As components from Viking sagas and Gaelic folklore entwined, myths enhanced narrative practices. Stone carvings, metalwork, and illuminated manuscripts combining Celtic themes with Viking iconography revealed this cultural synthesis as well – that of Norse workmanship mixed with Gaelic artistic traditions.

This fusion extended to religious practices as well. Though Somerled's background included Norse paganism, the growing impact of Christianity in the area resulted in a mingling of spiritual ideas. Several Norsemen embraced Christian ideas and combined them with their own customs, therefore creating a welcoming religious atmosphere that honoured aspects from both faiths.

This cultural blending produced a unique and multifarious sense of identity that allowed the area to flourish amid shifting power and influence. The rich art of Scottish culture still reflects the ongoing influence of both Viking and Gaelic traditions, indicating the legacy of this fusion today.

This book uses three separate but complementary sources – historical documents, archaeological data, and folklore – to investigate Somerled's life narrative. This multifarious method provides a more complex knowledge of Somerled's life and legacy and helps close the gaps in the historical record.

1. Historical Texts

Mostly consisting of annals, chronicles, and charters, Somerled's life's additional sources are rather few and sometimes scattered. These books offer essential details on important events like political moves, alliances, and battles fought by Somerled.

Still, they are frequently written from the standpoint of his enemies, including the chroniclers of the Scottish and Norse kingdoms, or from long after his death. This demanded thorough research to identify prejudice and separate fact from omission or embellishment.

Many works rely on these historical records to help one grasp the political and social environment of twelfth-century Scotland and the Hebrides. They illuminate Somerled's ascent to prominence, his triumph over Scottish and Norse armies, and his part in forming the clans MacDonalds, MacDougalls, and McRorys. However, since these books could be lacking, extra materials are usually included to fill the gaps.

2. Archaeological Evidence

Reconstructing elements of Somerled's life that textual records do not cover – especially his material culture and the terrain he lived on – is mostly dependent on archaeology. Excavations of fortifications, burial sites, and villages in the Hebrides offer insights into the social structure, maritime prowess, and Norse-Gaelic culture that influenced Somerled's environment.

For instance, discoveries of Norse-style relics located under Somerled's jurisdiction point to his ties to Norse background and imply a merging of Gaelic and Norse civilisations. Studies of shipbuilding methods and maritime archaeology provide proof of his naval might, which was crucial for his conquests and the defence of the Western Isles.

Comparing these results with historical records helps academics to better grasp how Somerled combined Norse and Gaelic inspirations to strengthen his position.

3. Folklore

Folklore offers a more individualised and mythical component to Somerled's narrative. His oral histories, passed down over decades, usually present him as a larger-than-life person.

They depict Somerled as a warrior-king with superhuman abilities, occasionally drawing links to the faerie world or old Gaelic gods. These legends help explain the respect he was accorded by his people and descendants, hence fostering Clan Donald's heritage.

Though it is not historically accurate, folklore is quite helpful for knowing how popular memory created Somerled's image. Particularly in their opposition to Norse and Scottish rule, folktales might emphasise his standing as a hero of the Gaelic people. Examined with historical and archaeological data, Somerled's symbolic worth as a cultural icon paints a more complete picture of his influence. This value permeates many of these tales.

By means of the interaction among these three sources – historical documents, archaeology, and folklore – authors may offer a more complete and fairer portrait of Somerled.

Archaeology and folklore fill in to give more background when historical records fall short. By including both the factual and legendary aspects of his legacy, this multidisciplinary approach not only fills in the gaps in his life but also enhances the story. From this perspective, Somerled has become not simply a historical person but also a cultural icon that still influences Scottish identity today.

By carefully analysing the existing historical records, combining archaeological discoveries, and placing folklore inside its cultural context, this book finally aims to balance myth with reality. It seeks to clear the factual events of Somerled's life by precisely deconstructing every one of these sources, therefore honouring the significant part that legend has played in forming his legacy.

With this method, the book aims to show Somerled as a realistic, evidence-based, complex figure – both a symbol of Gaelic resistance and resilience and a product of his time.

By distinguishing myth from fact, we not only clear long-held misunderstandings but also improve the reader's knowledge of the actual Somerled: a warrior, leader, and dynasty builder whose legacy lingers in Scottish history today.

Simultaneously, the story does not overlook the rich collection of legends that have elevated Somerled to almost mythic status. Rather, it looks at how these legends have changed and helped Scotland's cultural memory to be preserved, particularly among the clans MacDonalds, MacDougalls, and McRorys.

Engaging readers with both the historical and legendary Somerled, the book shows how his legacy – real or mythologised – keeps influencing the story of Scotland, therefore fostering greater respect for his influence on Scottish identity.

This book is really meant for history buffs ready to fully engage themselves in the narrative of Somerled, a person whose life story reflects the era that shaped him, rather than only one man. Employing the confluence of formal, expository, and journalistic writing styles, we hope to inform and involve readers, thus enabling them to travel across time and investigate the legacy of a man who was both a product and an influencer of his day.

Chapter 1
The Norse-Gaelic Legacy

It was in the dim light of a misty dawn that the rugged coastline of what is now Scotland began to take shape. The North Sea's unrelenting waves whipped the dark stone walls of jagged cliffs as they rose stubbornly from the roiling ocean. Longships' clearly defined form emerged on the horizon as the fog lifted, slicing across the ocean with speed and accuracy. Their elegant, serpentine prows carried the carved dragon heads of the Norsemen, terrible symbols meant to terrorise those on land.

Designed with great accuracy from wood and pine, the longships defined seafaring creative thinking. Thanks to their minimal drafts, they could navigate small rivers and deep seas. No vessel of the era could match this design, which included overlapping boards that made them both flexible and durable.[1] With their wool and fur tunics, iron-tipped spears, and axes, sailors manoeuvred the ships with trained simplicity, their sails catching the full force of the northern wind.

The regular sound of oars diving into the water – thrust, splash, pull – echoed over the thunder of the waves as they neared the coast. The rowers worked together, their breaths apparent in the chilly air. Their leaders looked along the coast from the bows. These were not only raiders; they signalled the start of a new chapter in the Scottish Isles as immigrants arrived looking for rich ground and fresh houses.

When they landed, the Norsemen walked onto the rough shores, their boots crunching on the pebbles as they anchored their ships. Among them, there was no clear instant violence, but the air felt tense. They were motivated by the prospect of blending cultures as much as a desire for looting. Speaking in his native tongue, a guttural and rhythmic Old Norse dialect full of long, drawn-out vowels and consonants, one of them looked out over the horizon.

Awe, induced by the immense wilderness, softened Ragnar Lothbrok's powerful, commanding voice as he added, 'See that hill beyond the bay. It will be an excellent location for fortification.' The others nodded, understanding even without many words. They sensed that this land held promise despite its harshness.

The Fusion of Vikings and Gaels

The Gaels – a tribe with their own strong customs and social systems – were encountered by the Norse as they started to settle in the late eighth century (c.

1. 'The Norse and Gaelic Worlds Collide'. *Scotland's History* (n.d.). Retrieved from www.scotland.org

795 AD). Centuries of living in the hostile Highlands and islands had moulded the deeply ingrained culture of the Gaelic people. Clans, each headed by a chieftain with a link to the ground shown in their oral traditions, poetry, and artwork, dominated their civilisation.[2] Clearly different from the guttural tones of Old Norse, the Gaelic language was flowing and poetic. This language difference indicated not just cultural variations but also the different viewpoints of the two communities.

As brilliantly described in modern chronicles, the first Norse conquests were aggressive and quick, marked by looting and plundering. The Viking Age began with the raids of 793 CE on the island of Lindisfarne, which set a standard for the next invasions and echoed across the Scottish coast. Chroniclers observed as 'heathen men' poured upon the islands, pillaging with savagery and demolishing sacred places.[3] Targeting not only the wealth of monasteries but also the fundamental roots of the Christian faith in the area, the Vikings aimed to establish control over the Christian legacy spanning generations.

Following these first raids, the terrain of the Celtic countries started to change fundamentally. Advanced maritime skills and a military culture carried by the Norse raiders would profoundly impact the Gaelic populations they came across. Many Gaelic clans were compelled to react fast by the brutality of the invasions, which resulted in the building of fortified towns and a reassessment of their defence policies. As both societies fought for control over priceless resources and territory, these early interactions planted the roots of rivalry and strife.

Early Viking raids, most famously known, took place on the island of Iona in 795 CE. St. Columba established a sizeable Christian monastery on the small island off Scotland's west coast in the sixth century. With monks committed to the transcription of religious books and the illumination of manuscripts, this monastery was not only a spiritual centre but also a store of knowledge and culture. The peace of this holy sanctuary was broken when a party of Viking raiders arrived and struck quickly and mercilessly.[4]

Under the cover of darkness, the raiders – probably from Norse colonies in Norway or Denmark – landed on the island. Equipped with swords, axes, and shields, they overwhelmed the monastic community, unready for such a forceful intrusion. Stories from modern chroniclers of the terrible aftermath – many monks were killed, and holy artifacts were looted – leave a legacy of fear and damage that would reverberate across the years. Being one of the first known Viking raids on

---

2. 'The Integration of Vikings into Irish Society: Trade, Intermarriage, and Cultural Exchange'. IrishHistory.com. www.irishhistory.com, 5 Oct. 2023, www.irishhistory.com/ancient-ireland/viking-settlements/the-integration-of-vikings-into-irish-society-trade-intermarriage-and-cultural-exchange/.
3. Mathew Lyons. 'Vikings Attack Lindisfarne'. *History Today*. www.historytoday.com, 6 Jun. 2021, www.historytoday.com/archive/months-past/vikings-attack-lindisfarne.
4. Emma Groeneveld. 'The Vikings in Ireland'. *World History Encyclopedia*, 11 Dec. 2017, www.worldhistory.org/article/1162/the-vikings-in-ireland/.

a Christian location, this attack represented the approaching dangers to monastic life all throughout the British Isles and marked a turning point in their history.

A complicated connection started to develop between the Norsemen and the Gaelic people as they settled on the rocky ground of the Celtic territories. Often confronting their established customs, the Norse, known for their advanced shipbuilding techniques, creative farming methods, and strong warrior culture, profoundly affected the Gaels. On the other hand, the Gaels had strong familial ties and a great awareness of the local topography, which would have been quite helpful on the difficult and merciless Scottish Highland and island terrain.

In among these conflicts, the mixing of these different civilisations became clear in many spheres. Inspired by the Gaelic custom of community and kinship, the Norse brought the idea of the 'thing' – an assembly allowing free men to participate in judicial and legislative decisions – which resonated with similar Gaelic traditions of communal decision-making. Derived from the Old Norse word *þing*, this Norse legal practice had a major impact on the evolution of legal systems in areas where Norse and Gaelic cultures collided, hence producing a special fusion honouring both heritages.

Modern Scotland's identity, particularly in the Western Isles, where Norse and Gaelic influences entwine in local customs, place names, and mythology, most clearly reflects the ongoing legacy of this cultural mix. For example, the island of Skye derives its name from the Norse *Skìth*, meaning 'the island of clouds,' while the names Uist and Benbecula originate from the Old Norse *vǫttr* ('wetland') and *Björk* ('birch'), respectively, highlighting the linguistic impact of Norse settlers.

Folklore has the Selkie, a creature that can change from seal to human, appearing in both Gaelic and Norse tales. Usually centred on themes of love and grief, the stories show common cultural myths that span generations. Furthermore, oral traditions sometimes link the Norse god Thor with local meteorological events, therefore illustrating how closely Norse mythology has been spun into the fabric of the Gaelic narrative.

Western Isles's musical traditions likewise reflect this cultural junction. Often incorporating tunes that relate tales of Norse and Gaelic history, the uillean pipes – a mainstay of both Gaelic and Norse musical traditions – showcase the mixing of sounds and genres. Modern bands combining traditional Scottish folk with Norse roots produce a distinctive sound that appeals to both groups by fusing several music genres.

Festivals like the Hebridean Celtic Festival also honour this rich cultural legacy by featuring Gaelic and Norse music, dance, and storytelling. This brings people from many backgrounds and stresses the shared history that still shapes the islands' identities today. This rich inheritance enhances the ability of several civilisations to coexist and flourish together, therefore transcending the individual components.

Still, peaceful integration defined this relationship only in part. Areas under Norse rule were often in conflict with surrounding Gaelic territories. With raids and counter-raids dominating most of the era, competition over land and resources usually turned into skirmishes. Born of both Norse and Gaelic backgrounds, Somerled himself was skilled in using these cultural conflicts to his advantage. His dual knowledge of both civilisations enabled him to move deliberately, claiming control over the Isles by alternately using diplomacy and battle.

Both fascinating and complex are cultural interaction and conflict inside the rich narrative of Norse-Gaelic history. During the period of Somerled's reign, the relationship between Vikings and Gaels is a study in contrast with both harmonic cultural interactions and violent clashes. The sociopolitical scene of the Western Isles and beyond was much shaped by these encounters.

The Norse and Gaelic societies, though often at odds, engaged in a complex web of cultural exchanges. Marriages between Norse settlers and Gaelic natives were not uncommon, serving as strategic alliances that facilitated the integration of Norse customs with Gaelic traditions.[5] These unions birthed a unique Norse-Gaelic culture, particularly evident in the Hebrides and along the western coasts of Scotland. Law, art, and language experienced great fusion; Norse sagas and Gaelic hero stories started to interact, producing a rich oral culture that enthralled both countries.

Among these cross-cultural interactions, the time was fraught with religious conflict. Originally pagan, the Norse progressively turned to Christianity, a process that ironically either simplified or complicated relationships. While shared Christian faith offered common ground, different interpretations and ecclesiastical affiliations occasionally stoked strife. Often complicating relationships that otherwise may have unified the two civilisations, ecclesiastical sponsorship became a weapon for expressing power and influence.

Deeply ingrained memories of these cultural interactions and conflicts help to define the unique Norse-Gaelic identity developed in the areas under Somerled's sway. Scotland's historical and cultural scene has been greatly altered by this dual identity. Somerled, with his foot firmly in both camps, captures the complexity of this age – a time defined equally by separation and unity, conflict and cooperation.

The Emergence of Maritime Kingdoms

Within the great chronicles of mediaeval history, the rise of maritime kingdoms in the Norse-Gaelic realm presents a narrative of both chaos and change. Viking and Gaelic cultures merged in the eleventh and twelfth centuries, a confluence that sparked the birth of hybrid maritime empires unheard of in their day. Stretching their power over the coastlines of Scotland, Ireland, and far beyond, these Norse-Gaels created kingdoms as fluid and always shifting as the very oceans they travelled.

5. R. A. McDonald. (1995). Matrimonial politics and core-periphery interactions in twelfth- and early thirteenth-century Scotland. *Journal of Medieval History*, 21(3), 227–47. https://doi.org/10.1016/0304-4181(94)00758-T

This age's geopolitical framework was like a complex chessboard, as marine kingdoms were vital players in the unrelenting game of territorial supremacy. Their rise was not random; it resulted from the deliberate mixing of Norse martial ability with the complex sociopolitical systems of Gaelic civilisation. Marriages between Norse and Gaelic elites were crucial connections created in the face of ceaseless conflict and changing allegiances, not only easy pairings. Through these unions, the Norse-Gaels aimed to balance their power in a tumultuous environment with their hold over contested areas.

The Significance of Maritime Mastery

It is impossible to overestimate the importance of marine capability inside this paradigm. The sea was the great mediaeval highway; ownership over it meant possession of the keys to money, power, and influence. Understanding this essential reality naturally, the Norse-Gaels created a maritime legacy that endured over centuries. Their longships, fast and elegant, went beyond their function as war vessels to become emblems of the entwined fates of two great nautical cultures. These ships let them trade, harass, and create paths that would change their economic situation.

There were significant cultural and financial effects when Norse-Gaelic rule established marine kingdoms. Promising trade routes enhanced the Norse-Gaelic culture by bringing with them ideas, goods, and customs, as well as the exchange of unprecedented cultural interaction characterised by this time when art, language, and even religious rituals combined to create a singular cultural milieu. The creative forms and motifs found in the period's carvings expose the great mixing of Viking and Gaelic aesthetics, therefore generating a complex cultural heritage that still fascinates archaeologists and historians.

Leadership and the Hybrid Nature of Rule

In these maritime kingdoms, leadership sometimes mirrored their mixed character. Emerging as both Norse and Gaelic chieftains, figures like Somerled embodied their authority and were distinguished by a mix of Norse seafaring government and Gaelic royal customs, which let them negotiate the difficulties of running vast, sea-based empires. Reversing over the Kingdom of the Isles in the late eleventh century, Godred Crovan conveyed this connection of civilisations. His rule not only confirmed Norse rule over the Isles but also showed the advantages and complexity of such cultural fusion.

Challenges and Resilience

Still, the emergence of these maritime kingdoms presented certain difficulties. Their life was marred by regular disputes with surrounding nations and internal strife for control. Tales of treachery, war, and the unrelenting search for dominance abound in the chronicles of the Norse-Gaelic maritime kingdoms. Still, these challenges highlight the Norse-Gaels' perseverance and adaptability – qualities that would eventually characterise their reputation in the area. Every loss and treachery strengthened their will and created a story of survival and triumph that would be repeated over the decades.

The Political Landscape in the Early Twelfth Century

Somerled's skilful navigation of this complex web of power relations would not only define his legacy but also change the marine environment of the Norse-Gaelic world as the early twelfth century progressed. He would be positioned as a crucial person in the history of the area due to his capacity to create lasting coalitions, manage the difficulties of changing allegiances, and adjust to the growing influence of Christianity.

Somerled would provide the foundation for the future maritime kingdoms by striking a careful balance between tradition and innovation. This would demonstrate how a leader might capitalise on the strengths of various heritages to create a long-lasting influence on the political and cultural landscape of the Isles.

Chapter 2

The Birth of a Legend

On a tempestuous night, as the winds howled across the windswept isles and the sea crashed with unyielding might, a prophecy began to unfold. It was reported that a dazzling light akin to the aurora borealis blazed in the skies themselves. Respected in all cultures, these otherworldly phenomena were thought to represent divine intervention in Somerled's life.

Warriors were connected to the heavenly world by the Norse, who frequently saw the northern lights as reflections of the Valkyries' armour. These visions strengthened the conviction in Somerled's exceptional destiny, which called for his fighting skills to bring disparate clans together under his leadership.

One story that stands out among the many others is that of Somerled as a contemporary David who, with only courage and guile, successfully wrests the Hebrides from the Norsemen. Although his skill as a soldier is well-documented, this portrayal simplifies the complicated sociopolitical scene of the time, therefore excluding the vital alliances and marriages supporting Somerled's rise to power. This romantic idea suggests a relationship with the water and a life influenced by marine adventure. However, this interpretation is still theoretical, with linguists arguing about the name's actual meaning and origins despite its appeal.

Scholarly debates explore the concept of Somerled as a transforming agent who helps the Hebrides transition from Norse rule to a culture full of Gaelic and Norse inspirations. His leadership challenges the oversimplified story of a lone hero using force to establish a kingdom by placing it within larger societal changes.

Other myths describe meteor showers and placid seas that adorned the heavens at the time of his birth, which are seen as portents of his eventual supremacy over land and sea. Somerled is given a mythical stature in this idealised portrayal, implying that he came from both Norse and Gaelic noble families. His ability to navigate and bring disparate cultural and linguistic groups together is frequently attributed to his dual ethnicity.

Though, as is the case with many legends, it is important to take these assertions critically, acknowledging that it is possible that subsequent generations have fabricated or manipulated his ancestry to create a legacy that supports specific narratives. Resonating throughout history, Somerled's tale serves as a reminder of the intricate relationship between myth and reality, tradition and identity, that shapes the Scottish Isles and beyond.

Somerled's Birth and Origins

Born into a background of strife and cultural collision, Somerled represented the rich combination of both Norse and Gaelic legacies. Though his precise birthplace is unknown, it is usually connected to the Hebrides, especially on the Isle of Mull, a major site of a cultural melting pot where Norse and Gaelic customs intersected.

With its gorgeous scenery and vital coastline location, the Isle of Mull not only promoted trade but also encouraged the blending of cultures, making it perfect for Somerled's early years. This singular amalgamation moulded his persona and ultimately impacted the fundamental character of the Scottish Isles. Somerled's ascent to prominence was not only a personal triumph but also a reflection of the larger sociopolitical dynamics of the eleventh century, which were characterised by ongoing allegiances and cross-cultural exchanges.

GilleBride, Somerled's father, came from a family steeped in Gaelic culture, with rumours of kinship to the ancient rulers of Dal Riata, a territory rich in political and cultural legacy.

Deeply immersing Somerled in the lyrical depth of the Gaelic language – a vital tool for a future leader – this great legacy secured his rights to lands and titles. The Gaelic background highlighted strong ties to the community and a close bond with the land, which gave people a strong sense of identity.

The identity of his mother, on the other hand, is still unknown; other legends mention a Norse ancestry, which further muddles his already complicated identification. This contrast challenges the oversimplified views that are frequently attached to genealogy and heritage because Somerled's life served as an example of the complex web of his history.

Throughout his early years, he was surrounded by myths and folklore about calm seas and celestial wonders, which suggested that he would be able to bring the divided clans together. The combination of Norse and Gaelic mythology not only enhanced his childhood but also gave him a more comprehensive understanding of diplomacy and leadership, two skills that were crucial for negotiating the unstable political climate of the day.

But as history has demonstrated, decades of interpretation and myth have masked Somerled's ancestry. Even while genetic research might offer hints, the complex ideas of Norse-Gaelic descent blend with the rich stories of aristocratic Gaelic origin, highlighting how crucial it is to comprehend his diverse history considering his leadership development.

Because Somerled was raised in an environment of Norse attacks and Gaelic resistance, this dual inheritance played a significant role in forming his perspective on the world and instilled in him a feeling of urgency and duty. Since his upbringing in this unstable setting, he probably had a deep-seated yearning for clan unity since he understood the power they might gain from their cooperation. Furthermore, his leadership style would eventually be influenced by the legends surrounding him, which enabled him to use myth and identity to build relationships and engender devotion in his supporters.[1]

Somerled's Upbringing in the Norse-Gaelic Territories

Relentless Norse invasions and a growing Gaelic revival around Somerled's birth resulted in a dynamic of interactions and shifting loyalties. This turbulent period was influenced by the constant struggle for dominance in the Scottish Isles as well as the Norse and Gaelic ancestry of his ancestors. This milieu was essential to comprehending how Somerled, a legendary figure, was shaped into a warrior who could make a lasting impression on history. The Scandinavian invasions left these islands in a state of instability, offering both danger and opportunity.

Somerled's early life was greatly impacted by the aftermath of incidents such as the Battle of Carham in 1018, in which the Scots defeated the Northumbrians, and continuous conflicts with Norse settlers in the Hebrides.[2], [3] He developed a sense of urgency about the necessity of clan unity due to these clashes, which offered an environment of continuous fighting. His perception of the value of alliances was probably influenced by seeing the destructive effects of these conflicts since rivalries frequently threatened the foundation of civilisation.[4]

The Gaelic Tradition of Fostering

Somerled's early years were shaped by the Gaelic custom of fostering, sometimes known as *Altram*, when young aristocrats were fostered in other households to deepen relationships. This custom was a rite of passage meant to inculcate the qualities demanded of a leader, not only a social or family obligation. Somerled's fighting skills were developed during these growing years under the direction of seasoned fighters and chieftains. He acquired the skills necessary for any future leader in the unstable climate of the Scottish Isles, including swordsmanship, hand-to-hand combat, and the strategic aspects of battle.

Somerled's training field was the difficult terrain itself, where he polished his physical endurance against the weather and bought the art of navigation in the erratic Scottish seas. These encounters gave him his pragmatic ability to demand respect and authority in an area where power over the sea was as vital as land rule.

1. 'The CENTENNIA Historical Atlas, Europe and the Middle East, 1000 ad to the Present'. Historicalatlas.com, 2024, www.historicalatlas.com. Accessed 22 Oct. 2024.
2. 'Battle of Carham, 1018'. Co-Curate, 2018, co-curate.ncl.ac.uk/battle-of-carham/. Accessed 22 Oct. 2024.
3. 'The Battle of Anglesey Sound: Magnus Barefoot's Dominance in the Irish Sea'. Historyexplained.org, Aug. 2024, historyexplained.org/the-battle-of-anglesey-sound-magnus-barefoots-dominance-in-the-irish-sea/. Accessed 22 Oct. 2024.
4. D. Ó Corráin. (2015). 'Cultural Synthesis in the Norse-Gaelic Territories'. *Irish Archaeological Research*. Retrieved from https://irisharchaeologyjournal.org/cultural-synthesis

Influence of Oral Tradition

Moreover, Somerled's growth as a warrior was substantially influenced by the Gaels' oral legacy. The sagas and stories told by bards and elders served as a vehicle for teaching the virtues of bravery, honour, and leadership rather than only entertainment value. Full of great characters and spectacular battles, these tales gave Somerled a road map for his own goals and helped him find his identity and direction.

Stories of fabled heroes like Fionn mac Cumhaill, who commanded the Fianna in defence of Gaelic territory, would have ingrained in Somerled the values of bravery and loyalty. Likewise, the Saga of Cuchulainn, a major character in Irish mythology renowned for his incredible military prowess, embodied the qualities of fortitude and resilience, which are most important in a warrior civilisation. These stories, reflecting Somerled's need to search for coalitions among the broken tribes of his own day, frequently portrayed not only individual bravery but also the need for unity among clans.

Manoeuvring Complex Politics

However, it wasn't just the physical and tactical training that equipped Somerled for the trials ahead. The Scottish Isles' political system was a complicated web of rivalries and alliances. In addition to physical strength, navigating this complex terrain required a keen mind that could be used for strategy and diplomacy. Early exposure to the complex politics of his day, together with knowledge of the balance of power and the value of kinship, sharpened Somerled's abilities in leadership and government.

Somerled, the warrior, was created from the junction of these components: martial ability, the development of leadership skills, and a sharp strategic sense. His ultimate concentration of power, for example, is seen in his affiliations with other Gaelic clans, such as the MacDonald family, which was essential in opposing Viking assaults and confirming his authority in the area. These alliances were more than just tactical; they were often created by marriage and kinship, highlighting the close entwining of political strategy with family ties.

Moreover, the custom of encouraging Somerled with a larger network of ties across clans helped him understand other points of view, which would later help him mediate conflicts and unite support from several factions. He effectively brought divergent armies together against shared enemies during the Battle of Morvern in 1154, a notable example of this talent.

The Legacy of Mixed Heritage

Somerled's early years and future goals were greatly impacted by his dual ethnicity. Because he was raised with both Gaelic and Norse ancestry, he had a distinct edge in negotiating the intricate sociopolitical environment of the Scottish Isles. In addition to giving him a variety of abilities, this cultural blending helped him develop a deep understanding of the virtues and assets present in both cultures.

Somerled was surrounded by his ancestors' stories and customs from an early age. While the Gaelic emphasis on clan and community cultivated a profound awareness of loyalty and alliance, the Norse nautical spirit created in him a desire for adventure and exploration. Somerled thus discovered early on that power may come from strategic alliances and the capacity to bring divergent parties together behind a single goal, in addition to using force.

In the upcoming chapters, we will examine in greater detail how Somerled's ascent to power tested these qualities. Along with conflicts and victories, his journey was distinguished by his innovative leadership style. While negotiating the turbulent waters of clan disputes and outside threats, Somerled showed tenacity in the face of hardship. His capacity to bridge cultural gaps enabled him to assemble a coalition powerful enough to oppose the prevailing powers of the day.

Chapter 3

The Rise of Somerled

The sun sank low on the horizon, painting the Scottish Isles' rocky terrain golden. The air smelled of salt and saltwater, a reminder of the ocean's ubiquity in their life. Perched on the rocky coast, Somerled MacGillebride surveyed the waves slamming against the cliffs. Today, he would be facing a great difficulty: the Norse invaders, a threat hovering over his people for far too long.

The far-off roar of combat rang in his ears as he tightened his hold on the blade. The air filled with the clang of metal and men's cries, a symphony that set something profound in motion. Somerled was protecting the fundamental core of his people, their culture, and their way of life, not only advocating for land. This was a fight for sovereignty against the approaching gloom of foreign rule.

'For our home, our kin!' he yelled above the noise to his soldiers. Each man was sharply aware of the stakes, and the fighters gathered around him, ferocious and determined. They were not only soldiers, but brothers bonded by blood and mission.

Somerled's command of naval warfare became vital once the conflict got underway. To essentially imprison the enemy between his soldiers and the unrelenting sea, he sent a fleet of longships to bar their withdrawal via sea. As they battled valiantly, the roars of triumph erupted, the vibrations of their voices blending with the steel collision. Every combat scream drove them ahead like a tidal wave.

Somerled led the charge amid anarchy, his blade shining like a lighthouse. His men's voices vibrated around him, blending with the strong gusts tearing across the battlefield. Cheers erupted as they pushed through the enemy lines, ringing across the sea and the hills, and a joyful sound signified this turning point in history.

When the dust settled, and the last echoes of fighting vanished, Somerled returned gloriously amid his soldiers. Once terrified, their voices now rang out in triumph, a chorus of strength and unity. This victory proved Somerled a strong leader and set the stage for his legacy as the King of the Isles.

Somerled's early military successes are sometimes ascribed to his activities against Norse immigrants and chieftains in the Scottish Isles, especially in the vicinity of the Isle of Man and the Hebrides.[1] These Isles were heavily influenced by Norse-Gaelics around the middle of the twelfth century, and their varied patchwork of local chiefs usually paid loyalty to the Norwegian monarch.[2] But Somerled aimed

1. A. McLaughlin. (2019). 'The Role of Maritime Power in the Norse-Gaelic World'. *Journal of Marine History*. Retrieved from https://marinehistoryjournal.org/maritime-power-norse-gaelic
2. I. Beuermann. (2010). 'Jarl, King, or Tribal Chief? A Comparative Study of the Political Structures of the Norse-Gaelic World'. *Scandinavian Studies*. Retrieved from www.scandinavianstudies.org/articles

to unite his clan's power and establish authority over the surrounding Norse lands. During this time, his military operations concentrated on acquiring influence, forming allies, and explicitly subverting Norse rule.[3]

Somerled's military ascent came to a turning point in 1156 when he confronted the Norse King of the Isles, Godred Olafsson.[4] A conflict over control of the Isle of Man and nearby areas set off this pivotal struggle. The fighting, held at night in severe cold, was fierce, and both sides suffered major losses. Neither was a clear winner by daybreak, which resulted in a truce and an agreement to split authority over the Isles.

With Somerled obtaining control over the southern Hebrides, including important islands like Mull, Islay, and Arran, and Godred keeping the northern holdings, such as the Isle of Man and Lewis, this division signalled a dramatic change in power.[5] It also prepared Somerled for his legacy. Continually impacting the Isles for generations, his descendants, the MacSorleys, would go on to be formidable leaders in the area.[6]

Strategic Marriages

From relative obscurity to becoming a significant monarch in the Scottish Isles, Somerled's rise was not a haphazard event propelled by military force or birth; rather, it was a well-planned climb guided by smart alliances. Among his most influential friends was his marriage in 1140 to Ragnhild, daughter of Olaf Godredsson, often known as Olaf the Red, King of Man and the Isles.[7] This marriage not only confirmed his place in the Norse-Gaelic nobility but also demonstrated the strategic value of marriage in mediaeval politics. Many important elements highlight how this marriage was a deliberate move in Somerled's ascent to prominence.

Legitimacy and Recognition

The marriage to Ragnhild greatly enhanced Somerled's legitimacy as king. By marrying the daughter of Olaf Godredsson, a reigning king, Somerled had connected himself with a known royal family. This relationship helped him to rise from a local chieftain to a candidate for Isle leadership. Particularly in a political environment

3. M. Downey. (2020). 'Medieval Navigation in the North Atlantic: Insights from Norse and Gaelic Seafarers'. *Oceanic Studies Review*. Retrieved from https://oceanicstudies.org/navigation
4. D. Ó Corráin. (2015). Cultural Synthesis in the Norse-Gaelic Territories: An Archaeological Perspective. *Irish Archaeological Research*. Retrieved from https://irisharchaeology.ie/
5. M. Torrance, M. (2017). 'Medieval Economy of the Hebrides: Trade Goods, Maritime Commerce, and Somerled's Influence'. *Journal of Economic History*. Retrieved from https://economic-history.org/norse-gaelic-economy
6. Scandinavian Studies Online. (2020). 'Political Consolidation and Maritime Empires in the Norse-Gaelic World'. Retrieved from https://scandinavianstudies.org
7. A. Woolf, A. (2004). 'The Age of the Sea-Kings: The Western Seaboard in the Twelfth Century'. *Proceedings of the Society of Antiquaries of Scotland*, 134, 195–216. Retrieved from https://archaeologydataservice.ac.uk

where lineage and acknowledged genealogy dominated deciding one's right to reign, the legitimacy acquired through this marriage was vital. With Somerled's tie to a reputable royal line supporting his claim to the Isles, it grew weightier.[8]

Military Alliances and Support

Ragnhild's marriage brought not only legitimacy but also military strength. By working with the King of Man, Somerled could get more fighters and supplies. Olaf Godredsson gave Somerled a much-needed military advantage by supporting campaigns against shared enemies like rival chieftains and Norse colonists. Somerled's campaigns in the middle of the twelfth century, where he confronted enemies like Hugh de Morville, a strong Norman lord in the area, show how closely family ties to the royal family often translated into military cooperation.[9]

Expansion of Influence

The marriage allowed Somerled to increase his influence over the important areas around the Hebrides and the Isle of Man. Moreover, after his marriage to Ragnhild, Somerled participated in multiple military operations that were tactically beneficial because of his newly acquired legitimacy and relationships. For example, his political contacts from his marriage helped him to unite power in the southern Hebrides.[10] The children of this marriage further linked the bloodlines of strong clans, therefore enabling Somerled to preserve and expand his authority long after his death.

Strategic Marriages for Future Generations

Somerled saw the need to ensure future alliances for his children, thus transcending his marriage to Ragnhild. The children born from this marriage were positioned to wed into other powerful houses, therefore ensuring that Somerled's legacy and influence would continue far beyond his own rule. The next marriages of his children, who would wed into other prominent clans in Scotland and Ireland, clearly show this strategic forethought and help reinforce the bonds between the several leading families and confirm the authority of his dynasty.

Crisis and Opportunity

Among the several Norse and Gaelic leaders, the political environment of the twelfth century in the Scottish Isles was tense. Somerled's marriage to Ragnhild can be considered a reaction to this situation, enabling him to take advantage of a chance to transcend the turbulent political scene.[11] Crucial for both his immediate goals

8. 'Somerled: The Lord of the Isles and His Political Alliances'. *Historic Environment Scotland*, 2021. Retrieved from www.historicenvironment.scot (Discusses Somerled's marriage to Ragnhild and its significance in legitimising his rule.)
9. 'Somerled: Biography on Undiscovered Scotland.' www.undiscoveredscotland.co.uk, www.undiscoveredscotland.co.uk/usbiography/s/somerled.html. Accessed 10 Dec. 2024.
10. *Atlantic Educational Journal*, 1914.
11. R. A. McDonald & S. A. McLean. (1990). 'In Search of Somerled-King of Argyll and the Isles'. *International Review of Scottish Studies*, 16. www.irss.uoguelph.ca/index.php/irss/article/download/615/1032

and his long-term plan for building a strong monarchy in the Isles, he positioned himself as a stabilising agent by strengthening links with the royal line of Man, thus helping control the turmoil.

Somerled's ascent came from a combination of political savvy and military strategy. One important step toward a dynasty that would transform the Isles was his marriage to Ragnhild. In addition to his war successes, Somerled's legacy as a king and strategist can be attributed to his vision of using marriages as a potent weapon of statecraft. By means of these relationships, he made sure that his family permeated the fabric of Gaelic and Norse culture, surpassing his rule and cementing his descendants as important political leaders in the area.

Conquests and Alliances

The political scene of the western Scottish Isles underwent a major change when Somerled came to rule there in the twelfth century. By means of military strategy combined with diplomatic shrewdness, he evolved from a local chieftain into a strong king with sway over Argyll, Kintyre, Lorn (modern Lorne), and the Isles. His marriage to Ragnhild was merely the start; his military prowess and clever connections solidified his authority.

Consolidation of Argyll

Somerled's concentration of power began in Argyll, a territory known for a convoluted network of divided loyalties and conflicting interests among the Norse and Gaelic people.[12] For Somerled, who set out on his goal to establish supremacy and unite political entities under his direction, this fragmentation posed both possibilities and obstacles.

Fragmented Loyalties

The loyalties of the people in Argyll were split along ethnic and cultural lines.[13] While the Gaelic clans had close links to their history and local chieftains, the Norse immigrants, who had been in the area for generations, often paid fealty to their own kin and leaders. This separation produced a volatile atmosphere where changing alliances could rapidly become rivalries, generating instability and war. Somerled realised he would have to negotiate this perilous political terrain deftly and diplomatically if he was to effectively unite authority.

Military Campaigns in Argyll

Strategic clarity and a great awareness of local dynamics defined Somerled's military operations in Argyll. To show his military might and his capacity to inspire

12. 'Scotland's History: The Lords of the Isles'. BBC. www.bbc.co.uk/scotland/history/articles/lords_of_the_isles/. Accessed 10 Dec. 2024.
13. B. Durie. (2022). 'Clans, families and kinship structures in Scotland: An Essay'. *Genealogy*, 6(4), 88. https://doi.org/10.3390/genealogy6040088

allegiance among his subjects, he started a sequence of focused raids and fights against competing clans. By claiming domination by force, he sought to destroy current power systems that challenged him and substitute a centralised authority benefiting the people living in the area.

Unification of Clans

Uniting the many clans beneath his banner was Somerled's main objective.[14] Through military force combined with persuasive diplomacy, he started building alliances with important local leaders, providing protection and shared benefits in return for their loyalty. This strategy helped the Gaelic people to experience solidarity and positioned Somerled as a uniting person, therefore helping win over clans who had earlier been enemies.

Establishing Order

Somerled started solidifying power, putting policies in place meant to bring a violent and divided area back under order. He won over many groups by advocating a system of administration honouring both Norse and Gaelic customs. His approach of stressing the need for justice and stability connected with the local people, therefore fostering support for his reign.

Somerled effectively combined power in Argyll by means of wars, diplomatic policies, and the building of a unified government structure. His efforts to bring order to a fragmented region set the foundation for his subsequent expansion into Kintyre and Lorn as he sought to extend his influence further into the Scottish Isles.

Conquest of Kintyre and Lorn

Geographic location and rich resources made Kintyre and Lorn key areas. With its short isthmus, Kintyre was an essential land link between the Scottish mainland and the Isles. This made trade and military movement very important here. Conversely, Lorn gave access to important marine channels and fertile agricultural ground. Somerled sought to improve his economic basis by gaining control over these areas, which strengthened his position against other groups.

Building on this strategic basis, Somerled's military operations in Kintyre and Lorn were distinguished by a sequence of forceful acts displaying his tactical acuity. Using his past naval victories to launch coordinated assaults on other clans and Norse colonists threatening his aspirations, he combined land and naval troops.

---

14. A. Woolf. *(2020)*. *'The song of the death of Somerled and the destruction of Glasgow in 1153'*. *The High Council of Clan MacDonald.* Retrieved from https://highcouncilofclandonald.com/scholarly-papers/the-song-of-the-death-of-somerled-and-the-destruction-of-glasgow-in-1153/

Engaging his well-trained troops in fights meant to show his military prowess and threaten other clans into submission, Somerled started campaigns against local clans that had opposed his authority.[15] Securing successes helped him reduce opposition and provide the foundation for peaceful integration into his growing territory.

Moreover, Somerled was able to control the coastal seas with a strong fleet at hand, making it more difficult for his adversaries to mount a defence.[16] His maritime operations supported raids on enemy strongholds around Kintyre and Lorn, therefore undermining conflicting claims to these lands. By means of these calculated military moves, Somerled not only increased his authority but also became a major force in the area.

Although his military might have been vital for his growth, Somerled also understood the need for diplomacy to entrench his authority in Kintyre and Lorn. Often using marriage and diplomacy as main diplomatic weapons, he deliberately created ties with powerful local leaders and clans.

Somerled, therefore, arranged marriages between his kin and well-known Kintyre and Lorn households. These alliances not only guaranteed loyalty but also promoted cooperation among once-competing groups. Somerled improved his authority by including important local leaders in his network, therefore promoting a feeling of shared identity and goal.

Beyond weddings, Somerled used diplomacy to build partnerships grounded on mutual advantage. Attaching to the interests of local officials, he pledged shared economic benefits and protection against outside dangers. Many people connected with his capacity to express a vision for a more steady and rich future, thus facilitating his road of expansion.

Establishing Governance

Somerled prioritised the creation of a good government as he effectively united Kintyre and Lorn under his kingdom. He understood that keeping control needed not only military might but the capacity to rule fairly and successfully.

To guarantee the effective running of his recently acquired territory, Somerled instituted administrative changes. Combining traditional Gaelic and Norse customs to promote acceptability among the people, he picked local leaders who were devoted to him to handle the government. This strategy served to bring stability and silence criticism.

Somerled also gained respect from his new people by advancing a system of justice that honoured the customs of the Norse and Gaelic communities. His dedication to fairness and order helped to confirm his authority as a legitimate king, therefore strengthening his profile as a uniting man in the area.

---

15. 'Somerled's Military Campaigns and Strategic Alliances'. *National Record of the Historic Environment*, 2019. Retrieved from https://canmore.org.uk
16. 'Gaelic and Norse Dynastic Ties: Military Impacts in the Hebrides'. Norwegian Heritage Foundation, 2020. Retrieved from www.norwegianheritage.no

Somerled's rise from a provincial nobleman to a sovereign ruler in the western seaways reflects the intricacy of mediaeval politics in the annals of Scottish history. His ability to combine military might with diplomatic strategy not only increased his territory but also confirmed his legacy among both Gaelic lords and Norse earls.

Combining Somerled's military campaigns and strategic marriages with his awareness of the political terrain, he shaped the conditions for a major change in power relations within the Norse-Gaelic society. His legacy would continue to shape Scotland's political fabric and the Isles for the next generations.

Somerled's Ascendancy by 1150

For the Isles and Scotland, Somerled's concentration of power signalled a turning point by 1150. His increasing fleet, which was evidence of his military might, allowed him to control the vital seas. By use of vessels built from the rich forests of Argyll, Somerled maintained a strong marine presence that enabled trade and military operations, therefore transforming him into a major participant in the power dynamics of the area.

Key Supporters and Alliances

The loyalty of important supporters and the calculated connections Somerled created helped to assist his ascent even more. Through marriage and diplomacy, he built a network of relationships spanning conventional clan rivalry by including powerful local leaders. Along with providing military support, these partnerships helped the many people under his authority to develop a feeling of shared identity. His success depended critically on his capacity to unite various groups behind a shared goal, hence preserving stability inside his expanding territory.

Expanding Territories

By 1150, Somerled's domains were vast and included major areas of Argyll, Kintyre, and Lorn. His deliberate military operations and diplomatic initiatives successfully brought these regions together to form a coherent nation prepared to resist outside threats. This consolidation prepared him for his aim to question the dominant powers of the Norse and Gaelic realms.

However, Somerled's problems increased along with his power. Along with battling outside foes, he controlled the intricate internal dynamics of his growing territory. The balance of power between different clans and the ongoing threat of competing groups called for smart government and leadership.

These early years helped Somerled's legend develop, laying the groundwork for a dynasty that would significantly influence the history of the Isles and Scotland itself. His approach to creating a maritime kingdom that would challenge the reigning powers of the day revolved mostly around his conquests and alliances.

Chapter 4

The Kingdom of Argyll

Argyll was a meeting place of strong cultural forces where Norse and Gaelic identities mixed under the care of its lord, Somerled, not only a geographical dominion. His ascent in Argyll was not only a tale of victories but the building of a heritage that connected his people to a new Gaelic-Norse monarchy. This vision of unity, both fierce and visionary, brought forth a society like no other, rooted in kin-based loyalty and driven by the strength of seafaring prowess. Somerled did not aim to simply rule Argyll but to make it an icon of cultural resilience, a kingdom defined by purpose as much as power.

In building his realm, Somerled's leadership style diverged from conventional mainland rulers. His authority, anchored in both sea and land, brought with it an entirely new model of governance. Rivers were regarded not as borders but rather as lifelines linking areas and ensuring Argyll's trade and communication superiority was maintained. His domain was one fixed to the rhythms of the sea, where power ebbed and flowed as often as the tides, turning Argyll into a maritime bastion projecting authority across every inlet and shoreline.

Societal Innovation

Under Somerled, Argyll developed into a distinctive community, a smooth blending of Gaelic and Norse customs against the convention of mediaeval Scotland. Deeply committed to clan and blood, Gaelic kinship entwined with Norse ideas of maritime lordship created a civilisation honouring intellectual and military prowess, perseverance, and independence. It was a dynamic blend – less a coexistence than a powerful synergy – that enabled the Isles to resist external pressures and chart their own path.

Central to this fusion was Somerled's court. Unlike the strict hierarchies of the mainland, his court flourished in a flexible social scene where warriors, intellectuals, poets, and craftsmen interacted unhindered.[1] Birthright was honoured alongside talent and accomplishment to create a society valued for both intelligence and bravery. Here, scholars enhanced the court's cultural identity by combining Norse sagas with Gaelic myth; artists created exquisite works reflecting Norse and Gaelic design, and Gaelic bards wrote songs praising Somerled's successes. Somerled's

1. Wilson McLeod. 'Political and Cultural Background'. *Divided Gaels*, 15 Jan. 2004, 14–54, https://doi.org/10.1093/acprof:oso/9780199247226.003.0002. Accessed 4 May 2023.

court was a microcosm of his realm, where martial ability coexisted with knowledge and artistic ability.

The social system of Somerled's kingdom allowed for a movement that was not common in mediaeval civilisation. People grew in prominence not only by ancestry but also by deeds, knowledge, and domain contribution.[2] This was a place that rewarded intelligence in counsel and ability in work, heroism in battle, and artistic talent. Under Somerled's direction, government and society were inspired to innovate, so transforming Argyll into a melting pot of many ideas and skills.

Perhaps the clearest expression of this cultural blend was found in Somerled's legal system. Crafted from both Gaelic and Norse traditions, it was a living legal framework that resonated with his subjects. Local assemblies offered a communal setting where disputes were settled under the guidance of trusted representatives from the clans and the king. This strategy maintained Somerled's dedication to justice and trust by balancing the Gaelic focus on kin-based justice with the rule of law.

Somerled gained the allegiance of his people by encouraging this legal system, so displaying a great respect for their autonomy and legacy. His rule was evidence of the wisdom of respecting custom while wielding power, therefore balancing his kingdom's stability.

Somerled created a society that was as strong as it was flexible, where Norse seafarers' history blended with Gaelic kinfolk and justice, not only a kingdom under his rule. Drawn from both land and sea, his vision was reflected across the years as a Gaelic-Norse community that flourished in terms of diversity and unity.

Anchoring the Isles

For Somerled, the scattered islands of Argyll's lordship were vital to a greater, linked kingdom spanning the Norse-Gaelic world, not only remote outposts. Seeing their strategic value, he turned these far-off areas into centres of trade and culture. Every island became a vital component of a vast maritime system throbbing with life that connected Argyll to Ireland, Norway, and beyond.

His rule's real genius was his mastery of these seas. Once considered far-off havens, the Hebrides were quickly humming centres of activity under his direction. Recognising that these outposts were not only homes for his people but also vital links in a network, strengthening his idea of a maritime empire, he turned every island into a fortified stronghold. These islands became important components of a united Gaelic-Norse kingdom where trade, culture, and power all flowed through their harbours, thanks in large part to his forethought.

Anchored on his fleet of birlinns, warships known for their speed and agility, Somerled's naval might was made from Argyll's great oaks and imbued with Norse

2. 'Introduction to the Clan Donald Armorial'. *The High Council of Clan Macdonald*, New Media Colophon, 11 Jul. 2024, highcouncilofclandonald.com/introduction-to-the-clan-donald-armorial/. Accessed 6 Dec. 2024.

sailing wisdom; these boats were unparalleled in their agility.[3] Light enough to negotiate shallow waters and rough beaches, the birlinns were Somerled's pride, reflecting military force and strategic awareness. Their supremacy on the Atlantic became legendary; every ship represented his authority over the huge marine areas of his domain. For Somerled, his fleet served as an extension of his country, spreading might over the seas wherever they sailed, not only as a weapon of war.

Beyond military rule, Somerled's skill at sea paved the way for economic growth all over the Isles. Understanding the riches found in trade, he turned his seas into tradeable arteries connecting his people with far-off places. Markets in Argyll's ports hummed with activity as traders from Ireland, mainland Scotland, and as far afield as Norway traded products, ideas, and culture. Trading over furs, grains, handcrafted products, and even weapons, the sounds of Gaelic, Norse, and Latin filled the air. By means of his economic policies, Somerled spun a network of links that rendered Argyll strong against economic isolation and hunger.

Somerled's vision transcended mere military conquest; he fostered a thriving maritime society. By treating the sea as both a barrier to enemies and a conduit for trade, he built a kingdom as dynamic as the tides that defined it.[4] This self-sustaining maritime powerhouse merged prosperity with military strength, ensuring that Argyll was not only a formidable force but a flourishing, stable society. His fleet defended the shores while carrying the riches of Argyll to distant lands, bringing back wealth, influence, and a legacy that would endure long after his time.

In anchoring the Isles to his vision, Somerled cemented Argyll's status as a formidable kingdom on the mediaeval stage. Under his rule, the Isles became more than storm-battered fragments of land – they became the thriving heart of his legacy, evidence of the ruler who turned scattered islands into the lifeblood of a united kingdom.

Governance in Argyll

In Somerled's hands, governance in Argyll became a revolutionary force, blending the best of Gaelic kinship loyalty, Norse customs, and even elements of Norman feudal hierarchy. Where mainland kings often ruled with strict hierarchies, Somerled saw power as something more fluid and adaptable. He entrusted local chieftains with authority over their territories while maintaining a central power that united them under his vision. This balance allowed clans to retain autonomy while bonding them under a single banner, reinforcing loyalty through respect rather than sheer dominance.

At the core of Somerled's leadership was his vivid court, a rare cultural mixing pot where Norse creativity collided with Gaelic customs. Poets, craftspeople, and

3. 'Norse Rituals: Traditions, Ceremonies'. Vaia, www.vaia.com/en-us/explanations/history/viking-history/norse-rituals/.
4. I. Beuermann. (2012). 'Jarla Sögur Orkneyja: Status and Power of the Earls of Orkney according to their Sagas'. *Viking and Medieval Scandinavia*, 8, 99–143. Retrieved from www.brepolsonline.net

academics sought solace here among soldiers. Scholars compiled Norse sagas with Gaelic mythology, blacksmiths fashioned weapons inspired by both Norse and Gaelic motifs, and bards spun epic tales of Somerled's exploits, so producing a cultural synthesis of Argyll. Somerled's court was more than just a seat of authority; it was an intellectual and cultural centre that flourished on variety, a haven for all kinds of skill, and a venue where diplomacy was as valued as power.

Somerled took a similarly amazing approach to justice. Renowned for his honesty, he oversaw assemblies where conflicts were settled by a mix of Gaelic and Norse rules. Here, the people witnessed a king dedicated to justice and unity who equally appreciated law and loyalty. Somerled's style of government produced harmony and stability, which won his subjects' unflinching allegiance. His power was adored rather than feared since he created a culture in which authority was held with respect, and justice solidified loyalty.

The Economic Renaissance

Argyll became a vibrant maritime economy because of Somerled's economic vision, which turned a group of scattered clans into a kingdom. Understanding his kingdom's wealth of natural riches, he transformed conventional Gaelic customs and modified them as calculated financial strategies. Cattle-raiding, once a survival tactic, became a calculated form of economic warfare, weakening his rivals while boosting Argyll's wealth. Every attack was more than just a skirmish; it was an act of economic strategy showcasing Somerled's skill in applying cultural practices to fortify his territory.

Beyond such strategies, Somerled connected the Hebrides, Ireland, and even far-off Norway by using Argyll's geographical location to create vast trading networks. His ports turned into energetic hubs of trade, humming with the activity of traders trading everything from grain to skilfully made weaponry. The mixing of languages – Gaelic, Norse, even Latin – was evidence of Argyll's role as a centre of cultural interaction. Here, Somerled's vision of economic resilience came to pass, producing a linked, stable society.

But Somerled's influence transcended business; he invented marine and agricultural technologies, guaranteeing Argyll's long-term viability. He promoted the growth of hardy crops fit for the local temperature and crop rotation, therefore enhancing food security. On the maritime front, he backed shipbuilding businesses and the renowned Argyll birlinn craftsmanship. These ships were more than just warships; they were emblems of Argyll's military and financial might as well as of Somerled's vision and the fortitude of his realm.

Somerled's economic strategies promoted unity, strength, and independence rather than only financial success. As a marine power, Argyll flourished economically and culturally, and symbolised the transforming potential of a leader who saw beyond victory to the prosperity of his people.

Religious Patronage and the Spiritual Legacy of Somerled

To Somerled, the Church was not just an institution to support his rule; it was a deeply personal alliance, one he forged with both reverence and intent. His contributions to religious life in Argyll went beyond mere patronage. Investing in monastic sanctuaries and ecclesiastical sites, he produced locations of education, religion, and cultural unification. Under a shared faith, monasteries evolved as hubs where Norse and Gaelic Christians could pray side by side, hence healing cultural divisions. To his people, Somerled was a spiritual protector as much as a king.

Under his direction, Argyll's Christianity developed to reflect a special fusion of Gaelic and Norse customs, combining Celtic Christianity with Norse respect for the natural environment. This syncretic spirituality produced a kingdom rich in cultural variety yet united in faith. Somerled promoted this synthesis, therefore cultivating a faith that really connected to his subjects. His dominion covered the spiritual centre of Argyll, therefore fostering allegiance by a shared feeling of spiritual and cultural identity, not only of the physical kingdom.

The stone and mortar of churches and monasteries, as well as little but significant memorials honouring Somerled's dedication, shaped his religious legacy as well. Linking Argyll to the larger Christian world, these buildings grew centres of religious activity, drawing academics, clergy, and pilgrims. By his commitment to the Church, Somerled not only guaranteed spiritual cohesiveness but also securely rooted Argyll within the Christian landscape, therefore producing a legacy that would continue long after his rule.

Legacy of the Kingdom of Argyll

Argyll would have a legacy from Somerled that would be felt for centuries, representing freedom, tenacity, and cultural pride. To the Gaelic people, he was a hero who reflected their attitude, a leader whose resistance to outside demands strengthened their own feeling of identity. Argyll became a symbol of unity, power, and hope – a lighthouse for everyone who loved their history and yearned for autonomy rather than merely a kingdom of lands and titles.

Generations of Gaelic lords, most famously Clan Donald, built their foundation on the systems Somerled devised. Those who adopted his government model – which combined centralised power with kindred loyalty – were able to let Gaelic culture flourish even as it opposed the growing influence of the Scottish monarchy. With his name connected with Gaelic pride and resilience, Somerled's legacy became the guiding spirit for the next chiefs trying to maintain the independence of the Isles.

Under Somerled, Argyll's legacy transcended the aspirations of any one leader to become a territory able to withstand the demands of both Norse and Scottish armies. His vision of Argyll, where Norse legacy and Gaelic identity coexisted in peace, created a model for a civilisation that was varied and coherent. Argyll was more than just a territory to be governed; it was a legacy of unity, strength, and resilience that would inspire the people of the Isles going forward. This balance made that possible.

During his rule, Somerled created a kingdom beyond boundaries or conquests. He built a society anchored in shared cultural roots, respect, and loyalty. His legacy demonstrated that real strength comes from the depth of faith, from the love of the land they called home, from the unity of a people connected by purpose and legacy, not from dominance. Inspired by a Gaelic-Norse society that would last long after Argyll was gone, he was, and still is, evidence of a king whose influence stretched across seas and decades.

Chapter 5
The Battle for Islay

In the middle of the Hebrides lies the Isle of Islay, a vital tool for the Hebrides' power fight. Given its crescent form and rich agricultural ground, the island's strategic value increased dramatically in the middle of the twelfth century. Often referred to as the 'Queen of the Hebrides', Islay was ideally positioned to regulate military paths as well as trade across the area.

Its pivotal position gave control over important marine lanes connecting Norway, Ireland, and Scotland. Any king wanting to rule the Western Isles sought out the island as a target. To Somerled, Islay was a strategic basis and a symbol of the Gaelic rebirth he imagined, not only a territory. To rule Islay was to exercise influence over the seaways and so over the Hebrides' balance of power. Eliminating it was no little challenge. It was a task that tested Somerled's leadership, strategic mind, and resolve.[1]

Prelude To Conflict

Bound to the Norwegian kingdom, Godred Olafsson aimed to retain Norse dominance over the Hebrides. He commanded with an iron grasp and a flotilla of terrifying longboats. Somerled was a man stuck between two cultures with his Gaelic background and Norse ancestry. He sought to blaze his own road free from Scottish or Norwegian control.

Years of competition between the two had been growing. Ambition, treachery, and their divergent ideas on the Isles' future moulded it.

Early on, Somerled teamed up with Godred, believing that he could get a foothold in the Isles by working with the strong Norse-Gaelic ruler. For Godred, this union was also advantageous; Somerled's power over Argyll and his strategic acumen made him a useful friend. Taken together, they could repel invaders and provide stability to the area.

Still, their cooperation was precarious. It was grounded in a shared knowledge of the dangers they encountered rather than in faith or allegiance. Together, they faced competing chiefs, restoring authority over areas that had slipped toward independence. Their tense alliance persisted for a time, and both leaders prospered. Still, tensions fanned beneath the surface even then.

1. A. R. Johnston. (1991). 'Norse settlement in the Inner Hebrides ca. 800–1300; with special reference to the islands of Mull, Coll and Tiree'. (Doctoral dissertation, University of St Andrews).

With his birth and the approval of the Norwegian monarch, Godred felt he was the proper king of the Isles. But Somerled was motivated by a picture of a Gaelic comeback for the Isles. This ambition would finally collide with Godred's will for Norse supremacy.

As his strength developed, Somerled felt increasingly independent. His calculated victories in Argyll and partnerships with strong clans like the MacInneseses and MacDougalls raised his influence and reputation and helped him unite authority over a large area. For many, Somerled was a remarkable combination of Gaelic and Norse elements – a king able to unite the split Isles into a coherent territory apart from Norway and Scotland.[2]

Somerled's Vision: A Unified, Independent Gaelic-Norse Kingdom

For his day, Somerled's vision was innovative. His goal was to create a realm where the familial ties and clan loyalty of Gaelic civilisation mixed with the maritime ability of the Norse. In his perfect world, the Isles would be a strong, self-governing nation where Gaelic language, customs, and government moulded the community rather than cowering under foreign kings.

As a high king, he united the clans under a shared identity and goal while envisioning a distributed governmental system allowing local chieftains some authority. Using the advantageous location of the Hebrides to create economic independence, this Gaelic-Norse monarchy would flourish in trade. At its core, Somerled's vision was about freedom from outside rule. He saw the Isles as a land deserving of self-determination, a kingdom for its people rather than the prize of distant kings.

Godred's Vision: A Norse-Gaelic Kingdom Loyal to Norway

By contrast, Godred considered the Isles as an extension of Norway's authority, a territory whose legitimacy sprang from its links to the Scandinavian world. Supported by Norwegian history and the line of Norse kings who had ruled the Isles for centuries, he considered himself the legitimate king of Norse origin. To Godred, the Isles were a Norse cultural and influence stronghold in the western seas, a Norwegian outpost.

Godred envisioned a tightly controlled kingdom loyal to the Norwegian crown and unified under Norse authority. By preserving Norse cultural and political traditions, he believed he was upholding stability and honouring his ancestors. For him, any attempt to establish a Gaelic-led, independent kingdom was a threat to this order. He perceived it as a challenge that could unravel the very identity of the Isles.[3]

---

2. Andrew McDonald, *The Sea Kings: The Late Norse Kingdoms of Man and the Isles, c.1066–1275*. Review By: Simon Egan, 2020 VII.
3. Wilson McLeod. 'Political and Cultural Background.' *Divided Gaels*, 15 Jan. 2004, 14–54, https://doi.org/10.1093/acprof:oso/9780199247226.003.0002. Accessed 4 May 2023.

The First Betrayal

The first open break in their alliance came in 1153. At the time, a power struggle was underway on the Isle of Man, the hub of Godred's authority. The Kingdom of the Isles depended much on the Isle of Man. Its pivotal position enabled trade among Ireland, Scotland, and the Hebrides and helped regulate the Irish Sea. During this period, some Manx nobles became dissatisfied with Godred's rule. They began to support Somerled, hoping he might give them more autonomy and a voice in a newly unified Hebrides.

Somerled sympathised with these rebels. He quietly encouraged their dissent, hinting that his leadership might bring them a more inclusive form of governance. When Godred heard about the unrest, he viewed it as a direct betrayal. To him, Somerled's covert support of the Manx rebels was a clear challenge to his rule. Godred publicly denounced Somerled, accusing him of trying to undermine the Norse order in the Isles. This accusation marked the start of their breakdown. Godred saw any weakening of his rule over Man as a betrayal of both their alliance and Norse authority itself.

Somerled was furious in response. He had not meant to incite full rebellion; his goal had been to subtly shift the power balance. But Godred's reaction was swift and brutal. He crushed the Manx rebellion before it could gain strength. Godred intended his response as a warning to Somerled and anyone else who might challenge his rule. Instead, it only increased Somerled's resentment. Feeling betrayed by Godred's harsh response, Somerled turned his ambitions more openly toward independence, having realised that Godred would never share power.[4]

A Treaty in Bad Faith

Tensions between them peaked in 1155. Understanding the possibility of mutual devastation should they keep fighting, Somerled suggested a diplomatic conference. He suggested they meet on neutral ground to discuss dividing the Isles. The goal was to create a peaceful arrangement that recognised both of their powers. Somerled imagined a division where he would rule the southern Hebrides as a Gaelic lord. Meanwhile, Godred would retain control of the Northern Isles and the Isle of Man as a Norse king.

Godred was wary of Somerled's rising influence. He agreed to the meeting, but he never planned to share power. Instead, he saw it as an opportunity to trap his rival. Godred arrived with a large force, positioning his men strategically around the meeting site. This setup ensured Somerled would be isolated and vulnerable. Godred intended to either eradicate Somerled as a danger or force him into compliance.

4. Andrew R. McDonald. 'Images of Hebridean Lordship in the Late Twelfth and Early Thirteenth Centuries: The Seal of Raonall Mac Sorley'. *The Scottish Historical Review*, vol. 74, no. 198, 1995, 129–43. JSTOR, www.jstor.org/stable/25530679, https://doi.org/10.2307/25530679.

However, Somerled sensed the trap. As negotiations began, he observed the tense behaviour of Godred's warriors. Furious at the treachery, Somerled cut off the negotiations suddenly. He and his men retreated before Godred could act on his plans.

This failed negotiation was the last straw. Somerled now saw Godred as treacherous and incapable of true diplomacy. Godred, in turn, saw Somerled's withdrawal as defiance. To him, it showed that Somerled would never accept his rule. Men ready for battle had no place for compromise.

The Battle Lines Are Drawn

Played off the northern shore of Islay, the Battle of Epiphany in January 1156 was a pivotal turning point in the conflict between Somerled and the King of the Isles. Somerled's fleet lay hidden in the narrow bays and inlets around Islay when dawn's first light burst through the hazy horizon. His forces were poised to confront Godred's larger Norse fleet.

There was no standard naval conflict here. Decisive for the fate of the Hebrides, it decided whether the Isles would continue under Norse control or develop as a Gaelic-Norse kingdom. Despite his meagre numbers, Somerled used creative strategies, surprising and outmanoeuvring the Norse ships under the shelter of the inlets and shallow waters.

The Fog and Silence: Setting Up a Psychological Advantage

Somerled's fleet arrived off the northern coast of Islay early on 6 January under the cover of a heavy, wet fog. The timing was deliberate; the fog was thin enough to let his captains keep visual contact with one another but thick enough to cover the movements of his ships.

There was complete silence. Oars cut through the water with disciplined precision, each birlinn moving in near-soundless unison. Trained to avoid the loud, clanking noises sometimes indicating an incoming fleet, Somerled's warriors had developed a reputation for erratic leadership, and he exploited that. Already suspicious of Godred, his troops were driven into a state of anxious expectation.

Encirclement in Loose Formation: Creating Confusion and Fear

Somerled signalled his ships to spread out in a wide, loose formation, surrounding Godred's fleet on three sides. Somerled's fleet fanned out, with each birlinn approaching from a different angle instead of the customary Norse technique of building a compact, defensive line. This configuration gave Somerled's ships the ability to appear from several angles, therefore giving the impression that the enemy was everywhere.

Godred sensed it right away. Designed for simple, head-on conflicts, the Norsemen became confused about where the major attack would land. Godred's troops felt vulnerable as ships closed in from all sides. Before a single arrow had even been fired, some yelled in panic while others tried to relocate, causing anarchy on the Norse longship decks.

Hit-and-Run Attacks: The First Strike

The first hit came quickly and unexpectedly. Emerging from the mist on Godred's fleet's eastern side was a gathering of birlinns. At the closest Norse ship, warriors fired a volley of arrows. The Norsemen hurriedly built their defences, the arrows whirling against shields. The Norse crew was stunned when the birlinns vanished back into the mist before they could react.

Moments later, from the west, another group of birlinns attacked the exposed sides of the Norse ships with javelins and arrow fire. These strikes came in brief, rapid bursts from several directions each time. Godred's forces, used to open combat, struggled with these tactics. The Norse longships, built for strength, couldn't adjust quickly enough to defend against each new wave.

This strategy continued, with Somerled's ships striking and retreating before the Norse could respond. By attacking from multiple angles, Somerled kept Godred's fleet on edge and wore down their warriors with constant, small assaults.

Drawing the Enemy into the Shallows

Frustrated by these attacks, Godred tried to seize control. He ordered his fleet to advance, hoping to close in on Somerled's ships. The Norse longships surged forward, oars churning as they pursued the retreating birlinns.

Somerled had expected this move. His ships fell back in a controlled retreat, drawing Godred's fleet toward the shallow waters near Islay's rocky coast. Hidden reefs and sharp rocks lay just beneath the surface here. The birlinns, with their shallow drafts, navigated easily. The larger Norse longships struggled, scraping rocks and finding it hard to manoeuvre.

Caught in the shallows, Godred's ships became easy targets. Some collided with submerged rocks, causing panic among their crews. The tight quarters made it difficult for the Norse fleet to organise, stripping them of their advantage.

Flanking Manoeuvres and Harassment

With Godred's ships trapped, Somerled's fleet split into two lines. One stayed near the shore, using rocks for cover, while the other cut off any escape route. Somerled's birlinns darted in and out, firing arrows and javelins at the trapped longships. They withdrew before the Norse could counterattack.

This tactic deepened the Norsemen's helplessness. Somerled's forces struck from all sides, then pulled back in swift, coordinated movements. Each time the Norse tried to organise a defence, another wave of birlinns attacked from a new angle. Some Norsemen fell back, while others held their ground in desperation.

Somerled's plan worked perfectly. By keeping the Norse forces confined and off-balance, he wore down their defences without risking his own men.

Boarding Isolated Ships for Close Combat

Once Somerled had weakened the Norse formation, he signalled his warriors to board isolated ships. A group of birlinns closed in on a single Norse longship, hurling grappling hooks to tie the vessels together. Somerled's men, skilled in both Gaelic and Norse fighting, swarmed the enemy deck with axes, swords, and shields.

The Norse longships, usually mighty in open water, became liabilities in these tight quarters. Godred's men, with little room to manoeuvre, faced fast attackers skilled in hit-and-run and direct combat. Somerled's warriors struck with disciplined force, breaking through the Norse defences.

Each time they overpowered a ship, Somerled's men retreated before reinforcements could arrive. Godred's men watched their comrades' ships fall one by one, helpless to stop it.

The Assault on Godred's Flagship

With the battle in his favour, Somerled targeted the largest prize – Godred's flagship. Leading a vanguard of birlinns, he approached Godred's vessel, still anchored at the fleet's centre. The flagship was heavily guarded, but Godred's men were weary after watching their forces crumble.

Somerled's men launched grappling hooks, securing the birlinns to Godred's ship. Warriors leaped onto the enemy deck, axes flashing as they clashed with Godred's guards. The fighting was fierce and chaotic. Somerled's men pushed forward, aiming to reach Godred.

For a moment, it seemed the two leaders might face each other directly. But Godred's guards rallied, forcing Somerled's forces back before they could reach him. Somerled ordered his men to withdraw. His birlinns detached from the flagship and slipped into the fog, leaving Godred's forces battered and confused. Somerled's men regrouped while Godred's exhausted warriors struggled to hold their positions.

The Final Encirclement and Decisive Assault

As Godred's fleet tried to regroup, Somerled launched his final assault. His birlinns formed a tight crescent around the remaining Norse ships, blocking any escape. Scattered and disoriented, the Norsemen had no way to counter the organised assault closing in.

One by one, Somerled's warriors boarded the remaining Norse vessels, overwhelming the exhausted defenders in brutal, close combat. The Norse forces, worn down by constant attacks, began to collapse. Some ships surrendered, while others tried to flee, only to be intercepted and destroyed.

The final phase was swift and merciless. Somerled's forces moved from ship to ship, eliminating every remaining threat. By the end of the day, the waters around Islay were littered with the wreckage of Godred's fleet. Somerled's tactics had brought him complete victory.

Aftermath and the Shifting Power Balance

Somerled's victory at Islay did more than claim an island; it reshaped power across the Hebrides. After the battle, he and Godred reached a truce, dividing territories. Somerled took the southern Hebrides, including Islay and other key islands. This agreement began the Lordship of the Isles – a Gaelic-Norse kingdom that defied both Norwegian and Scottish rule for centuries.

Somerled asserted Gaelic dominance over Norse influence. His victory established a lasting Gaelic-Norse identity that would define the Isles for generations. Securing Islay was not only a military win but also a statement of cultural unity and resilience.

In the wake of Islay's conquest, its impact echoed across the Isles. This marked the start of a new era, where Gaelic culture and leadership began to regain prominence. Somerled's renown as an influential and visionary leader rose, and the vision of a Gaelic maritime kingdom emerged. This battle set the stage for the Lordship of the Isles, a realm that would contest Scottish and Norwegian rule for generations.

Chapter 6

Naval Dominance and Expansion

The narrative of Somerled's rise to power is incomplete without examining his military innovations and strategic skills. This blend enabled him to dominate the Scottish Isles and influence parts of the mainland. Central to his ascent was an inherent naval superiority. He was extremely knowledgeable about the Hebrides' perilous waters and possessed an unmatched command of marine technologies. In addition to being a narrative of conquering, Somerled illustrates how naval might revolutionised mediaeval combat.

Somerled's greatest weapon was his fleet. He created a distinctive design in contrast to his competitors, who depended on conventional Norse longships. He created ships known as birlinns by combining Norse and Gaelic construction skills. These were more agile, lighter, and quicker. Because of their shape, they were perfect for the Hebrides' rough beaches and restricted seaways. Somerled's fleet was a powerful force because of his inventiveness and flexibility. His vision of a maritime kingdom was emphasised by his dedication to naval supremacy.

Building the Fleet

Somerled made a prudent investment in building his fleet. He understood that establishing his dominion over the dispersed islands of the Hebrides required maritime might. Thus, Somerled devoted substantial resources to constructing ships that could navigate the region's complex waters.

Timber from the thick forests of Argyll was used to construct the birlinns. Each ship was expertly made by skilled shipwrights. Built to endure the severe, erratic conditions of the Atlantic, these ships were not only swift but also robust. They made navigation versatile by having both sails and oars, allowing for the use of labour when necessary and the wind when feasible. Somerled's fleet had a significant advantage over his adversaries because of this dual propulsion technology since their ships were frequently slower and needed larger crews.

The resources and experience required to assemble such a fleet demonstrated Somerled's leadership. His soldiers were more than just sailors; they were warriors trained to fight on land and at sea. This unique blend of combat readiness and marine expertise was uncommon at the time and demonstrated Somerled's creative strategy for fighting. He created a culture among his supporters that valued flexibility, tenacity, and unwavering devotion, creating a distinct identity that distinguished them from opposing forces.

The birlinn was not merely a vessel. Its design reflected the ethos of Gaelic culture, which prized freedom and solidarity, as well as the Norse seafaring prowess. Somerled solidified his position as a leader who symbolised the multifaceted identity of the Isles by constructing a fleet that reflected this dual ancestry.[1]

Battles Beyond the Isles

In addition to being a chieftain of the Isles, Somerled is regarded in the history of mediaeval Scotland as a fearless and imaginative leader whose military aspirations extended well beyond his immediate territory. His legacy is one of territorial expansion and naval might, revealing a man who used military prowess and strategic acumen to change the political climate along Scotland's west coast. Somerled's forays outside of the Isles tell an equally captivating tale of greater geopolitical ambition, even though the well-known battle for Islay represents a pivotal moment in his consolidation of power inside the Isles.

In the British Isles, the balance of power changed during the twelfth century. While local chieftains, Norman lords, and Norse rulers fought for dominance, Somerled became a commander in a rare position to use his Norse-Gaelic ancestry and deep knowledge of maritime warfare. His determination to increase his power along the western seaboard and beyond was demonstrated by his wars that reached into the Irish Sea and mainland Scotland. These conflicts demonstrated Somerled's prowess as a warrior and as a cunning tactician who was aware of the intricacies of mediaeval combat.[2]

Naval Campaigns in the Irish Sea

Somerled's fleet, an invention that distinguished him from other regional leaders, was the foundation of his dominance. The narrow canals and rugged coasts of the Irish Sea and the Hebrides were perfect for his birlinns. His idea of a marine Gaelic-Norse empire was strengthened by this fleet, which served as more than just a defensive weapon.

The Battle of Mann was one of the most famous campaigns in the Irish Sea. A crucial prize was the Isle of Man, which is situated in the middle of the Irish Sea. By controlling the island, Somerled would have access to the northern English, Scottish, and Irish shores as well as influence over the western trade routes. A strong Norse-Gaelic chieftain with close ties to the Norwegian throne, the King of Mann ruled the island. Somerled put together a fleet of birlinns – slim, nimble war galleys

1. J. Marsden. (2001). 'Norse-Gaelic Dynamics in the Isles: A Reinterpretation of Scandinavian Political Structures in Scotland'. *Journal of Historical Studies,* 15(4), 33–58. Retrieved from https://journals.sagepub.com
2. W. P. L. Thomson. (2008). 'The Norse Legacy in Orkney and Shetland: Political and Cultural Continuities'. *Scandinavian Journal of History*, 33(1), 45–68. Retrieved from www.tandfonline.com

that combined Gaelic and Norse shipbuilding techniques and were built especially for speed and agility in shallow waters – to subvert this authority.

Somerled employed a pincer plan to encircle the Norse forces after splitting his fleet into three groups in preparation for the conflict. Leading the core charge and immediately confronting the bulk of the Norse fleet was his flagship, a huge birlinn with a terrifying figurehead. Armed with swords, axes, and shields, Somerled's soldiers, who had been trained for close-quarters fighting on ship decks, boarded the enemy ships using grappling hooks. The conflict was intense, with Somerled's men defeating the bigger, slower Norse ships by using their agility and discipline.

Somerled became victorious in the Battle of Mann. Now that he controlled the Isle of Man, he could affect military and commercial activities across the Irish Sea. Beyond simply increasing his domain, this battle marked the beginning of a new Gaelic-Norse power that would challenge Norse dominance in the area. By forming alliances with local Gaelic chieftains who sought refuge from Norse overlords, Somerled was able to strengthen his control over the Irish Sea and bring about a significant change in the balance of power in the area. This was made possible by his victory at Mann.[3]

Off the coast of Ulster, Somerled's forces engaged Norse vessels in another major campaign in the Irish Sea. By exercising power here, Somerled was able to fortify his bonds with Irish friends and protect his western lands from possible Norse incursions. This was a strategically important region with historical ties to Gaelic Ireland.

Somerled gained the upper hand by being unexpected and using fast moves. As his fleet swept the coast, it captured important ports as bases for future development and struck Norse settlements with surprising fury. These efforts demonstrated his ability to use psychological warfare and naval tactics, as his quick and erratic strikes terrorised the coastal Norse-held communities.

Somerled had virtually eliminated the Norse menace in the area after his wars in the Irish Sea. He was able to establish alliances with Gaelic chieftains, gain economic dominance through commerce, and expand his influence into regions that had previously been under Norse rule thanks to his control over the sea lanes. Somerled's achievements in the Irish Sea were more than military victories; they were declarations of his ambition to create an independent Gaelic maritime kingdom free from Norwegian and Scottish oversight.

Mainland Expansion: Campaigns in Morvern and Ardnamurchan

After establishing his supremacy in the Irish Sea, Somerled shifted his goals to the mainland, concentrating on Morvern and Ardnamurchan. In addition to being resource-rich, these areas were strategically significant for strengthening his hold on

3. A. Woolf. (2007). 'The 'Sea Kings' Revisited: Political Continuity and Change in the Hebrides, c. 800–1200'. Scottish *Historical Review*, 86(2), 191–215. Retrieved from www.euppublishing.com

the Western Highlands. Somerled's adaptability as a military leader was demonstrated during the campaigns in Morvern and Ardnamurchan, which combined his nautical skill with his ability to adjust to land-based combat.

The Campaign in Morvern

The peninsula of Morvern was rocky and isolated, with steep slopes and thick forests. Additionally, Morvern was a stronghold of Gaelic culture, and Somerled could solidify his cultural connections with the local Gaelic clans while solidifying his authority on the mainland. He launched a series of quick, focused attacks against the towns and fortifications in the area to start his war in Morvern. Before reinforcements could be arranged, Somerled's fleet enabled him to swiftly send soldiers to the coast, where they could advance inland and fight local armies.

Using his ship as a base of operations, Somerled's soldiers would launch amphibious attacks against key strongholds. They often struck around dawn or twilight to add to the sense of surprise. His forces employed guerrilla warfare, striking swiftly before retreating into the dense forests or back to their ships to keep the enemy from putting up a fierce fight. These tactics were particularly effective in Morvern's difficult terrain, where traditional large-scale combat planning was challenging. Somerled's warriors used the natural environment by moving with accuracy and dexterity, accustomed to the rugged terrain of the Hebrides.

After seizing Morvern, Somerled expanded his domain and strengthened his influence among the mainland tribes. His campaign's success showed the local chieftains that he was a capable commander who could protect Gaelic territory from outside dangers. Somerled's influence on the mainland was further cemented when numerous clans in the Western Highlands began to view him as a defender of their culture and independence.[4]

The Campaign in Ardnamurchan

Ardnamurchan, a location characterised by its hilly terrain and slender coastline inlets, presented different difficulties. Here, Somerled modified his strategy, navigating the challenging terrain with his fleet and his knowledge of guerrilla warfare. Since Ardnamurchan was a gateway to the Western Highlands, gaining control of it ensured a vital point of entry for any inland march in the future.

A well-planned attack on a strategic fortification with a commanding view of the shore marked the start of Somerled's campaign in Ardnamurchan. When his armada led him to a remote bay in the dark, his warriors managed to disembark without being noticed. Then, they ascended the cliffs and unexpectedly overran the castle, defeating the defenders before they could signal for help. Somerled secured the surrounding areas and gained the favour of the local chieftains by using this castle as a base of operations.

4. S. Duffy. (2006). 'Irish and Scottish Mercenaries in Medieval Europe: Origins of Galloglass Warfare'. *Irish Historical Studies*, 35(138), 175–91. Retrieved from www.cambridge.org

Throughout the Ardnamurchan conflict, Somerled's soldiers employed hit-and-run tactics, quickly striking adversary targets and escaping into the highlands before counterattacks could be organised. This strategy demonstrated his in-depth knowledge of the terrain and his opponents' boundaries. Somerled's troops were trained to take advantage of the terrain, using flanking attacks and ambushes to outmanoeuvre and outthink the defenders, whereas conventional armies focused on open-field combat.

After the Ardnamurchan campaign, Somerled built a system of fortified fortresses to defend his coastal domains from Highland attacks. His triumph at Ardnamurchan showed that he was able to combine naval power with land tactics, something that few of his peers could match.

The Broader Impact of Somerled's Campaigns

The political landscape of the western British Isles was altered by Somerled's activities. He established himself as a force that could resist both Norse and Norman domination by extending into Mann, Morvern, and Ardnamurchan. By controlling the coastal seas with his fleet, he was able to forge alliances, conduct raids, and establish a network of trade that strengthened his empire. His power in the area was strengthened by these campaigns, which upended Norse rule and established ties with Gaelic lords in Ireland.[5]

On the mainland, Somerled's conquests were a clear message. Territories like Morvern and Ardnamurchan became strongholds supporting his maritime realm. His campaigns demonstrated his vision of a Gaelic-Norse empire that resisted outside attacks from both Norse and Norman forces and stretched beyond the Isles.

Somerled proved his command of both land and marine tactics in these engagements. His armies brought a versatility that his enemies could not match because they were equally proficient on land and at sea. In contrast to more inflexible armed units, his fervently devoted followers maintained a culture of flexibility, fortitude, and devotion to their leader.

Legacy of Somerled's Expansion

Warfare in the Scottish Isles and western Scotland was revolutionised by Somerled's campaigns in the Irish Sea and the mainland. His creation of the birlinn, a multipurpose, agile war galley, raised the bar for naval might in the area. The Hebridean environment was ideal for the birlinn's design, which was geared for both speed and shallow-water navigation. Other Gaelic and Norse chieftains were eventually impacted by this invention, which resulted in a move away from the use of big Norse longships and toward more nimble fleets with quick deployment and adaptable strategies.

5. W. P. L. Thomson. (2005). 'Political Interactions between Norway and the Isles during the Viking Age. Scandinavian Studies', 77(2), 145–67. Retrieved from https://muse.jhu.edu

The way wars were waged in the area was also altered by Somerled's style of warfare. He added a new dimension to military strategy with his emphasis on psychological warfare, intimidating opponents with the sight of his flagship and the disciplined precision of his fleet. He realised that winning meant more than just outlasting adversaries in combat; it also meant displaying strength in a way that discouraged resistance. Because his reputation alone frequently put an end to uprisings and discouraged competitors, this strategy allowed him to maintain control over large areas with a comparatively small military.

Additionally, Somerled proved the value of multi-terrain warfare by successfully combining land and maritime power. His ability to lead well-planned campaigns that combined guerrilla and naval tactics demonstrated a level of adaptability and skill uncommon for the time. He was able to create a solid foundation for his Gaelic-Norse kingdom by using this two-pronged strategy to control both the Isles and strategic areas of the mainland.

Somerled made a lasting impact on the history of the Scottish Isles with his land and naval campaigns. He established a Gaelic-Norse dominion that would eventually become the Lordship of the Isles with his naval warfare innovations, strategic footholds in Morvern and Ardnamurchan, and triumphs in the Irish Sea. His legacy is one of cultural synthesis, military innovation, and a fierce commitment to Gaelic independence.

In the centuries that followed, Somerled's descendants, particularly the MacDonalds, would carry forward his vision of a unified Gaelic-Norse kingdom. The Lordship of the Isles became a bastion of Gaelic identity, resisting both Norwegian and Scottish encroachment and preserving a unique cultural heritage. Somerled's life and campaigns remain a powerful example of how one leader's vision can reshape the political and cultural landscape, leaving a legacy that resonates through history.

Chapter 7
Religion and Patronage

According to the comprehensive record of Somerled's life, his legacy forged a profound way into the spiritual core of his people, reaching far beyond the blood-stained fields and the power struggles of the throne. In addition to being a warrior and a king, Somerled was a guardian of faith, a cunning Church ally, and a constructor of places of worship.

Somerled saw the Church as more than just a place of prayer in a time when religion and authority were intertwined; it was a source of power, a moral fulcrum, and a unifying force. His support of religious organisations was a purposeful, almost artistic, attempt to ground his power in something above mere piety. Through this alliance, he created a legacy that blended devotion with leadership, binding his people under a shared spiritual and cultural vision.

The Cross and the Crown

In the twelfth-century Scottish Highlands and Isles, faith was not just a matter of personal preference; it was the basis of existence, uniting clans, culture, and power in a harsh environment shaped by wild seas and even wilder emotions. In this context, having power meant more than merely employing physical force; it meant exercising a deeper kind of authority that influenced every facet of day-to-day existence. Here comes Somerled, a ferocious fighter, a cunning leader, and most importantly, a man who believed that faith was strong enough to stabilise and tame his chaotic world. Somerled saw that the Church was more than just prayer and repentance; it was a source of power, wisdom, and solidarity that he might join to purify and guarantee his authority.

Monks safeguarded the sacred writings that contained wisdom, history, and even power in the Church, which acted as a beacon in these places. It was a meeting point where Christianity blended with Norse and Gaelic customs, reflecting Somerled's own goal of a unified people under a single, potent vision. He acknowledged the Church's twin role as a cultural anchor and a moral compass, and his relationship with it was anything from passive. With his patronage, Somerled merged the role of the warrior with that of a sacred ruler, adding divine legitimacy to his authority and ensuring that his legacy would reach into the hearts and minds of his people long after his sword went silent.

The Church in Somerled's time had just undergone sweeping reforms – efforts to enforce celibacy among the clergy and cut back on secular interference, shifting the Church's power toward an independent, moral authority. Even the Highlands, wild and remote, felt the tremors of this shift. Somerled was able to harness this new moral power by aligning himself with the Church, which gave his authority a more expansive spiritual resonance. He encouraged the development of monasteries and churches that functioned as both political and spiritual strongholds by donating land and other resources. In return, the clergy joined him as friends, strengthening his power by associating it with divine favour; this collaboration extended throughout his domain and into the lives of his subjects.

Somerled's partnership with the Church was not without conflict, though. His goals frequently conflicted with the Church's own interests as he enlarged his sphere of influence. Gaining territory occasionally entailed intruding on church property, which led to disputes with influential church leaders who opposed any perceived challenge to their autonomy. Determining to maintain its position, the Church viewed Somerled as a potential ally against foreign powers as well as a challenger of the current quo. Somerled was at odds with both the Norwegian and Scottish monarchs because of his ancestry, which gave him roots in both Norse and Gaelic history. Because of this complex loyalty, Somerled frequently had to balance his own expansionist goals with the Church's desire for autonomy.

Nevertheless, Somerled's dedication to the Church continued to be a defining characteristic of his rule. Beyond simple gestures, his deeds revealed a vision of a society in which power and faith coexisted as foundations. He created a cultural stronghold and a place of prayer by founding religious institutions like Saddell Abbey in Kintyre, where monks could foster their religion and knowledge together.[1] Saddell Abbey served as a tribute to his political savvy as much as his piety. In this case, Somerled's investment in the Church was not merely an act of honour; rather, it was a calculated effort to increase his power, encourage allegiance, and present a sanctified image that appealed to his subjects.

Somerled's relationship with the Church was a delicate balancing act between calculation and devotion. His patronage was motivated by more than altruism; it was a way to exercise both the sword's power and the authority of the cross. Through his well-planned assistance, he converted the Church into a political tool and a collaborator, giving his rule legitimacy outside of the battlefield.

The Church in Somerled's world evolved into more than just a house of worship; it became the centre of a community united by common values and customs. By accomplishing this, Somerled did more than just establish a kingdom; he created a legacy, a place where the sovereign and the sacred coexisted, solidifying his authority and establishing a legacy of a country fashioned by both the crown and the cross.

Patronage of Monasteries and Churches

Somerled's backing of the Church in his realm was a brilliant leadership move that spoke directly to his people's hearts by fusing faith, diplomacy, and strategy.

1. Ian D. Whyte. *Scotland before the Industrial Revolution*. Routledge, 12 May 2014.

It was more than just a gesture of piety. Supporting the Church meant more to Somerled than sanctifying his reign; it meant incorporating the spiritual into his power. In an era when monasteries held immense power, both spiritual and social, Somerled's patronage was a calculated move to anchor his influence in something beyond the mortal plane – a divine partnership that added weight to his rule and brought cultural unity to the Highlands and Isles.

Somerled constructed bridges in addition to churches under his religious patronage. His endorsement was not merely symbolic; it strengthened his power in the eyes of a people who valued the sacred and guaranteed that the clergy would view him as a divinely favoured monarch. A communal identity that incorporated both traditions under a single faith was fostered by Somerled's nurture of the Church, which helped to soften the sharp boundaries between the Gaelic and Norse cultures within his territory. These monasteries developed into sites where Christian doctrine and ancient traditions blended to create a spiritual fusion that spoke to his people's deepest longing for a single kingdom.

Beyond Saddell Abbey, Somerled's support spread to other places of worship that were essential to the unity of his realm. In addition to being places of worship, these halls of religion served as educational institutions where monks recorded the rules and customs of Somerled's society, in addition to the Church's doctrines. These texts became invaluable documents that preserved the core of Gaelic and Norse tradition for future generations in a society where oral history predominated. Somerled's religious sites, therefore, became a storehouse of cultural riches and a testament to his dedication to a legacy that would endure beyond his lifetime.

Furthermore, Somerled's affiliation with the Church was not limited to his immediate area; rather, it placed him at the centre of a broad movement of religious reform that was revolutionising Europe. Somerled portrayed himself as a progressive ruler who upheld his own authority while respecting the Church's moral authority by supporting the Church's demands for clergy purity and independence from secular government. By demonstrating that his devotion to the Church was sincere and calculated – a tie woven from his care for the spiritual well-being of his kingdom as much as his political savvy – this balance improved him not only in the eyes of his own people but among the clergy and reformers outside his boundaries.

However, Somerled's ecclesiastical backing was about community, not merely establishing allies. Under his leadership, these monasteries served as hubs for social interaction among members of various clans and backgrounds, fostering a sense of unity via a common religion. In turn, the monks developed into Somerled's devoted followers, forming a network that spanned his kingdom from Kintyre to Argyll. In addition to influencing his subjects, his patronage had a cascading effect, encouraging local chieftains and noble families to support the Church, bolstering its presence throughout the Isles, and assisting it in serving as a unifying factor in a region where clan wars were frequent, and allegiances were often strained.

In a world that could be brutal and divided, Somerled's monasteries became havens of peace, culture, and learning. The monks under his protection preserved not only spiritual texts but also knowledge that grounded society and maintained order. Somerled created a civilisation in which the Church served as a moral compass and a barrier against the chaos of clan rivalry by endorsing these havens. His reputation as a king who valued religion and intelligence just as much as strength and power was cemented when his vision established a realm where the spiritual and secular supported one another.

Somerled's loyalty to the Church was a deep knowledge of leadership that went beyond merely governing territory; it was more than just a political decision. He viewed the Church as a source of unity and resilience, as well as a collaborator in the governance of his kingdom, rather than as an independent organisation. Today, his monasteries serve as enduring reminders of his dedication to a world that valued education, culture, and solidarity. Centuries later, the legacy of this kingdom, which flourished on faith and might, is still felt throughout the Scottish Isles. It was a place where the sword and the cross were used side by side.

Iona and the Abbots' Calling

Iona was not just any island in Somerled's thinking; it was Scotland's spiritual centre, pulsing with a centuries-old sanctity and history. A spot where faith and fortitude met in the face of Viking attacks and where St. Columba himself had sown the roots of Christianity that would spread throughout the Highlands and Isles, this small island off the western coast represented something significant to pilgrims, monarchs, and saints. As someone with both Norse and Gaelic ancestry, Somerled saw Iona as more than just a place of worship; it served as a link between the customs and values that influenced his life. When he sought to bring the esteemed Abbot Flaithbertach Ua Brolcháin to Iona in 1164, it wasn't just an act of respect; it was a bold statement of his devotion to faith, culture, and unity.

Somerled was aware that Iona was a symbol of prestige and identity in addition to its theological authority. Somerled was asserting his position as a warrior and a steward of the Gaelic-Christian legacy when he invited Abbot Ua Brolcháin, a man known for his insight and profound spirituality, to restore Iona as a thriving monastic centre. He made a brilliant choice in selecting Ua Brolcháin. This was more than just politics; it was about revitalising Iona's legacy, re-establishing a connection between the populace and a place they respected, thereby tying his authority to something enduring and admired.

The perfect leader to revive Iona was Abbot Flaithbertach Ua Brolcháin. He would guide the monks in meditation, learning, and conserving the wisdom of the ages. He was well-known for his commitment and scholarship. Somerled envisioned Iona as more than just a monastery; he saw it as a haven where culture, intellect, and faith could thrive despite the changing and evolving outside world. Iona would be a spiritual lighthouse to Somerled, shining its light on both the faithful and those who are lost in life's storms. Monks would preserve and disseminate religious knowledge here, transforming Iona into a location that inspired and taught.

Somerled knew the impact of restoring Iona would go beyond his lifetime. He saw that under the guidance of a leader like Ua Brolcháin, Iona would become a symbol of endurance – a living testament to the strength of faith. His goal was to leave something that would endure beyond his lifetime, a legacy of Christian unity and cultural resilience that would endure long after his conquests had diminished, rather than to secure his power or make quick gains. Somerled was able to firmly establish his legacy via Iona in a cause that would endure and lead the Isles for many centuries.

Somerled's respect for Iona's heritage conveyed a strong message to both his supporters and detractors. His reverence for the sacred was an indication of his humility and a reminder that his strength extended beyond the force of his weapon. Somerled realised that his greatest strength came from identifying with something that spoke to his people's hearts and souls. He could promote unity via Iona that transcended territorial divisions and clan rivalries, one based on respect for the spiritual foundations of the land and a common faith.

Somerled's plans for Iona extended much beyond his personal sphere of influence. He was confident that a revived Iona led by Abbot Ua Brolcháin would live on as a symbol of knowledge and optimism. In addition to being a gesture, his summons to the abbot was a statement of the kind of kingdom he wished to leave behind and a legacy-making act. He was creating a legacy of unity and faith that would last for centuries, not focusing on the fleeting glory. Somerled saw in Iona the soul of his land – a place where Norse and Gaelic hearts beat as one, bound together by the cross and the spirit of something greater than any single ruler could embody.

Chapter 8

The Somerled Dynasty

Stories of clan ancestry, struggles for supremacy, and the legacies of influential figures abound in Scotland's history. Somerled stands out among these. In addition to insurrection and conquest, his life was also about family and the dynasty he established. Somerled's legacy persisted for a long time after his passing because of the connections he made and the descendants who maintained his goals.

His ancestors were some of the most influential people in the Western Highlands and Isles. Somerled's sons, Dugall, Ranald, and Angus, inherited his goals and lands. They created clans through their deeds that would have a lasting impact on Scottish history.

Over time, his ancestry gave rise to the Lords of the Isles, a somewhat independent family of kings who held considerable authority and were revered throughout the Hebrides and portions of the Scottish mainland. The lives, ties, and legacies of Somerled's family are examined in this chapter, along with their enduring influence on Scotland.

Marriage and Alliances

It was not just his military skill that propelled Somerled from a local chieftain to a strong maritime tyrant. Strategic partnerships, often formed through marriage, were another foundation of his success. An important turning point in his rise was his marriage to Ragnhild, the daughter of King Olaf Godredsson of Man and the Isles. This union involved more than just love or a personal bond; through a strategic partnership, Somerled's power was extended over the Hebrides and Scotland's west coast.

By marrying Ragnhild, Somerled consolidated his claim to the Isles, which had long been disputed between Norse and Gaelic groups. His affiliation with the Isle of Man's dominant Norse-Gaelic dynasty placed him in a position of influence across the Irish Sea. In addition to bringing aristocratic ancestry, Ragnhild also provided legitimacy, solidifying Somerled's position as a monarch with claims to Norse-controlled lands. Thanks to this marriage, he had a better base from which to contend with the Norse lords who controlled the Isles and established his dominance over them.

Somerled and Ragnhild: A Union of Power and Strategy

During the Middle Ages, marriage was a potent political instrument. Matrimonial alliances had the power to establish coalitions, strengthen territorial claims, and forge ties of allegiance – all of which were critical for survival and growth. Somerled knew this very well. By marrying Ragnhild, he gained, in addition to a wife, an alliance with a strong dynasty which ruled over the Isle of Man and the Hebrides. This action gave him legitimacy with both Norse and Gaelic subjects by allowing him to associate himself with Norse objectives while maintaining ties to his Gaelic heritage.

The political situation was unstable at the time. Several chieftains, monarchs, and lords were fighting for control of Scotland's and the Isles' western coast. Somerled had a tactical edge over opponents who might have otherwise seen him as an outsider or danger by marrying into the King of Man's court. He was able to bring the Gaelic and Norse groups under his control by using his marriage with Ragnhild as a bridge between their cultures. Control over his territories, which extended throughout the Hebrides and into portions of mainland Scotland, depended on this unity.

A pivotal moment in Somerled's ascent to power was his marriage to Ragnhild. Historians estimate that Somerled and Ragnhild were married somewhere in the middle of the twelfth century, most likely between 1140 and 1150. With Norse-Gaelic kings ruling over sections of Ireland, the Isle of Man, and Scotland's western coast, this was the height of Norse dominance in the Isles. Somerled gained credibility and a strategic presence throughout the area by marrying Ragnhild and establishing a direct relationship with a strong Norse dynasty.

Why Somerled Chose to Marry Ragnhild

Somerled made a planned political move when he chose Ragnhild, not just out of personal preference. Olaf Godredsson, Ragnhild's father, centralised authority in the Irish Sea by ruling the Kingdom of the Isles from the Isle of Man. Getting married into this family gave Somerled a lot of benefits. In addition to gaining access to allies who held sway in Norse-controlled regions, this coupling gave him a distinguished Norse ancestry. He was able to garner support from groups that might have otherwise seen him as an outsider thanks to this marriage, which also enhanced his claim to the Isles.[1]

Strengthening His Dynasty Through His Offspring

Somerled and Ragnhild's marriage resulted in offspring who would continue their father's goals and increase his impact. Dugald and Ranald were two of their children who would later start their own lines and carry on Somerled's tradition. Due to their

1. 'Irish Dalriada, Dunseverick Castle and Ossain's Grave'. Macinnes.org, 2024, macinnes.org/dalriada/dalriada.html. Accessed 10 Dec. 2024.

dual Gaelic and Norse ancestry, Dugald and Ranald had the legitimacy required to govern a multicultural populace. Stability in an area with conflicting cultural influences depended on their capacity to demand respect from both Gaelic clans and Norse settlers, thanks to their mixed heritage.

Ranald and Dugald played crucial roles in the Isles. Later, Dugald would establish Clan MacDougall in Argyll, which grew to be one of the most powerful clans in the area. On the other hand, Clan Donald, which would grow to be one of the strongest and most resilient Scottish clans, was founded by Ranald. More than just inheriting his holdings, Somerled's sons broadened his perspective and influenced Scottish politics for many years. Somerled's legacy evolved into the influential line known as the Lords of the Isles through these successors, extending much beyond his lifetime.

Dugald: Founder of Clan MacDougall

A sizeable chunk of Somerled's territory was passed down to his eldest son, Dugald. Dugald seized Argyll, a rocky and strategically significant area that would eventually become Clan MacDougall's heartland following Somerled's passing. As the forerunner of this powerful clan, Dugald played a key role in establishing the family's dominance in western Scotland. To establish their dominance over neighbouring regions and defend their own territory, his descendants, the MacDougalls, constructed Dunollie Castle close to Oban.

Clan MacDougall developed into a powerful force under Dugald's direction. His family was heavily involved in the Wars of Scottish Independence, frequently siding with the English monarchy against Robert the Bruce. Although useful for retaining control over Bruce's army, this relationship with England eventually caused friction with other Bruce-aligned Scottish clans. Clan MacDougall suffered consequences following Bruce's triumph and accession to the throne, which made their standing in Argyll weaker. Nevertheless, the clan was able to endure and hold onto power, and Dugald's lineage's legacy is still felt throughout Scottish history.

The MacDougall family, Dugald's ancestors, are renowned for both their cultural achievements and military prowess. They helped maintain the local culture despite pressure from Norman and Scottish influences by supporting Gaelic customs and patronising the arts. Dugald's leadership and the fundamental role he played in establishing Somerled's dynasty are reflected in Clan MacDougall's heritage.[2]

Ranald: Progenitor of Clan Donald and Clan MacRuaridh

The second son of Somerled, Ranald, was the ancestor of Clan Donald, also called Clan MacDonald, which would grow to be one of the most influential clans in Scottish history. By establishing his own line, which would rule the political landscape

2. C. Ellis. (2020). 'Impressions of a twelfth-century maritime ruler – Somerled: Viking warrior, clan chieftain or traitor to the Scottish king'. *Northern Studies*, 51, 1–14. Retrieved from https://www.ssns.org.uk/wp-content/uploads/2022/02/01_Ellis_2020_Vol_51_pp_1-14.pdf

of the Western Isles for generations, Ranald inherited estates in the Hebrides and portions of mainland Scotland. In addition to extending their power throughout the Isles, Ranald's descendants established the basis for their title as the 'Lords of the Isles,' which gave them some degree of autonomy from the Scottish Crown.

Donald, Ranald's son, would later combine Clan Donald's territories, giving the clan its name and making it a powerful force in the area. Clan Donald gained notoriety for controlling trade routes and projecting influence over the Hebrides thanks to its vast lands and strong navy. By fusing Gaelic culture with Norse ancestry, the clan also forged a strong Gaelic identity that struck a deep chord with the Ilses' populace. Clan Donald made a substantial cultural contribution by supporting Gaelic poetry, music, and art, which helped revive Gaelic customs during a period when Norman influence was encroaching on Scotland.

A lesser-known branch of Ranald's family, the MacRuaridhs, were descended from his son Ruari. Clan MacRuaridh, often known as the MacRuaridhs, possessed the islands of Garmoran and Uist in the northern Hebrides. Despite not attaining Clan Donald's level of influence, the MacRuaridhs were important regional figures in their own way. They continued to rule over portions of the Isles, which bolstered Somerled's descendants' general power and sway. Their lands would eventually be assimilated into Clan Donald, extending Clan Donald's dominion and consolidating Somerled's heritage under a single, strong clan.

Angus: Guardian of the Southern Hebrides

Sections of Kintyre and maybe sections of Islay were among the holdings in the southern Hebrides that Somerled's youngest son, Angus, acquired. Angus was instrumental in preserving Somerled's power in the southern regions of his realm, although he was less well-known in history than his brothers. His dominion over Kintyre and Islay served as a vital connection in Somerled's family's network of lands, tying the southern Hebrides to the larger Norse-Gaelic realm.

Angus's successors remained in charge of the southern Isles, acting as regional chiefs and preserving Somerled's line's sway over Kintyre and the neighbouring islands. In the eyes of the local Norse-Gaelic aristocracy, Angus's line was revered even though they did not develop into a strong clan like the MacDougalls or the MacDonalds. They made sure Somerled's legacy persisted in these communities by managing relationships with nearby families and being actively involved in local government.

According to certain historical records, Angus's descendants eventually got embroiled in disputes with Somerled's other family branches. Somerled's heirs were divided and had conflicting interests, which resulted in rivalries which reduced their combined might. Nonetheless, the Angus line continued to exist, which helped Somerled's reign in the southern Hebrides remain stable overall.[3]

3. R. A. McDonald. (2006). 'The Western Gàidhealtachd in the Middle Ages. Scotland: The Making and Unmaking of the Nation, c. 1100', 1707, 65–89. https://doi.org/10.1515/9781474468862-010

Challenges in a Turbulent Norse-Gaelic World

It was not easy to form coalitions in the Norse-Gaelic civilisation. Somerled gained strong allies by marrying Ragnhild, but he also became entangled in a complex web of political rivalry and familial ties. With opposing chieftains and kings constantly switching allegiances and fighting for control, Norse-Gaelic culture was one of perpetual upheaval. Every marriage union has advantages as well as disadvantages. A family may become entangled in power struggles, disputes, and feuds that last for several generations.

Somerled found himself in precarious political ground because of his new familial links. He had to keep up his Gaelic relationships to keep the support of his own people, even though he was now obligated to the Norse lords of Man. It took a deft diplomatic technique to strike a balance between these two allegiances. Every choice he made ran the danger of offending someone, which could lead to conflict and undermine his authority. As Somerled sought to preserve peace and stability in an area that was always on the verge of conflict, this delicate balancing act became a crucial component of his strategy.

He also carefully considered the marital alliances he made for his children. Somerled wanted to guarantee his sons' positions and increase his family's power by marrying them into powerful households. Every marriage served to solidify his dynasty, increase his authority, and guarantee the continuation of his family. These coalitions weren't always reliable, though. Internal conflicts could easily result from shifting allegiances and familial strife, making it difficult to keep his own soldiers united.[4]

The Lords of the Isles: Semi-Autonomous Rulers of the Hebrides

The Lords of the Isles were the descendants of Ranald, particularly through Clan Donald. In mediaeval Scotland, this title denoted a special position. The Lords governed a maritime kingdom that included the Hebrides and portions of the western mainland, with a degree of autonomy comparable to that of the Scottish Crown. Frequently functioning as though they were sovereign princes rather than dependents of the Scottish monarch, they were semi-independent rulers with their own courts, ships, and alliances.

Somerled's own maritime skills had left them with a strong navy, which contributed to the Lords of the Isles' dominance. They had a strategic edge in both trade and combat thanks to their fleet, which gave them control over important sea lanes connecting Scotland, Ireland, and Norway. They were able to engage in long-distance trade, defend their borders, and have an impact on the politics of the larger British Isles thanks to their naval prowess. The Scottish Crown, which depended on the assistance of the Lords to preserve regional stability, found them important due to their control over the Hebrides' waters.

4. Hebridean Genealogy Society. (2020). 'Kinship and Clan Governance Under Somerled'. Retrieved from www.hebrideangenealogy.co.uk

The Lords of the Isles established a distinctive form of government by combining Norse and Gaelic traditions. They combined aspects of Norse maritime governance with Gaelic customs and rules. Poets, musicians, and intellectuals were honoured at their courts, which developed into hubs of Gaelic culture. During a period when Norman and Anglo-Saxon influences were encroaching on Scotland, the Lords helped to maintain and enhance the Gaelic cultural legacy by supporting monastic institutions and patronising the arts. As a symbol of defiance against outside pressure to adhere to the feudal standards enforced by the Scottish monarchs, their court on Islay became a focal point for Gaelic identity.

A Complex Relationship with the Scottish Crown

Despite having a great deal of autonomy, the Lords of the Isles frequently had a tense relationship with the Scottish Crown. They occasionally served as important allies, defending the Crown against rival Scottish aristocrats or outside threats. At other periods, they were enemies who challenged the Crown's authority by claiming their independence. The careful balance of power that Somerled himself had perfected – loyalty when it was convenient, independence when it was required – was represented in this fluctuating relationship.

The early fifteenth century saw one of the most prominent battles between the Scottish Crown and the Lords of the Isles. A strong Lord of the Isles, Donald of Islay, claimed the Earldom of Ross, a position that would greatly increase his power on the mainland. Tensions turned into an open clash because the Crown perceived this as a direct challenge to its authority. Donald led an army to the Battle of Harlaw in 1411, where he engaged in a brutal conflict with royalist soldiers. Despite the lack of a clear winner, the conflict demonstrated the Lords' overwhelming strength and determination to oppose the Scottish monarchy.

For centuries, the Lords of the Isles were able to maintain a considerable amount of independence despite these disputes. The Scottish Crown was unable to completely incorporate their lands into the kingdom, therefore continuing to rule the Hebrides and maintain their naval superiority. But because of their independence, they were also singled out by the Crown's expanding desire to consolidate control. To weaken the Lords' power, succeeding Scottish kings used economic pressure, military conquest, and political ties.[5]

Governance and Cultural Patronage: A Dual Legacy

Somerled's dynasty was not solely successful because of its military might. Even during stormy times, the Lords of the Isles maintained a stable society by using a governing model that blended Gaelic and Norse features. They acknowledged

5. W. D. H. Sellar. (1966). 'The Origins and Ancestry of Somerled'. *The Scottish Historical Review*, 45(140), 123–42. https://doi.org/10.3366/shr.1966.45.140.123

the Lordship but adopted a decentralised system of governance that permitted local chieftains to hold onto their positions of authority. Clan chiefs who looked to the Lords of the Isles for protection and guidance were more loyal because of this governance structure, which struck a balance between local autonomy and centralised leadership.

Additionally, the Lords of the Isles were well-known for supporting monastery establishments, especially those in the Hebrides. To preserve the region's spiritual and cultural continuity, they provided funding to churches and monasteries. Monastic communities served as learning hubs, created manuscripts, and protected the Gaelic language. By giving the Lordship a degree of stability and reaffirming the position of the Lords as guardians of Gaelic culture, this religious patronage improved the social structure of the Isles.

The Hebrides developed into a hub for Gaelic poetry, music, and art during the Lords' reign. They brought intellectuals, poets, and bards from all over the region to their court on Islay. By strengthening their allegiance to the Lordship and conserving customs that were in danger of being eclipsed by Norman and Anglo-Saxon influences on the mainland, this cultural blossoming helped the Isles' residents develop a feeling of shared identity. The Lords' support of Gaelic arts strengthened their position as guardians of the area's distinctive cultural character and protectors of Gaelic heritage.

Decline and Fall: The End of the Lordship of the Isles

The Lords of the Isles gradually but inevitably began to fall. The increasingly centralised and strong Scottish monarchy viewed the Isles' independence as a barrier to total authority over the realm. The Crown used various tactics, such as military operations, political scheming, and alliances with rival clans, to undermine the Lords during the fifteenth century. As a result of this constant pressure, the Lords' independence progressively diminished, and their authority steadily decreased.

The last straw was delivered in 1493 when Scotland's King James IV called the last Lord of the Isles, John MacDonald, to stand before him. John lost his titles and estates because of his refusal to submit to the Crown's authority. This put an end to Somerled's successors' nearly four centuries of semi-independent control over the Isles by essentially dissolving the Lordship of the Isles. A unique chapter in Scottish history, when a Gaelic-Norse dynasty ruled over an area that defied feudal conventions, came to an end with the dissolution.

Somerled's Enduring Legacy

The loss of the Lordship did not diminish the influence of Somerled's dynasty. His descendants have continued to have important roles in Scottish history, especially through Clan Donald. Clan Donald and Clan MacDougall continued to play a significant role in Scottish politics, culture, and identity throughout the Highlands and Isles. Even after the Lordship itself had collapsed, the customs that the Lords of the Isles had established – their support of Gaelic arts, their naval might, and their dedication to Gaelic identity – persisted.

The Long-Term Impact of Somerled's Marriage to Ragnhild

As crucial to Somerled's success as his military victories was his union with Ragnhild. He acquired the political clout required to lay the groundwork for his future reign through this union. The union created the foundation for a long-lasting dynasty that would rule Scotland with authority and respect. Somerled was able to secure his family's affluence for generations by transforming personal relationships into potent instruments of influence through his ability to negotiate the political complications of marriage alliances.

This alliance's impact reverberated across the centuries. Through Ranald, Somerled's descendants became the Lords of the Isles, strong, semi-autonomous kings who ruled over western Scotland and the Hebrides. Within their realm, they operated as autonomous princes, frequently contesting the Scottish Crown's authority. Despite pressure from the Scottish monarchy, their control created a distinctive culture that persisted by fusing Norse maritime skills with Gaelic customs.

The Lords of the Isles continued to represent Somerled's foresight and strategic thought despite their eventual downfall. Even though their influence eventually waned, they made a lasting impression on Scottish history.

Somerled's Legacy in Mediaeval Scottish Politics

The significance of strategic alliances in mediaeval Scottish politics is underscored by the legacy of Somerled's marriage ties. These unions were more than just personal connections; they were deliberately constructed arrangements that aided in securing lands, winning allegiance, and fortifying claims to power.

The tale of Somerled serves as a reminder of how important partnerships were to the mediaeval struggle for dominance. To succeed, leaders required more than just fighters; they also needed strategic alliances that could bring disparate regions together and establish support systems. Marriage was as important to Somerled's success as any military operation. With the help of his connections, he was able to establish a kingdom, and his children would continue his legacy under his direction.

Looking at Somerled's life, it is evident that his achievements came from both his own strength and his capacity for networking. He had an ambitious plan for a united Norse-Gaelic monarchy, which he put into action through his marriage to Ragnhild. His alliances were more than just short-term agreements; they were long-lasting ties that influenced Scottish politics for generations. Somerled's legacy extended beyond the territory he subjugated; it also included the family and relationships he formed, which would have a lasting impact on history.

Chapter 9
The Final Campaign and Fall

In mediaeval Scotland, the year 1164 was a turning moment marked by territorial conflicts and mounting power struggles. Scotland was a fractured territory split between the semi-independent Highland and Isles rulers and the monarchy's centralised aspirations. Under Somerled's authority, the western seaboard functioned as a separate political and cultural arena, combining Norse maritime customs with Gaelic clan systems. Here, Somerled had become powerful, confronting the ambitions of the Scottish Crown to unite its dominance as well as the Norwegian rulers claiming the Isles.

The Scottish king Malcolm IV had great difficulties establishing control. Years of internal turmoil and outside threats had undermined his country. Beginning at the age of twelve, Malcolm's rule concentrated on restoring order and fortifying the Crown. The Highlands and Isles stayed essentially outside the reach of the monarchy to the north and west. Often seeing royal participation as a danger, the lords of these areas – including Somerled – operated with great freedom. Norway's claims to the Isles dramatically changed the political scene and added still another level of stress to an already delicate situation.

The growing power of Somerled made him a major challenge to Malcolm's objectives. By means of alliances and conquest, he had united a maritime kingdom, therefore challenging the power of the Crown. His leadership gathered several Gaelic clans and Norse immigrants under one banner. This togetherness made him a tough opponent who would not be readily subdued. Malcolm's government started arranging reliable allies like Walter Fitz Alan, the High Steward of Scotland, to guard crucial areas like Renfrew by 1164. This campaign sought to control Somerled's impact and stop his spread onto the mainland.

That year, the mounting conflicts between Somerled and the monarchy reached a breaking point. Seeking to increase his authority, Somerled prepared for a bold war against the Scots. The political climate had got to a breaking point, and both sides were preparing for a forceful clash over western seaboard authority. Against a landscape of fractured loyalties and regional aspirations, this collision signalled the end of Somerled's rule.

Early in 1164, Somerled started getting ready for his assault on the Scottish mainland. His aspirations were now beyond defending his realm. Too great to overlook was the chance to challenge the Scottish Crown, increase his influence, and establish rule over the Clyde area. Driven to deliver a fatal blow, he called men from all around his large territory, from the Norse colonists of the Isles and the Gaelic clans of the Highlands. Argyll, Skye, Islay, and beyond were among the places where the call to arms rang. Men lured by loyalty, mutual ambition, or the promise of riches gathered behind Somerled's banner by land and water.

The fleet formed was among the biggest ever seen in the western oceans. Along the shore, several dozen longships, sleek and battle-ready, lay waiting. Designed for speed and power, these ships embodied the height of Norse-Gaelic workmanship by fusing local inventiveness with Scandinavian ideas. Equipped with swords, axes, and spears, warriors filed onto them in groups. Defending the sides of the ships, glinting in the weak sunlight, were shields. The sound of preparation permeated the air: gruff directions from captains, clashing metal, and a rhythmic chant of sailors getting ready for their vessels. With measured accuracy, Somerled supervised the mobilisation to make sure soldiers, supplies, and weapons were ready for the trip ahead.

This was not a raid; it was an invasion. The army, said to be thousands strong, gathered on the western seaboard. Norse and Gaelic fighters united forces, each seasoned by years of fighting on land and sea. From the Isles, the force sailed east toward the Clyde, cutting across the frigid Hebrides. Emblazoned with clan and kin insignia, the sails billowed in the great winds. A symbol of Somerled's might and ambition, the sight of the fleet coming across the waves was both terrible and magnificent.

Arriving near Renfrew, Somerled's army rushed swiftly to seize control. The troops advanced with regimented, exact motions and a trained degree of efficiency. While leaders guided their soldiers inland, ready for the confrontation defining the campaign, warriors locked the perimeter. Scouts were sent ahead to survey the terrain while Somerled consulted with his commanders. His plan was clear. The aim would be Renfrew, the home of Walter Fitz Alan, High Steward of Scotland. Retaking it would severely damage the Scottish Crown's power over the West and undermine its influence in the East, therefore strengthening Somerled's position.

Somerled's army was strong, but the Renfrew defenders were not unprepared. Walter Fitz Alan had used the time to bolster his position after being advised of Somerled's aims. His tiny but disciplined troop had scoured the nearby ground, spotting natural advantages fit for counteraction against Somerled's bigger army. Familiar with the territory, Fitz Alan's troops had selected positions meant to impede and disturb an oncoming force.

Tension started to rise as Somerled's troops started their march toward Renfrew. From the margins of the battlefield, scouts on both sides observed one another's motions. Confident, Somerled proceeded; his warriors were battle-hardened and orderly. But Fitz Alan waited silently, his soldiers hidden in a defensive posture. The struggle deciding the course of the western seaboard was about to start.

The Battle of Renfrew

The fight started at daylight, Somerled's army moving upon Renfrew in precisely ordered rows. Before them, the ground opened out, a combination of low hills, marshy meadows, and small pathways. The morning air was silent and heavy, just the muffled noises of footsteps on damp ground and the odd weapon clang. With their banners hoisted high and their shields creating a glistening steel wall, the army moved with assurance. The Renfrew defenders had already set up their positions far away. Though he had a weaker army, Walter Fitz Alan had picked the ground deliberately, knowing its benefits.

The first clash struck as Somerled's fighters arrived. From the surrounding forests, a concealed number of Fitz Alan's soldiers burst with arrows into the oncoming troops. The attack forced Somerled to reorganise since it upset their front lines. As Gaelic fighters raised their shields to create a defensive barrier against the missiles, shouts resounded over the field. Somerled himself urged his soldiers forward from the front. His voice carried across the field, commanding discipline and courage. The archers retreated into the trees, but the disruption had delayed the main advance.

Somerled's forces pushed forward toward the heart of the battlefield. The terrain slowed their progress. The recently moist, swampy ground made it difficult for the heavily equipped fighters to stay on their feet. Seizing this, the Renfrew defenders launched another attack while Somerled's troops battled to move. From higher ground, Fitz Alan's knights charged with exact lance aim. Steel rang out as Somerled's men faced the charge head-on, their axes and swords slicing through the columns of mounted attackers. Though resilient, Somerled's forces started to suffer from the uneven ground and constant assaults.

Amid the mayhem, the tide of war started to change. More Scottish recruits surfaced, hiding behind hills and natural barriers. On several fronts, Somerled's army discovered they were surrounded. Under the constant strain, his army started to lose cohesion. Trying to retreat to safer areas, groups of fighters broke ranks. Sensing the threat, Somerled worked to inspire his troops. He stayed between the lines, his presence a counterbalance. His shield showed fresh marks from the combat, and his blade darkened with enemy blood. While some were motivated by his efforts to reorganise, the advantage was gone.

Somerled's posture grew more hazardous as the fight waged on. There are different stories of the last minutes. Some claim he drove a charge across the Scottish ranks, his weapon slashing foes as he advanced. Others say he was struck down in the turmoil of a retreat, his body surrounded by devoted fighters who fought to the death to guard their master. Though these remain unproven, there are rumours of treachery and of comrades who left him at the pivotal point. Somerled apparently collapsed on the battlefield, and his death rocked his troops.

The morale of Somerled's army crumbled with his absence. What had been a precisely ordered invasion turned into a disorderly rout. To get to the protection of the ships, the warriors dropped their positions and ran back toward the coast. Renfrew's defenders hunted them down, clearing stragglers and making sure the invading army couldn't reorganise. By midnight, the field was covered in corpses, once-proud Somerled army banners trampled across the ground, soaked in blood.

The Division of Somerled's Kingdom

Along with ending an era, the fall of Somerled in 1164 started a period of great conflict and disintegration that tore apart the cohesive kingdom he had laboriously created. For decades, Somerled had been the pillar of a strong Norse-Gaelic kingdom, balancing the conflicting forces of the Scottish Crown, the Norwegian monarchy, and the fiercely autonomous clans of the Western Highlands and Isles. His passing left a power vacuum in that his successors lacked the vision and uniting authority he had personified, therefore making it impossible to fill. With long-lasting effects on Scotland's western coast, the political, cultural, and territorial cohesiveness of his kingdom rapidly gave way to strife.

Held together by Somerled's great leadership, military might, and strategic diplomacy, Somerled's realm had been a fascinating mix of Norse and Gaelic traditions. By means of a mix of conquest and well-planned alliances – including his marriage to Ragnhild, daughter of Olaf Godredsson, King of Man and the Isles – he had extended his rule. Along with supporting his claim in important areas, this marriage helped him to establish himself as a strong middleman between Norse and Gaelic groups. His authority over the Hebrides, Argyll, and portions of the Scottish mainland had been further cemented by his naval might and capacity for command of loyalty from several factions. But this careful equilibrium hinged totally on Somerled's power. The weak unity he had attained started to fall apart with his death.

Somerled divided his lands and titles among his three sons, Dugald, Ranald, and Angus. Although each son claimed a piece of the kingdom, the divisions went beyond mere geography. They mirrored different allegiances and priorities, as well as mounting conflict between the Norse and Gaelic identities Somerled had painstakingly reconciled. These cracks would shape the Western Highlands and Isles for generations.

Dugald and the Rise of Clan MacDougall

Dugald, Somerled's eldest son, inherited Argyll's tough heartlands and strategically important coastal areas. From these areas, Dugald would build one of the most powerful clans in western Scotland, Clan MacDougall. Subsequently, Dugald used Oban, Dunollie, and areas of Lorn as power bases to establish his control. Though his brothers disputed his rule over the islands, he also claimed several of the Inner Hebrides. Dugald tried to preserve his father's heritage of independence from both the Scottish Crown and Norwegian influence, but conflicting family groups and outside influences regularly threatened his position.

Clan MacDougall grew well-known over time for its involvement in the Wars of Scottish Independence, usually supporting the English Crown against Robert the Bruce. After Bruce's triumph, this loyalty finally resulted in their fall in importance; nonetheless, Dugald's descendants carried great power in the Highlands for decades.

Dunollie Castle, built based on Dugald's authority, is evidence of the ongoing legacy of Somerled's eldest son.

Ranald and the Foundations of Clan Donald

Ranald, Somerled's second son, inherited much of the Hebrides, including important islands like Islay, Jura, and portions of Skye. He started Clan Donald, often known as Clan MacDonald, which would develop into one of the strongest clans in Scottish history. Ranald's branch kept its Norse-Gaelic background and developed strong maritime ties, which helped them control trade routes and project a great naval force. Eventually, his successors would create the semi-independent Lords of the Isles, who controlled Scotland's western coast with great autonomy from the Scottish Crown.

Though their relationship with the Scottish king remained tense, Clan Donald's grip over the Hebrides and their naval might helped them sustain Somerled's ambition of a maritime empire. Combining Gaelic and Norse customs, the Lords of the Isles created a unique cultural identity that reverberated over the Highlands and Isles. Clan Donald grew to be a formidable force under Ranald's descendants, yet they could not quite preserve the unity their ancestors had attained.

Angus and the Southern Hebrides

The youngest of Somerled's sons, Angus, was given charge over the southern Hebrides, covering probably Islay and Kintyre. Unlike his brothers, Angus's area was less than that of a well-known clan such as the MacDonalds or the MacDougalls. Still, his key locations linked the islands with the mainland. Apart from pressure from their more powerful siblings, Angus's descendants fought to retain their position from outside forces, including the Scottish Crown and Norwegian invaders.

Eventually, Angus's line became caught in conflicts with the other branches of Somerled's family, feeding the internecine struggle and weakening the kingdom. Over time, Clan Donald took over parts of Angus's possessions, showing how challenging it was to keep autonomous control in an erratic territory.

The Aftermath of Somerled's Demise

The split of Somerled's dominion among his sons signalled the start of a stormy chapter for the Western Highlands and Isles. Somerled's diplomatic and leadership skills had produced cohesiveness which was lost and replaced by a fractured political scene where rival groups fought for influence. This segmentation of power had several key consequences:

Resurgence of Norwegian influence: When Somerled left, the Isles saw a fresh drive from Norway to retake authority over the area. Taking advantage of Somerled's weakened realm, Norwegian leaders reclaimed territory once under their control. Once a cohesive maritime empire, it started to break apart into a patchwork of smaller, less stable territories, each more susceptible to outside control.

Scottish monarchy's westward expansion: Under Malcolm IV and his successors, the Scottish Crown grabbed the chance presented by Somerled's death to spread their authority into the West. Though largely accomplished through deliberate alliances and military operations, the fragmentation of Somerled's kingdom made it simpler for the monarchs to exert authority over the Highlands and Isles. Local autonomy began to progressively fade in the years following Somerled's death as the Scottish king consolidated its hold on the territory.

Internal rivalries and clan feuds: Somerled's dominion was divided among his sons, fostering the seeds of enduring conflicts. Seeking to unite their authority, Dugald, Ranald, and Angus each caused territorial and influence disputes. These conflicts not only undermined the Isles' cohesiveness but also took funds and focus away from resisting outside threats. Generations of rivalry among the descendants of Somerled would continue to cause instability that marked the area in the years that followed.

Cultural Shifts and the decline of religious patronage: Somerled's passing had cultural and theological effects as well. He had supported monastic establishments, using his patronage of the Church to confirm his authority and advance cultural unity. The momentum for such initiatives dropped without his guidance. New religious centre buildings stagnated, and the Church's influence got caught in the power conflicts of Somerled's heirs. This drop in religious attendance signalled a change from the coherent cultural vision Somerled's rule had defined.

The Battle of Renfrew: A Turning Point

A turning point in Scottish history, the Battle of Renfrew saw Somerled meet his death. The campaign had been painstakingly scheduled, Somerled gathering a powerful force of ships and fighters to attack the Scottish Crown. Along with increasing his realm, he wanted to establish his authority over Malcolm IV and the mainland. Under Walter Fitz Alan, however, the Scottish defenders outmanoeuvred Somerled's army using topography, strategy, and local knowledge. For Somerled's troops, who were more used to sea warfare and island skirmishes, the swampy ground around Renfrew proved challenging.

Somerled died from the mayhem of the combat, along with probable betrayals among his troops. His fall signalled the end of his war and the moral breakdown of his army, which compelled a retreat. Apart from a personal tragedy, Somerled's death on the battlefield marked a symbolic turning point toward the end of an era. It was the turning point that allowed the Scottish king to increase his authority over the western coast, therefore changing the political scene of mediaeval Scotland.

The memory of Somerled's leadership was invoked in many ways in the next centuries. To some, he stood for a golden period of freedom and unity when the Western Highlands and Isles were a potent force opposing outside control. For others, his passing and the division of his kingdom underlined the frailty of charismatic leadership and the difficulties of a large and varied territory.

The divisions among his heirs and the return of outside powers finally guaranteed that the united kingdom he had created would not last. His political and cultural impact, though, continued. His vision of a Norse-Gaelic maritime kingdom went on through the ascent of Clan Donald and the Lords of the Isles, even as it changed to suit the demands of modern society.

Chapter 10

The Legacy of the Sea King

Harp in hand, a Gaelic bard is performing in a smoky firelit hall beside Argyll's bleak coastlines. The wall shadows created by the flickering illumination of the hearth freeze the room in quiet. Around him sit chieftains, clansmen, and fishermen. Sea breezes and conflicts have worn their faces. The bard starts his reading. His voice swings like waves breaking on the coast outside.

He relates to Somerled, the great Sea King, whose adventures resound over the islands even centuries after his death. His voice quakes with desire. He describes the amazing birth of the leader who brought the broken Hebrides together, confronted the Norse invaders, and opposed Scottish Crown aspirations. In the songs of the bard, Somerled transcends mere man. He starts to be a legend. He stands for cultural pride, tenacity, and freedom. The bard guarantees that Somerled's legacy will never fade by addressing the memories of a hero.

For the Highland and Isles Gaels, Somerled represents more than just historical significance. His name conveys leadership and the enduring power of defiance. It represents the enduring strength of Norse-Gaelic culture. Through the words of bards like this one, his story remains part of the cultural fabric of Scotland.

Legends of Somerled

Beyond historical records, Somerled enters the world of legend and leaves a cultural legacy that persists long after his death. Although his life took place in the harsh reality of mediaeval power conflicts, his legacy has expanded well beyond the total of his achievements. Earlier chapters have detailed his fights against Norse invaders and the Scottish Crown, his ascent from a regional chieftain to a strong maritime monarch, and his attempts to unify split clans.

The narrative of Somerled has endured centuries of oral history. Through bards, poets, and storytellers who turned his life into a heroic and leadership narrative, generations have maintained it. In Highland Gaelic melodies, he is regarded as a fierce warrior and guardian of his people. Poems and stories depicting the values and hardships of the Gaelic and Norse-Gaelic societies help to capture his life. These legends have made sure Somerled is regarded as a symbol of resilience and cultural pride as much as a leader.

Examining how his influence has been spun into the cultural fabric of the Highlands and Isles, this chapter transcends the physical successes of his rule into the intangible world of memory. Somerled's legacy lives not because of the countries he conquered or the wars he waged but through the way his narrative inspires people who came after him. Deeply ingrained in Scotland's cultural consciousness, he speaks for ideas of tenacity, independence, and cultural strength.

A Birth Shrouded in Prophecy

Among the most enduring stories in Gaelic culture is the prophecy around Somerled's birth. According to his mother, Ragnhild, wife of Gillebride of Clan Gabran, she dreamed and saw visions predicting the remarkable fate of her unborn son. A druidic seer is said to have foreseen Somerled as a saviour of the Gaelic people, destined to unite dispersed clans and oppose foreign tyranny. In some variants of the story, celestial events, including a comet or brilliant star, showed up on his birth night. These omens were taken as divine signals approving his future brilliance.

Along with narratives of celestial events around his birth, this vision gave Somerled's life a sense of divine direction. Although his family was modest yet honourable, the prophecy raised him beyond others of his day. For his supporters, this confirmed him as a destined leader. In mediaeval Gaelic society, where kings and fighters were sometimes presented as chosen characters whose lives were directed by divine will, these stories were rather prevalent.

Heroes in Celtic mythology sometimes had miraculous or predetermined births. These tales align with mythical people like King Arthur and Cú Chulainn, whose fates were moulded by prophecies. The fables around Somerled presented him as more than just a mortal king. They made him a figure of heavenly significance, therefore strengthening his power in an era when legitimacy and leadership were sometimes challenged.

Modern historians think these stories might have been political propaganda used to support Somerled's ascent during the twelfth century. The picture of divine favour appealed to Christian communities in the Isles and the Gaelic people, who appreciated their druidic background. Combining Celtic and Christian ideas, the prophecy story represented the coming together of Norse-Gaelic identities under his direction.

The Battle of Largs: A Posthumous Tale

Though factually untrue, one of the more fascinating legends about Somerled ties him to the Battle of Largs in 1263, a key war between the Norse under King Hákon Hákonarson and the Scots under King Alexander III. Oral history holds that this struggle, which occurred about a century following Somerled's death, is occasionally retroactively linked to him. Somerled is shown in these tales as a valiant man guiding the Gaels in their fight against Viking invaders. The narrative emphasises Somerled's status as a champion of sovereignty and a symbol of Gaelic resistance, even though historical records show this to be unachievable. Representing not only his own era but also later efforts for independence and autonomy, this mythic link shows how his significance grew beyond life.

The Magical Galley

As a nautical king, Somerled's mythos revolves mostly around the legend of his magical galley. Built of wood claimed to have been blessed or enchanted by the spirits of the Otherworld, this ship was supposedly faster and nimbler than any other vessel of its day. It was claimed to be able to easily traverse turbulent waves, allowing Somerled to rule the western coast of Scotland and the Hebrides. In other variants of the narrative, the galley appeared nearly alive and answered Somerled's orders immediately, directed by magical forces.

Somerled's nautical inventions are historically somewhat well recorded. His fleet brought Norse longship ideas along with Gaelic workmanship. These hybrid boats were faster, lighter, and more fit for both raiding and troop transportation. They let him seize vital maritime trade routes and outmanoeuvre more sizeable Norse fleets.

The story of the magical galley gives these technical developments divine favour. It captures the Gaelic perspective whereby control over nature, especially the erratic seas, symbolised divine or supernatural power. The magical ship stood for both Somerled's unparalleled maritime might and his capacity to shield his people from alien dangers.

The Fairy Banner

Among the most intriguing and often recounted stories of Somerled is the Bratach Sith, sometimes known as the Fairy Banner. The fairies bestowed upon Somerled the banner, identifying him as the selected guardian of the Isles. The banner was supposed to have a magical ability, giving its bearer military triumph. Still, its authority could only be called three times. It is stated that Somerled revealed it during two pivotal conflicts, each time displaying amazing success against insurmountable challenges.

One story has the banner raised during a naval conflict between a Norse force. Somerled raised the banner, facing almost defeat, and set off an unexpected and strong storm. While his own fleet remained unharmed, the storm wrecked the enemy ships. The last application of the banner is still unknown. Some accounts of the narrative assert it was never utilised again, wasting its ultimate power.

Historians speculate that the Bratach Sith might have been a real object, perhaps a highly ornamented banner representing Somerled's power and motivating his fighters. The concept of a strong relic with limited use reflects ideas in Celtic folklore, where circumstances typically restrict magical talents. This myth captures the way Somerled's historical advocacy of Gaelic independence combined with spiritual ideas.

The Elemental Summoner: Commanding Nature

Another common motif in the stories around Somerled's life is his capacity to rule the elements. Stories tell how he called storms to disperse enemy fleets or quieted choppy waves to guarantee his own ships could pass safely. In one such story, Somerled conjured up a tempest that destroyed the enemy ships before they could land from standing on a cliff overlooking an incoming Norse fleet and with a raised hand and a Gaelic prayer.

This myth links Somerled to old Celtic customs, in which druids and leaders were thought to have a magical relationship with the natural world. Particularly, the sea was a holy and terrifying power in Norse-Gaelic society. Somerled is shown as not only a master of naval warfare but also as a person with a strong spiritual link to the land and sea he governed by commanding the elements.

The background of this myth is Somerled's naval plan. Knowing the coastline topography of the Isles helped him take advantage of tides and weather, outmanoeuvring less experienced enemies. The mythologising of these strategies into superhuman achievements captures the wonder his colleagues felt toward his leadership.

The Duel of Wits with a Viking Sorcerer: A Clash of Cultures

In one of the more esoteric stories, Somerled is claimed to have engaged a Norse sorcerer in a wits and magic combat. To create a storm that would wipe out Somerled's fleet, the sorcerer tried to curse Somerled by writing runes on a stone and throwing it into the sea. But Somerled, drawing on old Gaelic spiritual traditions, performed a holy prayer and threw blessed herbs over the sea to fight the curse. The storm passed, and the sorcerer fell from his own magic and turned against him.

This story represents the spiritual and cultural struggle between the Norse and Gaelic worlds during Somerled's lifetime. While Somerled's counter-spell captures the oral and ceremonial customs of Gaelic spirituality, the sorcerer's use of runes illustrates the Norse belief in the magical power of written symbols. The narrative supports Somerled's position as guardian of Gaelic identity and unifier of its cultural legacy.

The Vision of Iona: A Divine Mandate

One of the most spiritually important stories is about Somerled's trip to Iona, the historic Christian monastery established by St. Columba. Disturbed by questions about his authority, Somerled supposedly prayed at the shrine of the saint and had a vision. Appearing to him, St. Columba urged him to go on his task of bringing the Isles under fair and holy control. Inspired by this idea, Somerled sponsored the building of monasteries such as Saddell Abbey, hence increasing his patronage of the Church.

Somerled's allegiance to the Church was historically a calculated step toward power consolidation. Aligning himself with the Church helped him to validate his authority and win the acceptance of Christian communities in the Isles. But the narrative of the vision at Iona presents Somerled as a divinely directed leader who matched martial desire with religious dedication, casting this union in a spiritual light.

Supernatural Powers and Druidic Connections

Legends about Somerled transcend earthly leadership by attributing to him supernatural powers that confirm his role as both a warrior and a spiritual leader. Among these stories, those of his control over nature stand out the most. Somerled is reported to have been able to call storms to fight his foes or quiet the waves to guard his fleet during campaigns. These narratives imply a link to pre-Christian spiritual beliefs of the Gaelic culture, therefore influencing ancient Celtic druidic traditions.

Celtic druids were held as middlemen between the natural and supernatural spheres. They were said to know the elements, the earth's cycles, and the forces of the invisible universe. Though Somerled lived during a period when Christianity had taken over Scotland, remnants of ancient pagan customs persisted, especially in the rural and coastal regions where Gaelic culture bloomed. By the twelfth century, druids' mysterious powers assigned to persons of great significance had been absorbed into mythology.

Legends of Elemental Control

One well-known myth holds that Somerled called a tempest to wipe out a rival chieftain's fleet trying to raid his territory. This story has Somerled climbing a coastal ledge and praying for divine or supernatural aid as his enemies advanced across the open sea. Moments later, the heavens darkened as a strong storm broke out, dispersing the opposing ships and compelling them to flee. Although there is no historical record of such an incident, the narrative mirrors a recurrent theme in Gaelic legend: the leader who orders the natural world as an expansion of his authority.

Another narrative relates how Somerled's fleet encountered choppy waves that would have capsized his ships on a dangerous journey to Islay. Rising from the prow of his ship, the chieftain yelled phrases purported to be old incantations while lifting his arms. According to the story, the winds stopped, and the waters calmed down so his fleet could approach Islay without incident. Such tales highlight the sea's symbolic function in Norse-Gaelic society. To command the waves was not only a mark of power but also an assertion of divine favour or mystical insight.

Historical Context: Druidic Symbolism in Gaelic Society

The cultural and theological setting of the period informs the traditions of Somerled's elemental control. Although Somerled was a devoted Christian, his position as a

Norse-Gaelic king put him in a cultural setting that had not quite abandoned its pre-Christian customs. The Highlands and Isles kept close ties to Celtic mythology, and local stories frequently combined Christian ideas with more ancient pagan beliefs. Leaders were sometimes revered as spiritual guardians of their people, as well as military or political leaders.

Somerled did not have a unique concept of a king endowed with superhuman ability. Reflecting their function as middlemen between the human and divine realms, monarchs and fighters were sometimes blessed with magical powers in folklore across Celtic and Norse cultures. In Gaelic society, the idea of *geis* – a forbidden or magical obligation – often encircled leaders, underscoring their relationship to the spiritual domain. Their power was reinforced by these magical links, which presented them as beings selected especially to lead their people.

Somerled and the Natural World

Somerled's deep connection to the natural world went beyond mythological reference. Modern sources document his ability to negotiate the waves precisely, especially in difficult circumstances. Designed using a mix of Norse and Gaelic shipbuilding methods, his fleets were renowned for their flexibility and robustness. This knowledge of the sea environment most certainly helped stories about his authority over the elements grow.

According to some stories, Somerled used his knowledge of the tides, winds, and star patterns to schedule his naval operations – a talent sometimes ascribed to magical insight in folklore. These useful skills, along with his military achievements, could have motivated the conviction that he had superhuman ability. Surrounded by the frequently erratic powers of nature, these tales helped the people of the Isles to improve Somerled's reputation by presenting him as a defender able to command the very elements influencing their lives.

Connections to the Druidic Legacy

Somerled lived in a mostly Christian environment. However, aspects of his myth link him to the druids, the spiritual elite of pre-Christian Celtic society. Druids were supposed to be quite knowledgeable about the natural world, including herbalism, astronomy, and meteorology. They were also supposed to arbitrate between people and the gods, therefore guaranteeing peace between civilisation and the powers of nature. Although by Somerled's day, the druidic class had virtually vanished, their legacy lived in the mythology and cultural memory of the Gaelic people.

Some variants of Somerled's story have him instructed by wise men from far-off locations, such as the holy Isle of Iona or the mountains of Argyll. Often presented as keepers of old knowledge, these people combine Christian and Druidic traditions. Through these stories, Somerled transforms into a link between two realms, representing the spiritual power of a Christian monarch as well as the mystical wisdom of the past.

Symbolism and Political Power

Somerled's affiliation with supernatural talents strengthened his political influence in addition to enhancing his personal legend. Leaders in the mediaeval Gaelic society were sometimes assessed not only on their military prowess but also on their capacity to live according to their cultural values. Somerled's tales of commanding storms or soothing the waters presented him as a guardian especially suited to shield his people from both physical and psychological dangers.

These stories also mirrored the close spiritual relationship the Gaelic people had with their surroundings. Particularly important to the Norse-Gaels' lives was the sea, which shaped their cultural identity, economy, and warfare. Emphasising his responsibility as a defender of both his people and their country, Somerled's presentation as a master of the elements links his leadership to the natural world.

Cultural Legacy of the Legends

The stories of Somerled's supernatural powers continue to resonate in the cultural memory of the Highlands and Isles. Poems, songs, and oral histories honouring his life and accomplishments have been spun from their retelling. Though surely distorted, these stories offer insightful analysis of the ideals and beliefs of the Norse-Gaelic people.

Through these narratives, Somerled's legacy has been maintained not only as a historical person but also as a symbol of spiritual connectedness, resilience, and leadership. His capacity to link the earthly and divine domains guarantees that his memory lives as a legendary character as well as a cultural hero. Somerled is an everlasting representation of the power and mystery of the Scottish Highlands and Isles, whether as a warrior calling storms or a king soothing the waves.

Somerled's Lasting Influence on Gaelic Culture

Poetry: The Bardic Tributes

In mediaeval Gaelic society, bards were essential historians assigned to preserve the memory of leaders and singly narrate significant events in song. With bardic poetry, Somerled turned his accomplishments into compelling stories that brought him an almost mythic reputation. These songs honoured his martial prowess and strategic sense and function as a clan unifier.

Most certainly performed in the years following his death, one famous lyric describes Somerled as the 'An Sgiath nan Eilean' ('Shield of the Isles'). The ballad praises him as a defender of the Hebrides, a warrior whose valour challenged Norse rule and preserved the Gaelic legacy. Inspired by 'a shoal of whales gliding across the black seas', Somerled's fleet is vividly depicted, and its relationship to the natural world – a frequent topic in Gaelic literary tradition – is emphasised.

Bards explored moral leadership and sacrifice in their works as well. Somerled is shown in one kept piece as a king weighed down by hiås obligations. The verse mourns his passing with sombre reverence:

Who now will hold the seas?
Who will steer the clans through storms?
He who calmed the tides is gone.

These lines illustrate how Somerled was seen not only as a warrior but also as a stabilising force whose death left a void in the hearts of his people.

Songs of the Isles

Songs inspired by Somerled have persisted through oral tradition, finding their way into Highland music festivals and local gatherings even centuries later. Commonly told in traditional Gaelic ballads are his maritime adventures, battles, and Isle unity. Still sung in the Hebrides, one such ballad honours his resistance against Norse persecution with a refrain that suggests:

Raise your oars, sons of the Gael,
For Somerled's banner leads the gale.
Through storm and fire, we hold the seas,
To guard the land and claim it free.

Reminding the Gaelic-speaking people of their common past and identity, these musical creations were not just festivals but also cultural monuments. They connected Somerled's legacy to the ongoing ideas of pride in the face of outside dangers, independence, and resistance.

Visual Art: Carvings and Symbols

Although oral traditions dominated mediaeval Gaelic society rather than visual art, some physical objects have been related to Somerled and his descendants. Longships and armed warriors, emblems firmly linked with Somerled's legacy, abound in carved stone crosses and effigies in locations like Iona and Saddell Abbey. These sculptures show not only the individual but also the values he embodied, therefore blurring the line between historical depiction and symbolic exaltation.

A relatively well-known relic connected to Somerled is the so-called Bratach Sith (Fairy Banner). The legend goes that this mystical flag, given by the Otherworld, assured success in battle but could only be raised three times. Though no physical proof of the banner exists, its tale lives in art and narrative, signifying Somerled's relationship to the earthly and spiritual spheres. Artists influenced by Celtic

Revivalism have painted the Fairy Banner in modern times, therefore reaffirming its significance as a symbol of Somerled's legendary strength.

Shaping Scottish Cultural Identity

The Gaelic Identity and Somerled's Symbolism

As a symbol of Gaelic resilience and identity, Somerled's life and accomplishments really speak to me. Central to the history of the Highlands and Isles, his unity of the Hebrides and opposition to outside control reflect the ongoing struggle for cultural and political autonomy. For the clans – especially Clan Donald and Clan MacDougall – whose ancestors are him, he is a patriarchal figure, a model of leadership, and a cause of communal pride.

For generations, Somerled's legacy was upheld by his successors, the Lords of the Isles. Despite mounting pressure from the Scottish Crown, they continued to practise a distinctive Norse-Gaelic culture. Gaelic study and culture were centred in their courts on Islay. Through their creations, poets, singers, and artists praised Somerled and portrayed him as a mythological hero as well as a historical leader.

The National Narrative: Resistance and Independence

Outside the Gaelic sphere, Somerled's narrative has come to symbolise Scotland's more general fight for sovereignty and independence. His defiance of the Norse invasion and his refusal to surrender to Scottish royalty reflect the larger story of Scotland's resistance to dominance, whether from England or another outside power. Somerled has, therefore, been knitted into the fabric of the Scottish national narrative, his legacy emphasising issues of leadership, autonomy, and cultural preservation.

Somerled in Modern Culture

Somerled is seen nowadays not just in historical research but also in artistic creations and cultural activities. For example, the Hebridean Celtic Festival frequently features readings of traditional songs and poems about him, bridging the link between past and modern identity. Everything from whisky brands to local legends bear his name, ensuring that his story lives in contemporary awareness.

The life of Somerled still inspires painters and writers. Works of fiction and drama set in mediaeval Scotland often draw on him as a resilient and wise leader. Documentaries and historical reenactments examine his fights; musicians adapt songs about his achievements for contemporary audiences. These honours highlight the ongoing attraction with Somerled as a person who embodies the junction of myth, history, and culture.

Somerled's legacy is evidence of the force of memory and the way myth interacts with history. Inspired by his experiences, he remains a vivid part of the cultural identity of the Highlands and Isles through his poems, music, and artworks. More than merely a mediaeval chieftain, Somerled is a symbol of a people that negotiated the violent tides of history and the rough waters of the Hebrides, therefore reflecting the continuing spirit of Gaelic perseverance and ingenuity.

Generation after generation, his impact on Gaelic culture has ingrained him in the hearts of the Scottish people as a liberator, a unifier, and a cultural figure. Somerled's narrative reminds us of the shared histories and values that bind Scotland's people over centuries, therefore inspiring pride, independence, and a feeling of identity as it celebrates its varied past.

Chapter 11

Unearthing Somerled's World

Digging into the past is sometimes a voyage with many discoveries and difficulties. Researching someone like Somerled, sometimes regarded as the Sea King of Argyll and the Isles, adds still another level of complication. His life spans the junction of cultural memory and historical truth. Archaeologists and historians who examine centuries of sediment, scattered relics, and worn-out ruins will help us discover his world and legacy. By means of the analysis of archaeological relics, scholars have started to create a better picture of Scotland in the twelfth century. This time is defined by cultural mixing, political aspiration, and the confluence of Norse and Gaelic traditions.

This chapter examines key archaeological finds that clarify Somerled's universe. It focuses mostly on the excavation of religious structures, ship remnants, and towns. The discussion also covers how best to interpret these results and their significance in clarifying Somerled's life, reign, and legacy.

Unearthing History: Excavations Across Somerled's Realm

Archaeologists have focused on important sites throughout the Hebrides and the western coast of Scotland to reveal the mysterious world of Somerled. These historically significant areas act as physical linkages to Somerled's life and legacy. Employing painstaking digs, scientists have unearthed an abundance of material evidence illuminating the political, cultural, and religious dynamics of the twelfth century. Notwithstanding difficulties, these revelations provide a great understanding of the field over which Somerled controlled and the legacy he left behind.

Once the administrative and ceremonial centre of the Lords of the Isles, Finlaggan on the Isle of Islay is among the most important archaeological sites. Though Finlaggan is mostly connected with Somerled's successors, evidence points to its importance starting either during or soon after his lifetime. A sophisticated network of stone-built buildings, including what is thought to be a mediaeval hall, perhaps used for council meetings, feasts, and ceremonial occasions, has been unearthed by excavations. The site offers peeks into the political landscape of the Isles, where Norse administrative methods combined with Gaelic customs mingled together. Stone crosses and carved slabs unearthed here show a fusion of religious and cultural influences, therefore highlighting the twin identity of the Norse-Gaelic society.

Beyond Finlaggan, Iona is unique in the archaeology of Somerled's period. Renowned for its ecclesiastical background, Iona was a spiritual and cultural lighthouse in the Gaelic society. On the island, excavations have turned up a wealth of religious relics, including well-carved burial markers with both Gaelic and Norse inscriptions. Together with ornamental patterns combining Christian imagery with pagan themes, these inscriptions show how Somerled and his descendants utilised religion not just as a source of legitimacy but also as a means of uniting many cultural aspects within their dominion.

The archaeological perspective also includes the military acumen of Somerled, reflected in fortified towns. Smaller fortified duns strewn around the Isles and Dunadd in Argyll expose a strategic network of fortresses keeping control over important areas. Weapons, tools, and household goods unearthed from Dunadd excavations highlight the daily life of both soldiers and colonists. These relics suggest a society firmly ingrained in both local defence and more general trading routes. Underwater archaeology is still a topic of great interest as well. Corresponding with historical records of Somerled's naval might, the seas around the Hebrides have exposed the remnants of Norse-style longships. Designed for quick travel and shallow coastal navigation, these boats represent the marine technologies underlined by his might. Dates for fragments of clinker-built hulls, iron rivets, and hardwood planks span the twelfth century, providing unique and priceless information on the design and purpose of Somerled's fleet.

Excavations at other important sites, including Mull, Jura, and Skye, underline the geographical complexity of settlement patterns during Somerled's rule even more. Originally bustling hubs of activity, these islands have produced artifacts ranging from luxury goods reflecting a rich and linked culture to domestic tools. Evidence of coastal trade centres, fortified farmhouses, and ceremonial buildings highlights the complex nature of Somerled's time, which combines religious and commercial activity with subsistence needs.

Significant Finds: Artifacts of Power, Faith, and Culture

Fortifications and Settlements

Among the most vivid and permanent signs of Somerled's authority are fortified locations. They represent his strategic attempts to unite power in a divided and competing political environment and the stormy character of his rule. Archaeological digs at hillforts, duns, and fortified homesteads in the Hebrides and mainland Scotland offer details on the defensive tactics Somerled used to keep control over his domains. Many of these places, such as Dunadd in Argyll, were deliberately placed on high ground or next to important rivers to guarantee they provided military strongholds as well as symbols of power. Excavations at Dunadd, a place connected with Gaelic kingship long before Somerled's time, have found proof of its ongoing significance during his lifetime. Finds point to its dual function as a centre for government and warfare, including moulded clay crucibles used for metallurgy, tools, and ceremonial objects. This suggests that locations like Dunadd might have been strengthened or rebuilt during Somerled's expeditions to guard important strongholds all around.

Similar defence networks supporting Somerled's dominion are shown by smaller duns and brochs strewn throughout the western seaboard. Usually constructed using dry-stone techniques, these buildings were probably employed to guard minor towns and impose authority over important coastal roads and harbours. These sites yield finds of iron weapons, including swords, spears, and axes, as well as bronze pins and brooches, therefore suggesting the existence of both warriors and local nobility.

Among the most important relics from these fortified communities are objects that capture the cultural mix of the day. From a fortified site on Islay, one remarkable discovery is a bronze brooch with Celtic knotwork and Norse animal designs. This relic powerfully shows the blended identity of the Norse-Gaelic people under Somerled's control. These functional and beautiful objects not only highlight the martial lifestyles of the residents but also their creative traditions, therefore implying a civilisation that appreciated both utilitarianism and exquisite workmanship.

These towns have also shown evidence of domestic life. Animal bones, hearth remnants, and broken pieces of clay pottery point to a diet heavy in locally grown seafood, cattle, and grains. These discoveries offer a window into the daily life of the people who lived at these fortified places, therefore capturing a picture of a society that flourished among the political and military changes of Somerled's day.

Maritime Legacy

Somerled's legacy is most intriguing in part because of his unmatched maritime ability, which allowed him to claim authority over the Isles and the nearby seas. Longship recovery is still ongoing, and maritime relics help clarify the naval technology that was fundamental for his military and political success. Crucially important for both conquest and rule, these ships represent the Norse-Gaelic synthesis that defined Somerled's rule. Fragments of clinker-built hulls, hardwood planks, and iron rivets unearthed from submerged sites close to Mull, Islay, and Skye date to the twelfth century, matching Somerled's supremacy. These ships blended local adaptations to negotiate the conditions of the Hebridean seas with Scandinavian shipbuilding techniques, including overlapping planks for increased speed and durability. Combining Norse marine customs with Gaelic inventiveness, this hybrid building captures the creative energy of Somerled's realm.

One cannot overestimate the significance of longships in Somerled's campaigns. They were emblems of power and prestige as much as weapons for battle. Found at places like Iona and Saddell Abbey, stone carvings and burial monuments showing galleys underline the ongoing cultural value of seafaring. Emphasising their part in pragmatic navigation and the cultural imagination of the Isles, these carvings frequently portray ships with lofty prows and rows of oars.

Outside military uses, longships promoted trade and communication over Somerled's territory. The Hebrides rivers were lifelines, linking remote villages and allowing the flow of ideas, people, and products. The recovery of fishing tools and anchor stones from coastal communities emphasises the sea's prominence in daily life and economic activities in Somerled's realm even more.

Coins and Trade

Finding trade commodities and coin hoards in places under Somerled's authority emphasises the economic complexity and interdependence of his empire. Found on Skye, Mull, and Islay, coins carrying inscriptions in Gaelic and Norse expose the way Somerled's economy combined several cultural components. Reflecting a realm that was at once strongly anchored in history and connected with the larger mediaeval world, these coins commonly include Christian crosses, Gaelic knotwork, and Norse motifs.

Reflecting the great trade networks linking the Isles to Ireland, England, and continental Europe, one amazing collection discovered on Skye comprised silver coins of Anglo-Norman, Irish, and Scandinavian origin. These coins were probably employed in trade, honour, and political alliances; they were also emblems of riches and status, perhaps utilised in payment.

Apart from money, archaeological data indicates the trade of valuable objects, including imported ceramics, glassware, and weapons. While Scandinavian weapons discovered in the Isles confirm the ongoing impact of Norse workmanship, French ceramic fragments discovered in trading centres point to ties with European markets. The discovery of weights, scales, and balance beams at trading sites suggests the presence of complex market systems, therefore refuting traditional presumptions that the Hebrides were isolated or economically inert.

Religious Artifacts

Religious objects offer a great window into the political and spiritual aspects of Somerled's rule. Along with seats of prayer, the monasteries and abbeys he supported – Saddell Abbey in Kintyre and the holy sites of Iona – were centres of learning, cultural preservation, and political legitimacy. Carved stone crosses, chalices, and remnants of illuminated manuscripts unearthed during excavations at Saddell Abbey attest to the way Christianity was woven into the social and political fabric of the Isles. These objects capture the patronage of Somerled and his successors, who united their territory and established their influence inside the Church.

One especially remarkable relic is a tomb slab from Iona that shows a galley together with a Celtic cross. This twin picture reflects Somerled's dual identity as a marine warrior and a Christian king. Combining religious dedication with the maritime customs supporting his authority, the stone represents the Norse-Gaelic synthesis that defined his rule symbolically. Apart from physical relics, the design and building of monastic sites provide hints on the function of religion in Somerled's realm. Local stone and ancient building methods point to a conscious attempt to ground Christianity within the Isles' cultural setting, therefore making it relevant and accessible to a people steeped in Norse paganism and Gaelic spiritual traditions.

The Challenge of Piecing Together the Past

Interpreting archaeological data about Somerled's reign presents a special set of difficulties. Though sometimes fragmented and vague, the material culture discovered from important Hebridean and Western Scottish sites provides an insightful analysis of the twelfth century. Reconstructing his life and rule from archaeological evidence calls for careful interpretation, methodological rigour, and a multidisciplinary approach. The main difficulties archaeologists and historians have in deciphering the data related to Somerled's time are listed here.

The Fragmentary Nature of Evidence

The scant and incomplete character of the archaeological record presents one of the biggest challenges in learning about Somerled's period. Somerled's time was more than 850 years ago. Potential sites and artifacts have been either destroyed or changed by natural events, including erosion, soil deterioration, and human activity. Important to Somerled's maritime realm, coastal towns have seen tides, storms, and increasing sea levels, leaving just faint remnants of what they previously were.

For example, longships and fortifications unearthed at some sites are sometimes unfinished, which makes it challenging to precisely recreate their design or ascertain their relationship to Somerled. The work has been further complicated by many locations connected to his rule being used or repurposed over the decades. Archaeologists sometimes depend just on what the material evidence can imply without written documents from his period.

The Blurring of Chronological Contexts

Finding the precise date of some relics or buildings is challenging. Many places connected to Somerled, including Dunadd in Argyll and Finlaggan on Islay, were active centuries before and following his rule. Thus, the strata of habitation at these sites sometimes cross one another. Separating artifacts and traits from Somerled's rule from those from previous or later times can prove difficult.

Over hundreds of years, Somerled's Norse-Gaelic society changed. Things like jewellery, tools, and ships can seem the same over eras. Norse-style fortresses or carvings, for instance, might have existed decades before Somerled. Although dendrochronology and radiocarbon dating can assist in determining the age of objects, even these techniques cannot always prove direct links to Somerled's actions. Later kings' changes, notably those of the Lords of the Isles, further obfuscate the historical setting. Rebuilding a fortification in the fourteenth century could hide its original design, therefore making it challenging to credit Somerled personally with the construction.

Distinguishing Somerled's Influence from Broader Trends

Living in the Hebrides and Highlands during a time of major political and cultural transformation, Somerled mixed Norse and Gaelic customs over the area, producing a shared material culture reflecting their blending. Another difficulty is separating what especially comes from Somerled's rule from more general regional patterns.

Longships seen in the Hebrides, for example, mirror centuries of Norse maritime customs. These boats could not always indicate Somerled's naval supremacy, even if he had historical ties to marine might. Likewise, Norse and Gaelic designs on sculptures and jewellery typically reflect a more general cultural synthesis than any conscious policy Somerled adopted. The artifacts and architecture of the period also reflected the relationships the area had with surrounding nations, such as Norway and the Scottish Crown. This confluence of influences hinders attempts to pinpoint Somerled's particular contributions.

The Absence of Direct Inscriptions or Attributions

Unlike later mediaeval leaders who left behind records, monuments, or seals bearing their names, Somerled's time was mostly dependent on oral traditions. Few objects or buildings may be exactly connected to him personally. Although sites like Saddell Abbey are linked to his patronage, historical writings rather than tangible physical evidence usually form the link here.

Ships and crosses carved in grave slabs from Iona and other sites reflect Somerled's reign. None of these, meanwhile, specifically names him or his contemporaries. Coins found in areas under Somerled's authority shed light on trade and economics, although their designs mirror more general cultural norms than policies linked to Somerled personally. Without inscriptions or markers, most of the archaeological record is left to be interpreted in any way one chooses.

The Impact of Modern Development

Modern development has complicated archaeological research much further. Agriculture, building, and tourism have all had an impact on coastal and island locations connected with Somerled. For example, urban development on Islay has upset regions close to Finlaggan, a site of great importance to the Lordship of the Isles. While excavations have produced priceless relics, much of the surrounding terrain has been changed, possibly hiding or destroying more evidence.

Similar difficulties confront underwater archaeology in the Hebridean seas. Fishing, shipping, and other maritime operations have shifted or destroyed underwater relics. Even with technological developments, recovering shipwrecks or harbours connected to Somerled's naval might remain a challenging and resource-intensive process.

Balancing Historical Narratives with Archaeological Objectivity

Archaeologists' interpretation of data depends on historical accounts of Somerled, penned centuries following his death. Many tales of his life, moulded by political or mythological goals, highlight his military and maritime successes or show him as a uniting Gaelic hero. These stories offer important background, but they run the danger of biasing interpretations of archaeological results.

The romantic picture of Somerled as a maritime ruler, for instance, would cause researchers to give naval finds top priority over land-based data. On the other hand, his defence of Gaelic culture may eclipse the Norse elements equally fundamental to his authority. Archaeologists must go gently to prevent forcing these preconceptions onto the facts. Their work calls for an emphasis on empirical facts and a recognition of the doubts about Somerled's life.

The Complexity of Interdisciplinary Approaches

Examining Somerled calls for cooperation among archaeologists, historians, geneticists, and other experts. Although every field offers different approaches and ideas, harmonising these might be difficult. Archaeological data, for example, can show family life or trade, whereas historical records centre on political events. Although they might not fit exactly with tangible objects, genetic studies of Hebridean people may expose trends of migration or ancestry.

LiDAR scans and underwater remote sensing are among the technological developments that have broadened the field of research, but they require knowledge to examine challenging datasets. LiDAR has found, for instance, concealed fortifications and town layouts, yet interpreting these results calls for cross-referencing with environmental data and historical sources. Likewise, dendrochronology has dated ship remains discovered in the Hebrides, providing information on Somerled's maritime operations; nevertheless, more study is required to verify direct links.

Ongoing Efforts and Future Potential

Archaeological studies have clarified Somerled's rule despite these obstacles. Advances in residue testing and isotopic analysis let researchers extract data from even the smallest objects. Isotopic study of human bones from burial sites, for instance, could expose information on nutrition and geographic locations, offering hints about the varied composition of Somerled's realm. These results enable placing his rule in the larger social and economic setting of the twelfth century.

Furthermore, community archaeology efforts in the Hebrides have been very important. Local participation in excavations has resulted in the discovery of fresh sites and enhanced respect for the area's legacy. These partnerships guarantee that, while supporting academic research, Somerled's legacy stays an active component of Scotland's cultural identity.

How Archaeology Has Shaped Our Understanding of Somerled

Notwithstanding the difficulties, archaeological research keeps revealing crucial information on Somerled's life and surroundings. Whether a basic domestic item or the remnants of a major construction, every discovery offers an insightful analysis of his time. Though often lacking, these results contribute to creating a more accurate image of the twelfth century. The labour is slow and demanding, needing accuracy and patience. Much of the process is realising what we do not know and yet working to keep learning. This harmony of humility and will drives the research of Somerled's past, attracting not just archaeologists and historians but also individuals greatly interested in Scotland's legacy.

The attempt to put Somerled's narrative together captures the general essence of archaeology itself. Interpreting the traces left behind in the ground and the ruins of past civilisations helps one to discover the history of mankind. The work calls for meticulous attention to detail and critical thinking, along with the knowledge that interpretations could evolve with fresh data. Rebuilding events that occurred hundreds of years ago requires archaeologists to combine science, reason, and imagination. This approach calls for resilience since many solutions stay elusive or vague.

Still, the goal is well worth the work. Even the slightest finding provides a window into the life of those who lived in Somerled's day. While a fragment of a ship can offer proof of naval technology and travel across the oceans, a shattered piece of pottery can expose specifics about daily life and trade networks. These objects help us bridge the distance between their experiences and our knowledge of their environment, bringing us closer to the individuals who shaped history.

The search for Somerled's past emphasises again the need for location in comprehending history. The scenery abounds with clues to the lives of people who once lived in the Highlands and Islands. Ruins of forts, remnants of prehistoric communities, and relics buried under the ground link us to a time of warriors, chieftains, and sailors. The places Somerled's people lived, battled, and worshipped let us better understand the forces sculpting their world and follow the outlines of their society.

The narrative of Somerled and his age keeps developing through every excavation. Every fresh piece of data adds to improved knowledge by providing flashes of a period influencing the political and cultural bases of the area. This continuous process reminds us of the close relationships between past and present and deepens our respect for history. Examining Somerled's life is evidence of the human yearning to know our background and how the deeds of those who lived centuries ago still affect our lives now.

Chapter 12

Reassessing Somerled's Reign

From an unknown child to the height of power as the founding father of the Kingdom of the Isles, Somerled's life's narrative arc creates a gripping chronicle that powerfully links with the greater saga of mediaeval Scottish and Norse history. Examining the layers of history, myth, and current interpretation helps us expose a picture of a leader whose legacy has been both enlarged and confounded throughout the years.

Modern Interpretations: A Reassessment of Somerled's Legacy

Scholars and historians have reassessed Somerled's life and impact in recent years, illuminating this mysterious personage of mediaeval Scotland. Beyond conventional narratives, these reinterpretations examine his martial successes as well as his responsibilities as a political strategist, cultural ambassador, and innovator. The outcome is a more complex picture of a leader whose relevance goes beyond mere legend.

From Warrior to Statesman: A Multifaceted Leader

Somerled was generally shown as a heroic Gaelic warlord fighting centuries of Norse rule. Although his fighting skills are indisputable, contemporary research highlights his statesmanship and negotiating skills. Somerled's ascent to prominence called for a thorough awareness of the convoluted political terrain of the twelfth-century Isles, not only of might.

His leadership shows his capacity to bring several factions under his flag. Somerled centralised authority over areas long entangled in internecine conflict in a time of fractured loyalties. He developed friendships with Norse leaders and ties with Gaelic clans. This flexibility shows a pragmatic king who gave stability and government priority over ideological struggle.

For example, his agreements with Norse kings – often read as acts of servitude or betrayal – were calculated relationships meant to protect his sea territory. These ties were erratic, depending on the political environment, with Somerled alternating between cooperation and opposition. Such pragmatism helped him negotiate the complexity of Gaelic-Norse politics and positioned him as a leader who aimed for integration rather than alienation.

Cultural Fusion: Bridging Gaelic and Norse Worlds

Among the most amazing features of Somerled's rule is his contribution to a distinctive cultural synthesis between Norse and Gaelic traditions. Somerled personified the double identities that distinguished the Western Isles in his day. His rule became known for this mingling of civilisations, which affected everything from art and social systems as well as government.

The Western Isles developed foci of cultural interaction under Somerled. Norse maritime customs mixed with Gaelic clan government produced a hybrid system that balanced local clan loyalties with nautical dominance. This cultural synthesis encompassed language, art, and even religious rituals, so forming a unique identity that would survive in the Isles for the next centuries.

For instance, the record of archaeology shows evidence of Norse-style longhouses coexisting with Gaelic defences, therefore showing the blending of architectural ideas. Furthermore, the oral histories of the Isles sometimes combine aspects of Gaelic and Norse narratives, implying that cultural fusion took place in daily life as well as at the political level.

This mixing of customs was not only a result of Somerled's background but also, a calculated tactic meant to unite his domain. He developed a shared identity by including Norse and Gaelic aspects, helping heal divisions within his domain. One of the most persistent features of Somerled's rule, its cultural legacy, shapes the Isles' identity long after his passing.

Maritime Power: Innovation and Strategy

Central to Somerled's legacy is his mastery of the sea; his naval prowess is sometimes recognised as one of his most distinguishing successes. Modern studies have broadened our knowledge of his maritime tactics and clarified how he used the sea for diplomacy, trade, conquest, and government.

Although historical narratives honour Somerled's fleet as a sign of his might, more recent research explores the logistical and technological features of his naval supremacy. Evidence points to his ships combining indigenous improvements to align with the difficulties of the Hebridean seascape with Norse design characteristics, including clinker-built construction. These hybrid boats could hold their own in open-sea operations and negotiate small coastal seas; they were lightweight but robust.

Somerled's fleet's efficiency let him project power over his maritime kingdom and manage key trade routes. Given their rocky shores and scattered towns, the Western Isles needed a commander who could travel swiftly and forcefully by water. Somerled's consolidation of power depended critically on his capacity to maintain control over these seas.

Furthermore, his naval tactics transcended conflict. Using his fleet to enable trade and guarantee the movement of resources between his domains, Somerled realised the financial value of managing the sea. This twin concentration on military and financial management emphasises his strategic sense and the value of naval might in the mediaeval Isles.

Religious Patronage: Piety and Politics

Many times, his funding of monastic establishments such as Iona is cited as proof of Somerled's piety and dedication to the Gaelic Christian heritage. Although this view has validity, many historians contend that his religious patronage had political as well as spiritual goals.

Somerled legitimised his authority by associating himself with the Church and building friendships with powerful ecclesiastical leaders. Particularly in Gaelic communities, where monasteries sometimes functioned as hubs of education, culture, and diplomacy, the Church possessed great power in the twelfth century. By helping these establishments, Somerled was able to establish himself as a defender of Gaelic Christianity, therefore strengthening his reputation among his Gaelic subjects and negating the impact of Norse pagan customs.

Somerled's support of the Church also indicates the larger part religion played in mediaeval politics. Sponsoring religious organisations helped him show his dedication to the spiritual welfare of his domain, therefore strengthening his reputation as a fair and moral leader. His favour of monasteries, at the same time, probably had pragmatic advantages since it gave him access to the diplomatic and administrative tools these establishments usually possessed.

Historians like William McLeod contend that Somerled's sponsorship of the Church helped him to establish his power. Aligning himself with reputable ecclesiastical establishments helped him to project a picture of a legitimate king and defender of the Gaelic people.

Mediaeval leadership often repeated this dual function of religious patronage, combining political tactics with spiritual devotion. The case of Somerled emphasises his capacity to negotiate the junction of spiritual and temporal power, thus strengthening his reputation as a multifarious leader.

Reevaluating the 'Liberator' Narrative

Somerled has been revered as a liberator who opposed Norse rule and brought Gaelic freedom back to the Isles throughout most of history. Although this story has truths, contemporary research has shown a more complicated picture of his motives and behaviour.

Although Somerled's operations against Norse leaders were surely important, their motivations were not only those of supporting the Gaelic cause. Rather, they seem driven by a mix of pragmatic needs and personal desires. Rather than pursuing an ideologically driven battle, Somerled tried to secure his personal power base and increase his influence by contesting Norse dominance.

This re-reading situates Somerled's accomplishments in the larger framework of mediaeval politics rather than lessening them. The reality of his day, where friendships and rivalries sometimes cut over ethnic and cultural barriers, affected his behaviour. The pragmatic attitude that defined Somerled's leadership, which let him adjust to the changing dynamics of the Gaelic-Norse society, reflects the flux of these links.

Debates and Controversies

The reign of Somerled has long been a rich field for intellectual discussions and different readings of events. He is one of the most revered yet mysterious characters from mediaeval Scotland, his life and legacy living at the nexus of myth, history, and cultural memory. Modern academics have worked to disentangle Somerled's narrative to reveal a leader whose motives, achievements, and influence are still captivating and divisive. The primary arguments on Somerled's ancestry, the nature of his power, the scope of his dominion, and his more general political and cultural influence are explored in this part.

Ancestry: Fact or Fabrication?

Among the most hotly debated elements of Somerled's life is his background. Traditional tales have Somerled descended from Norse royalty via his mother, from a noble Gaelic family on his father's side. Rich in oral history, these assertions were later recorded and spread by chroniclers closely associated with Somerled's descendants, the Lords of the Isles. This double background has sometimes explained his capacity to combine the cultures of the Gaelic and Norse worlds into the composite identity that distinguished his rule.

Modern genealogical and historical study, however, calls into question the veracity of these assertions. Some academics believe that the following generations trying to support their legitimacy may have inflated or even created Somerled's Norse links. Rising semi-autonomously for centuries following Somerled's death, the Lords of the Isles were vested in presenting their ancestor as a man of both Gaelic and Norse importance. This story let them take control over a varied population, including Norse immigrants and Gaelic clans.

Mediaeval cultures sometimes used genealogies to fit political demands, retrospectively creating lineages supporting the legitimacy of a ruler. Somerled's supposed connection to a royal dynasty may have been a deliberate construction – designed to align his descendants with the powerful Norse seafaring legacy while maintaining their Gaelic cultural roots. Modern descendants' genetic investigations have not yet produced clear proof either supporting or rejecting these assertions, thus leaving this side of Somerled's biography unresolved.

The Nature and Extent of Somerled's Power

According to conventional narratives, Somerled was a unifier who created a coherent maritime kingdom in the Western Isles and areas of the mainland. These images show a strong leader combining scattered areas into a single polity and subverting Norse rule as well as the newly established Scottish Crown. Recent research, however, has called into doubt this story by implying that Somerled's kingdom might have been less centralised than before.

Direct government would have been almost impossible given the Hebrides' geographical and cultural dispersion. To keep his power, Somerled most certainly forged arrangements with local chieftains and used a network of alliances and vassalage. This view places Somerled not as the only builder of a cohesive kingdom but as a skilled negotiator who controlled sway over a varied and sometimes divided territory.

More challenging to measure is Somerled's degree of power. Often penned by monks or chroniclers with limited access to accurate information, historical texts tend to idealise his accomplishments. Although he surely dominated most of the Hebrides, including Argyll and Islay, the precise limits of his influence are unknown. His capacity to inspire allegiance from several clans and factions attests to his leadership, but it also emphasises the dispersed character of power in the mediaeval Gaelic-Norse society.

Another issue of dispute is whether Somerled's domain can really be termed a 'kingdom'. Unlike a centralised monarchy like the Scottish Crown, Somerled's control seems to have been erratic, depending on marine mobility and localised government. Although successful throughout his lifetime, this decentralisation might have helped his realm to break apart after his death, as his sons and supporters fought for control of his legacy.

Motivations: Liberator or Opportunist?

Another important argument questions Somerled's motives and the larger importance of his campaigns. Particularly based on Gaelic oral history, traditional stories show Somerled as a heroic liberator who opposed Norse rule and brought Gaelic liberty back to the Isles. Central to Somerled's ongoing legacy is this picture of him as a champion of the Gaelic language and identity.

Modern historians have questioned, meanwhile, whether this representation oversimplifies the complexity of his rule. Some academics contend that Somerled's activities were motivated more by personal ambition than by nationalistic or cultural ones. Often presented as attempts to eradicate Norse influence, his military operations can equally be seen as calculated steps to strengthen his position and expand his realm.

It is worth noting that Somerled worked in a society where political alliances and rivalries cut beyond ethnic and cultural divides. Key to his success was his capacity to negotiate the convoluted web of Gaelic and Norse ties, but it also implies that pragmatism rather than idealism influenced his initiatives. He was ready to work with old rivals when it suited his needs, both by forming alliances with Norse chieftains and Gaelic clans. This duality of Somerled as a liberator and an opportunist adds complexity to his rule and gives his character dimension.

Naval Achievements: Myth or Innovation?

Although one of the most praised features of Somerled's legacy is his naval ability, it is also a subject of great controversy. According to historical records, he was a master of marine warfare, commanding a fleet that let him rule the North Atlantic. Often seen as technological wonders, his ships combine Norse design with Gaelic inventiveness.

Scholars have questioned, meanwhile, whether these accounts exaggerate the fleet's size and sophistication. Although archaeological data points to the presence of sophisticated shipbuilding methods in the area during his lifetime, it is not clear how much of this creativity Somerled personally can be ascribed. Recent research indicates that rather than innovative ideas, his fleet most certainly drew on known Norse nautical customs.

Notwithstanding these doubts, Somerled's use of naval force is nevertheless a major accomplishment. His success mainly depended on his capacity to project power over a large and divided marine area. Through the management of coastal fortresses and important sea lanes, he guaranteed the military and economic stability of his area. Though not particular to Somerled, these techniques highlight his flexibility and strategic insight in a time of ongoing strife and rivalry.

The Man Versus the Myth

Within mediaeval Scottish history, the figure of Somerled occupies a special and difficult place. He bridges the junction of fact and fantasy between historical documents and the legendary tales moulded by centuries of oral tradition, bardic poetry, and cultural memory. Examining his reign's notable events, key achievements, power conflicts, and cultural development reveals this dualism particularly clearly. Still, much of his legacy is unknown, further distorted by the appeal of mythology. Examining Somerled's rule calls for differentiating the legendary leader developed by folklore and inflated narratives from the historical leader.

Historical Legacy: The Realities of Leadership

Through his military feats, challenge to Norse supremacy in the Hebrides, and founding of a lineage that would eventually define Scottish history via the Lord of the Isles, Somerled's historical relevance is firmly established. He was not just a warrior but also a clever strategist and statesman who masterminded alliances and conquests with exactitude. His deliberate marriage to Ragnhild, the daughter of Olaf Godredsson, King of Man and the Isles, validated his aspirations and gave him a vital claim to Norse-owned territory. However, this marriage emphasised not only a political move but also the duality of his background and his function as a link between Norse and Gaelic civilisations.

The military operations of Somerled are further evidence of his historical sense. Combining force with diplomacy, he united several Gaelic clans using their common animosity against Norse masters, consolidating control. Supported by a fleet shaped by both Norse design and Gaelic inventiveness, his naval supremacy enabled him to impose authority over Scotland's western seaboard. These acts present Somerled as a man who grasped the complicated interaction of loyalty, ambition, and political pragmatism – a man firmly anchored in the power dynamics of his day.

Still, these successes are not without controversy, even if they are well-documented. Some historians contend that Somerled's dominion was less centralised than usually portrayed, hence exaggerating his image as a unifier. His dominion might have been a patchwork of semi-autonomous territory kept together by personal ties and the promise of protection, not a coherent kingdom. This reading emphasises the fractured character of Gaelic-Norse politics and encourages more research into Somerled's actual achievements.

The Creation of a Mythic Persona

For historians, the layers of myth covering Somerled's legacy present both opportunities and difficulties. On the one hand, these legends have ensured that Somerled stays a major player in cultural memory, honoured as a hero of Gaelic resistance and inventiveness. Conversely, they risk turning the historical figure into a larger-than-life caricature, therefore overshadowing his complexity.

Somerled's mythic profile has been primarily created by oral traditions and bardic poetry. Often lyrical and joyful, these accounts show him as a warrior of unparalleled ability, a liberator of his people, and a king graced with heavenly favour. Stories of his maritime successes over the Norse, for instance, are often inflated to highlight his almost superhuman talents. His fleet is said to be not only a set of ships but an unstoppable force, expressing his leadership and inventiveness. These stories grab the imagination but can hide the strategic and logistical reality underlying his achievements.

Another component of Somerled's story is his divine destiny and miraculous birth. Some stories hold that Somerled was born under unusual circumstances and was regarded from infancy as a figure of immense significance. Alleged prophecies of his ascent to prominence would have raised his profile to that of a selected hero. Though gripping, these tales also serve a more general cultural function since they support Somerled's representation of Gaelic identity and opposition against outside control.

Archaeology and Historical Documents: Grounding the Myths in Reality

Archaeological finds and careful study of historical records have strengthened attempts to separate the man from the myth. Sites connected to Somerled's dominion, notably Finlaggan on Islay, have yielded physical proof of the political and cultural scene he once oversaw. Remains of shipbuilding, domestic tools, and Norse-Gaelic weapons provide hints of his daily life and the pragmatic reality of his rule.

Though they have certain limits, historical records such as the Annals of Ulster and the Chronicles of Man offer still more insights. Usually penned by religious scribes, these records capture the prejudices and priorities of their writers. They might minimise Somerled's successes, for instance, to highlight the power of the Church or the Crown. On the other hand, they might embellish his actions to draw attention to the supposed threat he presented to established authorities.

One can interpret even these true sources in any way one likes. While historical records demand a critical approach that considers their inherent prejudices and gaps, archaeological finds must be thoroughly contextualised. For example, although Somerled is reported to have funded monastic establishments like Iona, his degree of piety is unknown. Was his patronage motivated by sincere religious commitment or by a deliberate attempt to validate his authority and get ecclesiastical approval? Such questions highlight the difficulty in piecing together Somerled's life and reign.

The Role of Folklore in Shaping Identity

Though the stories about Somerled sometimes blur the boundaries between history and fiction, they are also quite important for forming cultural identity. In the years after his death, Somerled came to represent Gaelic pride and resilience. Particularly in times of outside threat or cultural marginalisation, these stories help the Gaelic-speaking people of Scotland to feel a shared identity.

Somerled's myth's versatility is what makes it always appealing. His story has been understood by many generations and groups in ways that speak to their own hopes and experiences. For some, he is a champion of independence, someone who battled Norse and Scottish rule to protect Gaelic autonomy. For others, he is a unifier – a leader who united Norse and Gaelic traditions to build a legacy of cooperation across cultural boundaries.

This myth-making process is not exclusive to Somerled; it is a phenomenon noted in many civilisations and times. Still, Somerled's story emphasises how dynamically historical memory and cultural identity interact. The legends about him reflect the ideals, anxieties, and hopes of the civilisations that have preserved his narrative rather than simple fiction.

Reconciling the Man and the Myth

Examining Somerled's rule makes it abundantly evident that the distinction between the historical person and the legendary character is both hazy and important. Although it would be easy to concentrate just on the facts of his life, the stories that have developed around him are equally vital.

Understanding Somerled calls for a comprehensive approach that welcomes both the man and the myth since it reveals how he was seen in his own time and how his legacy has been understood and reinterpreted over the years. Examining the historical data in concert with the cultural narratives helps us to better understand his influence and relevance. Somerled was not only a product of his period but also a person who went beyond it to permanently change the Western Isles' history and character.

A Legacy Beyond Time

Within the rich fabric of mediaeval history, the tale of Somerled offers evidence of the dynamism and complexity of the era. By means of the previous chapters, we have travelled across the hostile terrain of the Norse-Gaelic society, disentangling the layers of a man who was both a product and a shaper of his time.

The story of Somerled is enhanced by the cultural mix that defined the Norse-Gaelic age, not only by a record of victories and monarchy. His narrative clarifies the complexity of identity in a period when loyalties and legacies were always changing.

Even after centuries, the figure of Somerled never fails to enthral and fascinate. His narrative provides insights into the government, social conventions, and cultural developments of the time, thereby bridging a bygone age. Though difficult, the archaeological projects covered in this book have started removing the layers of myth, revealing a more complex picture of Somerled's environment. These discoveries not only expand our understanding but also draw attention to the obvious links to the past still scattered over Scotland's and the Isles' landscapes.

It is sufficiently evident from considering Somerled's ongoing significance that his influence went much beyond the battlefield. The man emerges from the myth not as a one-dimensional figure but rather as a multifarious leader deftly negotiating the demands of his time with intelligence and foresight. Somerled's narrative finally represents the larger human experience of striving, adjusting, and finally affecting the currents of history rather than merely a chronicle of one man's desire. Closing this chapter on Somerled, we hope his path highlights the lasting impact one person may have on the globe and fosters a greater respect for the complex fabric of human history.

Chapter 13
The Norse-Gaelic Maritime Empire

Somerled's ascent to power and his legacy were closely entwined with the dynamic hybrid culture known as the Norse-Gaelic world produced throughout centuries of interaction between Viking colonists and Gaelic inhabitants in the British Isles. This world was one of changing borders, shifting identities, and dynamic interconnections of ideas, technology, and customs. By the twelfth century, coastal regions of Scotland, the Western Isles, and the Isle of Man had become cultural melting pots where Norse seafarers and martial traditions mixed with Gaelic kinship structures and political systems.

Analysing the nuances of this political, cultural, and financial environment that shaped Somerled's rule, and the regional order of his time helps one to properly value his achievements.

Cultural Synthesis in the Norse-Gaelic World

Viking assaults on the British Isles began in the late eighth century and produced the Norse-Gaelic civilisation. Arriving originally as raiders, the Norse settled in the ninth and tenth centuries in the Hebrides, Orkney, and the Isle of Man. They mixed with populations who spoke Gaelic over time and embraced local norms to produce a new, mixed society. By the time Somerled rose in the middle of the twelfth century, the Norse-Gaelic world had evolved into a coherent, yet adaptable culture marked by cultural interaction.

Language and Place Names

Language, especially in the region's place names, shows one of the most obvious aspects of Norse-Gaelic cultural fusion. Many of the Hebridean islands and communities have Norse and Gaelic elements. For example:

- Names like 'Uist' and 'Skye' have Norse roots, deriving from Old Norse words characterising the topography or natural elements of the terrain.
- Conversely, places like 'Tir nam Beann', Land of the Mountains, and 'Ardnamurchan', High Point of the Sea, highlight Gaelic traditions of lyrical descriptions of place.

These names show how Norsemen blended into Gaelic society without totally eradicating its customs. While Gaelic-speaking groups assimilated Norse vocabulary pertaining to seafaring, trade, and government, linguistically, many Norse immigrants chose Gaelic as a second tongue.

Legal and Social Structures

Another result of synthesis was the legal and governmental structures of the Norse-Gaelic society. While Gaelic society was established around clan systems run by hereditary chieftains, Norse immigrants brought their own legal traditions, including the Gulathing Law. The Norse legal traditions changed with time to fit Gaelic kinship-based government structures.

Norse-Gaelic marriage customs, which grew essential for forming alliances and preserving stability, also mirrored this pragmatism. Families of both Norse and Gaelic heritage held positions of authority in both societies. Claiming a Gaelic father and a Norse mother, Somerled himself epitomised this fusion, so appealing to both groups. His political legitimacy in both Gaelic and Norse spheres was enhanced even more by his marriage to Ragnhild, the daughter of the King of Man, Olaf Godredsson.

Political Landscape of the Norse-Gaelic World

Politically scattered, the Western Isles and their environs shared authority among chieftains, minor kings, and regional powerbrokers. Usually vowing allegiance to more powerful nations, including the Scottish king or the Norwegian crown, these commanders oversaw local strongholds. Somerled's political genius was in his ability to negotiate this broken terrain, combining force and diplomacy to unite his authority over the Western Isles and portions of the mainland.

Fragmentation and Fluid Alliances

Shifting loyalties and opportunistic alliances defined the political milieu of Norse-Gaelics. Depending on what would best serve their interests, leaders sometimes changed allegiance from the Scottish Crown to the Norwegian monarchy. Emphasising his Norse background to win the faith of Norse settlers, Somerled deftly entered this dynamic as a Gaelic chieftain to his Scottish allies.

The rise of Somerled started in a fractured setting under semi-autonomous control by local chieftains. Presenting himself as a uniting agent, he drew adherents looking for stability and defence in an environment of upheaval. He distinguished himself from other leaders by being able to close the distance between Norse and Gaelic identities, therefore enabling partnerships spanning political and cultural boundaries.

Norse Influence on Military Strategies

The military tactics of the Norse directly correlated with Somerled's political triumph. Raiding, a key component of Norse expansion, had long been a tool for claiming control and gathering resources in the area. But by the twelfth century, Norsemen were moving toward more orderly governments. Using raiding strategies as needed, Somerled embraced this change while concentrating on creating a coherent, maritime-based kingdom spanning important commerce routes and territory control.

Economic Foundations of Somerled's Realm

Somerled's kingdom had an essentially maritime economy, with the water acting as both a resource base and a highway. The riches of the area came from fishing, trading, and resource extraction; the Hebrides' rocky topography forced a reliance on coastal and marine businesses.

Trade Goods and Markets

Linking the Western Isles to a large network of commercial centres around the Irish Sea, Scandinavia, and the British mainland, trade was the pillar of the Norse-Gaelic economy. Typical trade items were:

- **Fish**: Major exports, herring and dried cod fed communities in mainland Scotland, Ireland, and beyond.
- **Wool and textiles**: The Hebrides traded their premium wool, which was spun into textiles and sold for products such as wine and spices.
- **Salt and grain**: Coastal towns that farmed salt exchanged grain with areas devoid of arable land.
- **Luxury items**: Reflecting their position and ties to foreign markets, wealthy elites imported luxury items such as silks, jewellery, and excellent weapons.

Somerled dominated this commercial network by commanding critical sea routes. Securing choke points like the Sound of Islay and the Minch, he guaranteed that businesses and fishermen fell under his jurisdiction, collecting income through tolls and tributes.

The Importance of Sea Power: Ships, Navigation, and Maritime Challenges

Somerled faced great difficulties depending on naval might and marine trade. Navigating the Hebridean shore was dangerous because of the choppy waves and erratic weather, so one needed both knowledge and creativity. Additional dangers came from Raiders and pirates, which called for ongoing alertness and fleet maintenance.

In Somerled's time, sea power was not only a means of mobility or combat; it was the foundation of political influence, economic growth, and survival in the fractured Norse-Gaelic world. Because of their steep topography, land-based travel was slow and ineffective in the Western Isles and coastal Scotland. Therefore, control of the seas defined control of trade, communication, and military growth as well as of the oceans.

Somerled's command of the sea marked his leadership success. His supremacy over the Hebrides, Clyde, and surrounding seas set him above his competitors and gave him unmatched power. Examining the kinds of ships he utilised, the navigation methods he applied, and the difficulties he encountered in his nautical activities will help one grasp this.

Ship Types: The Backbone of Maritime Dominance

Somerled's fleet of ships was vital for his capacity to negotiate, attack, and rule over his region. Inspired mostly by Norse longship design, his boats exhibited a fusion of local Gaelic adaptations and Scandinavian inventions. This mix produced a fleet exactly fit for the special needs of the Hebridean seascape.

Clinker-Built Longships

Somerled's fleet was based on the Norse shipbuilding classic clinker-built style. Under this building technique, a lightweight but strong hull was produced by riveting overlapping wooden boards together. The final ships were quite nimble and could negotiate the choppy North Atlantic waves.

Key features:

- **Shallow draft**: Allowed ships to sail in shallow waters, approach beaches for raids, and even navigate riverways. This feature made Somerled's fleet versatile and capable of striking inland targets.
- **Symmetrical shape**: An advantage during fighting or retreat that enabled longships to change direction without turning around.
- **Dual propulsion**: Equipped with both oars and sails, these ships could move independently of weather conditions, so they were dependable for trade as well as for combat.

Advantages in battle:
Clinker-built longships were perfect for the hit-and-run strategies preferred by Norse and Norse-Gaelic fighters. Their agility and quickness let Somerled's army ambush foes, strike quickly, and withdraw before suffering major reprisal.

Hybrid Gael-Norse Vessels

Somerled's fleet probably comprised vessels that combined Norse longship traits with Gaelic adaptations to fit the local conditions. These hybrid designs were developments catered to Hebridean water conditions.

Adaptations to local conditions:

- **Shorter keels**: Ideal for navigating the rocky coastlines and narrow channels of the Western Isles.
- **Broader hulls**: Provided additional cargo space for transporting goods or warriors, combining military and economic functions.
- **Lightweight construction**: Enabled ships to be carried overland when necessary, bypassing treacherous waters or gaining access to inland regions.

Economic utility:

These hybrid ships were not only employed for battle but also crucially for trade assistance. Their effective goods carrying guaranteed the flow of resources between the islands and the mainland, therefore strengthening Somerled's economic strength.

Birlinns: A Local Evolution

Often regarded as the successor to the Norse longship in the Hebrides, the birlinn was a particular kind of ship that arose during or soon after Somerled's lifetime. Smaller and more agile than the usual Viking longship, the birlinn demonstrated the continuous blending of Norse and Gaelic nautical customs.

Characteristics:

- A single square sail augmented for propulsion by oars.
- Smaller scale, which suited for negotiating the Hebrides' small sea lochs and inlets.
- Simplicity and durability, so that Somerled's armies may utilise them widely, and repairs would be simple.

Later, the birlinn would come to represent Gaelic maritime strength and a mainstay of the Lordship of the Isles, hence proving the ongoing impact of Somerled's ideas.

Navigation Techniques: Mastery of the Hebridean Seas

For sailors, the Western Isles' waters provided great difficulty. Navigating was dangerous, given strong tides, rugged coasts, and erratic weather. Success in this setting needed not only cutting-edge technology but also a great deal of information handed down over decades.

Sunstones and Celestial Navigation

While written records of Somerled's specific navigation techniques are scarce, it is likely that his mariners used tools and methods inherited from Norse traditions. One such tool was the sunstone, a crystal that could detect the position of the sun even on overcast days.

How sunstones worked:

- Sunstones polarised light, allowing mariners to locate the sun's position by observing how light passed through the crystal.
- This technique was especially useful in the often cloudy and stormy skies of the Hebrides.

Local Knowledge and Oral Traditions

Perhaps even more critical than tools was the deep local knowledge possessed by Somerled's mariners. Generations of sailors had committed the minute features of the local rivers to memory, including:

- **Tidal patterns**: Knowing the tides' ebbs and flows let sailors safely negotiate hazardous waterways.
- **Landmarks**: Navigating from natural elements, including mountains, islands, and cliffs, navigation found guidance.
- **Weather indicators**: Early storm warnings came from knowledge of cloud formations, wind patterns, and bird behaviour.

Often passed down orally, this expertise created a collective reservoir of nautical wisdom that made Somerled's fleet particularly adept at negotiating the challenging seas of his dominion.

Dead Reckoning and Coastal Piloting

Dead reckoning – a navigation method whereby one estimates a ship's position depending on its speed, direction, and elapsed time from its last known location – probably was the method Somerled's seamen used. This approach allowed seamen to cover great distances with amazing accuracy when combined with coastal piloting, navigating by sight of shore.

Maritime Challenges: The Perils of the Sea

Somerled's reliance on waterpower came with great hazards and difficulties, even with modern ships and trained sailors. The seas of the North Atlantic were as great a threat as any human rival.

Unpredictable Weather

Strong winds, abrupt storms, and changing tides define the Hebridean waters. These conditions may easily capsize even the toughest ships, so every trip is a risk.

- **Winter voyages**: For sailors, frigid, choppy waves in winter presented great risk, including hypothermia and frostbite.
- **Storms and swells**: Sudden gales might strand workers far from home by driving ships onto rocks or out to open sea.

Treacherous Geography

Narrow canals, secret reefs, and craggy coastlines – all of which made navigation dangerous – define the Western Isles.

- **Shallows and rocks**: Many places needed exact direction to keep clear of shipwrecks.
- **Sea lochs and fjords**: While these provided safe havens, entering and exiting them could be dangerous, especially under pursuit.

Piracy and Rival Fleets

The scattered political terrain of the Norse-Gaelic society meant that opportunistic pirates and rival chieftains regularly threatened Somerled's fleet. Maintaining naval supremacy needed constant alertness and a swift reaction to invasions. Somerled himself on raids, but he also had to guard his territory from other raiders who wanted to pillage it of resources.

Logistical Challenges

Maintaining a sizeable fleet needed supplies, including provisions for workers, lumber for shipbuilding, and trained craftsmen for maintenance. Ensuring his fleet ran continuously taxed Somerled's administrative and financial processes.

Somerled's success as a maritime commander was evidence of his adaptability and strategic vision as much as his technical prowess. His capacity to harness the force of the sea helped him establish a coherent, vibrant kingdom in one of the most difficult maritime settings of mediaeval Europe. Long after his death, this legacy of sea power would continue to shape the political and cultural character of the area for generations to come.

Trade Goods and Economic Systems in Somerled's Realm

Somerled's realm's western seaboard of Scotland and the Hebrides' economy was closely entwined with their maritime character. Apart from acting as barriers, the North Atlantic's seas were essential commerce channels linking Somerled's territory to a greater Norse-Gaelic world and beyond. His mastery of the oceans enabled him to rule trade routes and create a vibrant economic structure, bolstering his military aspirations. This section examines the trade items that passed through Somerled's territory and the systems of operation for his economy.

Key Trade Goods in Somerled's Realm

Trade commodities imported from farther-off locations as well as things reflecting the natural resources of the Western Isles and their environs in Somerled's day. These items helped the Gaelic and Norse worlds to trade culturally and materially, hence sustaining local economies.

Fish and Marine Products

Fish were among the most valuable goods in Somerled's domain since the Hebridean seas were among the greatest fishing grounds in mediaeval Europe.

- **Dried and salted fish**: Drying or salting helped cod, herring, and other species be traded across great distances. Particularly prized in Norse and Gaelic communities, dried fish – especially stockfish – was a basic food supply.
- **Shellfish and kelp**: Mussels, oysters, and other shellfish were consumed locally and occasionally traded. Kelp, harvested from the shorelines, was used as fertiliser or in the production of soap and glass.
- **Whale products**: While not a common industry, stranded whales provided valuable resources such as meat, blubber (used for oil), and bones, which were crafted into tools or decorative items.

The abundance of marine resources not only supported local populations but also made the Western Isles a key player in the regional fishing economy.

Timber and Shipbuilding Materials

Though most of the Hebrides lacked deep woods, lumber remained a vital building and shipbuilding tool. Somerled's mastery of trade channels allowed him to import timber from Scandinavia, Ireland, and mainland Scotland.

- **Oak and pine**: These woods were particularly prized for constructing ships and buildings. Oak provided durability, while pine was lighter and easier to work with.
- **Iron nails and rivets**: Necessary for shipbuilding, these were either produced locally or imported from Norse regions with more abundant iron resources.
- **Tar and pitch**: Used for waterproofing ships, these materials were likely imported or locally produced through primitive tar kilns.

Control over timber supplies and shipbuilding materials gave Somerled a strategic advantage, allowing him to maintain and expand his fleet.

Agricultural Products

Though the Hebrides' terrain was difficult, agriculture was essential in maintaining local populations and bolstering trade.

- **Barley and oats:** These grains were staples of the Gaelic diet and were used to produce porridge, bread, and ale. Surplus grain could be traded with regions less suited to farming.
- **Cattle and sheep:** Livestock were central to the Gaelic economy. Cattle were used as a measure of wealth and a form of currency, while sheep provided wool for clothing and trade.
- **Dairy products:** Cheese, butter, and milk were produced locally and occasionally traded with nearby regions.

The combination of subsistence agriculture and trade in surplus goods ensured the economic stability of Somerled's domain.

Luxury Items and Imports

Somerled's control of maritime trade routes allowed for the import of luxury goods, which symbolised wealth and status in Gaelic-Norse society.

- **Silks and fine textiles:** Imported from the Mediterranean and traded through Norse networks, these items were highly prized by the Gaelic elite.
- **Jewellery and precious metals:** Silver arm-rings, brooches, and other ornaments were popular among both Gaelic and Norse aristocracies. These items were often crafted locally using imported silver.
- **Spices and wine:** While rare, these luxury items reached Somerled's realm via long-distance trade networks connecting the Hebrides to the broader mediaeval world.

These goods not only enriched Somerled's court but also reinforced his status as a powerful and cosmopolitan leader.

Slaves

Although a terrible feature of the mediaeval economy, slave trafficking was rather important in Norse-Gaelic society. Slaves sold to other areas or used as labourers were gathered during raids or bought through trade. Though exact records are rare, Somerled's domain most certainly engaged in trade at the junction of Norse and Gaelic cultures.

Economic Systems in Somerled's Realm

The interdependence of the Norse-Gaelic world, dependent on a mix of subsistence farming, local trade, and long-distance commerce, influenced Somerled's economic institutions.

Subsistence Economy

The foundation of Somerled's economy was local subsistence farming and fishing, which supported most of his population.

- **Clans and kinship networks**: Gaelic society was organised around kinship groups that controlled local resources. These clans produced food, clothing, and tools for their own use, with any surplus used for trade or tribute.
- **Barter and tribute**: In the absence of a widespread monetary system, goods were often exchanged through barter. Tribute payments, often in the form of livestock or agricultural produce, were made to local chieftains or to Somerled himself as the overlord.

Trade and Marketplaces

Maritime trade connected Somerled's realm to neighbouring regions, creating opportunities for economic growth.

- **Regional trade hubs**: Ports and marketplaces in Islay, Mull, and other key locations facilitated the exchange of goods. These hubs likely attracted traders from Scotland, Ireland, and Scandinavia.
- **Merchant fleets**: Local merchants and shipowners played a crucial role in transporting goods between the islands and beyond. Somerled's control of the seas ensured the safety and profitability of these ventures.

Economic Role of the Church

Monastic institutions, such as the monastery at Iona, were not only centres of religious activity but also economic hubs.

- **Landownership**: The Church controlled large tracts of land, which were worked by tenant farmers. The produce from these lands supported both the clergy and local trade networks.
- **Craft production**: Monasteries often produced high-quality goods, including manuscripts, metalwork, and textiles, which were traded or gifted to secure alliances.

By supporting the Church, Somerled reinforced his political power while also benefiting from its economic influence.

Taxation and Tribute

As the ruler of a maritime kingdom, Somerled relied on a system of taxation and tribute to fund his administration and military campaigns.

- **Tribute from clans**: Local chieftains were required to pay tribute in the form of goods, livestock, or military service.

- **Customs duties**: Traders passing through Somerled's territory likely paid customs duties, either in money or goods. Control of key ports allowed Somerled to regulate and profit from this trade.

The economic success of Somerled's realm was rooted in its integration into a larger Norse-Gaelic trade network and its ability to harness the natural resources of the Hebrides. His control of the seas ensured the flow of goods, while his governance created a system that balanced local production with regional and long-distance trade.

By commanding land and water, Somerled created a flourishing economy to finance his military and political aspirations. This economic basis not only kept him in power but also had a long-lasting effect on the Western Isles, shaping their cultural and economic character for centuries.

Shaping the Future of the Region

Apart from defining his rule, Somerled's maritime policies helped to establish the course of the Western Isles for the next generations. His focus on naval power, trade, and cultural integration laid the foundation that survived even as the political scene changed.

Enduring Economic Networks

The trade routes and economic systems established during Somerled's time continued to support the region's economy, linking the Isles to a broader North Atlantic world.

- **Integration with emerging powers**: The maritime focus of the Western Isles allowed them to maintain relevance as Scotland and other neighbouring kingdoms consolidated power.
- **Adaptation to change**: The economic resilience fostered under Somerled's leadership enabled the region to adapt to shifting political and economic conditions, including the eventual decline of Norse influence.

Legacy of Maritime Identity

The cultural and technological innovations introduced during Somerled's reign became defining features of the Western Isles.

- **Symbol of independence**: Somerled's maritime legacy reinforced the Isles' identity as a region that thrived on its connection to the sea. This sense of independence and resilience persisted in the face of external pressures.
- **Inspiration for future generations**: Somerled's story, both historical and mythical, inspired subsequent generations to embrace the sea as a source of strength and opportunity.

Somerled's marine emphasis was not only a strategic need; it was a visionary approach that turned the Western Isles into a vibrant nautical force. His command of the sea helped him to unite his kingdom, promote economic development, and produce a legacy of culture still felt today.

Somerled moulded the future of his domain and made a lasting impression on the Hebrides by seizing the chances and difficulties of the North Atlantic. His nautical ideas and techniques established a model for the success of the area, guaranteeing that the Western Isles stayed a key component of the Norse-Gaelic society and a lighthouse of maritime culture for the next centuries.

Chapter 14

The Lords of the Isles: Somerled's Enduring Legacy

A legacy of Somerled, the lordship of the Isles became a potent political force in mediaeval Scotland. Established by his heirs, it broadened the idea of a unified maritime rule across the western seaboard and the Hebrides. Rooted in the Norse-Gaelic cultural mix defining Somerled's rule, the Lordship functioned as a semi-autonomous territory dependent on its own character and maritime might.

With Somerled dead in 1164, his successors carried on a legacy that was greatly important in forming the political and cultural identity of the Western Isles of Scotland. Consolidating dominance over the Hebrides and western seaboard, Somerled's sons and grandsons left a legacy that laid the groundwork for the establishment of Clan Donald, the major family ruling the Lordship for centuries.

The Immediate Division of Somerled's Realm

Somerled's three sons – Dugald, Ranald, and Angus – divided his lands upon his death. Every inherited specific area of Somerled's vast marine domain, comprising territories in Argyll, Kintyre, the Inner Hebrides, and the outer territories encompassing Skye and Mull. This split followed the Gaelic custom of tanistry, whereby multiple heirs shared power instead of one person being in charge. Although this method first led to fragmentation, it also guaranteed that Somerled's successors stayed in authority over the Western Isles, therefore preparing the ground for future Clan Donald-led consolidation.

Dugald MacSomerled (MacDougall)

The eldest, Dugald MacSomerled (MacDougall), inherited large tracts of Argyll and Lorn. Under sovereignty over mainland strongholds and portions of the Inner Hebrides, his branch of the family evolved as the Clan MacDougall. Rising to prominence, the MacDougalls lost popularity later because of their allegiance to the English Crown during the Wars of Scottish Independence.

Ranald MacSomerled (MacRuari)

Ranald MacSomerled (MacRuari) seized Islay, Jura, and portions of Skye. Eventually, his family produced the lesser-known Clan MacRuari, a force in the northern Hebrides. With Ranald personally sometimes recognised as a major player in uniting the Isles under his banner, Ranald's descendants were essential in cementing marine power.

Angus MacSomerled (MacAngus)
Angus inherited Kintyre and the southern Hebrides but was killed alongside his sons in clashes with different factions, most likely due to internal strife with his brothers or opponents trying to take advantage of the power vacuum left behind Somerled's passing. Ranald's heirs absorbed most of his territory with his passing.

The Rise of Clan Donald

Ranald's son Donald was the main uniting force in Somerled's family; he was the Clan Donald (Macdonald) namesake. Donald rose to become the clan patriarch, ruling the Hebrides for centuries. Particularly Aonghas Óg (Angus the Younger) and later John of Islay, his descendants, created the Lordship of the Isles into a semi-independent maritime kingdom, challenging the authority of the Scottish Crown.

The Lordship of the Isles first became a cohesive political entity under Donald's descendants. By use of strategic partnerships, military operations, and a strong maritime infrastructure, the MacDonalds effectively brought together divided areas. Established in Finlaggan on Islay, the administrative hub of the Lordship was governed under guidance from a council of clan chiefs and clergy leaders. Reflecting the double legacy acquired from Somerled, the MacDonald kings kept their power by combining Gaelic clan customs with Norse maritime techniques.

Key Descendants and Their Contributions

Donald MacRanald (d. late thirteenth century)
Donald's identity and his supremacy in the Western Isles made him indispensable. Consolidating power turned his family into the central focus of the Lordship of the Isles.

Aonghas Óg (Angus the Younger, d. 1314)
Aligning Clan Donald with Robert the Bruce, Aonghas Óg was instrumental in the Wars of Scottish Independence. Especially at the Battle of Bannockburn (1314), his support confirmed the clan's importance as major Scottish Crown supporters. The MacDonalds were thus allowed to keep their autonomy while increasing their impact on the Isles.

John of Islay, First Lord of the Isles (1326–1386)
Formally establishing the Lordship of the Isles, John of Islay produced a semi-autonomous realm functioning apart from the English and Scottish Crowns.

Through the Council of the Isles, a legislative assembly including clan leaders and clergy officials, he centralised power at Finlaggan and enhanced the government of the Isles. John's rule confirmed the Lordship's naval dominance in the North Atlantic, attesting to its height of influence.

Domhnall of Islay, Second Lord of the Isles (1362–1423)

Domhnall claimed authority over Ross and other lands of the Lordship, therefore broadening its influence. Though he retained the Lordship's autonomy and power, his reign was beset with difficulties, including disputes with the Scottish Crown.

Alexander MacDonald, Third Lord of the Isles (d. 1449)

Alexander kept enhancing the governmental and financial system of the Lordship to guarantee its supremacy as a marine kingdom. Rising tensions with the Scottish kingdom during his rule prepared the ground for later strife.

Political Structure and Governance of the Lordship of the Isles

Established by Somerled's ancestors, the Lordship of the Isles was an extraordinary illustration of semi-autonomous government in mediaeval Scotland. Covering more than three centuries, from the late thirteenth century to its loss in 1493, the Lordship was a distinctive political structure combining local government, Norse marine power, and Gaelic clan traditions. The political system and government of the Lordship were distinguished from those of the central Scottish Crown in that they showed creativity and flexibility in administering varied and sometimes divided areas.

A Hybrid System of Governance

The Lordship of the Isles was governed by aspects of Norse maritime customs mixed with Gaelic clan structures. This hybrid political structure let the Lords keep power over a large and physically demanding territory, including the Inner and Outer Hebrides, portions of mainland Scotland, and occasionally areas as far-reaching as the Isle of Man and Ireland.

Clan leadership on a federated basis dominated the Lordhood's government. The Lords decided not as absolute kings but rather as leaders depending on the allegiance of subordinate chiefs from strong clans such as the MacLeods, Macleans, MacNeils, and MacKinnons. These clans were connected to the Lordship by allegiances comprising tribute payments, military service, and council attendance, even while they kept their autonomy in local matters. This paradigm reflected the Gaelic idea of family and reciprocity, which prized group responsibility and mutual protection.

The Council of the Isles: A Mediaeval Parliament

Among the most distinctive aspects of the Lordship's governmental system was the Council of the Isles. Acting as a proto-parliament, the council advised the Lord and made judgments on issues of government by gathering clan chiefs, ecclesiastical leaders, and other powerful people. Meetings usually took place on the Isle of Islay at Finlaggan, the administrative and ceremonial centre of the Lordship.

The council tackled a spectrum of concerns, including military strategy, taxation, resource allocation, and clan conflicts. The Lord serving as a mediator also provided a venue for conflict resolution. This cooperative approach to government strengthened the power of the Lordhood and helped the clans to unite.

The Lords retained ultimate power in decision-making, while the council guaranteed representation and influence from local officials. This harmony between centralised authority and communal administration depended on maintaining peace throughout the Lordship's scattered areas.

Legal and Judicial Systems

Operating its own legal system based on Gaelic customary law (Brehon law) and inspired by Norse customs, the Lordship of the Isles emphasised arbitration and compensation instead of punitive actions for dispute settlement. This legal system, often known as brehons, stressed that judges were crucial in guaranteeing justice and diffusing disputes.

The legal system extended to maritime matters, with rules controlling the use of sea channels, fishing rights, and the distribution of gains from raids or trading operations. This attention to maritime law reflected the Lordship's economy and the primacy of the sea in its way of life.

Though it was autonomous, the Lordship sometimes acknowledged the general power of the Scottish Crown, especially in legal affairs outside of its domain. However, the Lordship maintained great autonomy inside its own borders, which allowed it to function as a sort of quasi-sovereign state.

Territorial Administration

Regional territories covering the Lordship were under the control of subordinate chiefs or taoiseachs (leaders). Acting as local governors, these chiefs managed their various domains while still serving the Lord of the Isles. They oversaw raising troops, paying taxes, and guaranteeing the Lordship's policies' execution.

The Lords depended on a network of castles and strongholds placed deliberately over the Isles and mainland areas to keep control over this scattered system. Administrative hubs, military bases, and marks of the Lordship's power were castles, including Dunyvaig on Islay, Ardtornish in Morvern, and Dunstaffnage in Argyll. These strongholds let the Lords respond fast to internal strife or outside dangers and project force over their territory.

The Lords also funded their military operations and government through a tribute and taxation system. Clans and areas under their authority gathered tribute payments, often in the form of cattle, grain, or fish. Maintaining the Lordship's economy and guaranteeing the allegiance of subordinate leaders depended critically on these resources.

Military Organisation

The military structure of the Lordship was a major component of its government. The Lords kept a strong naval fleet of birlinns. These ships let the Lords rapidly react to opportunities or threats and project force across the sea.

The devotion of the clans, who sent fighters for campaigns and defence, strengthened the military capability of the Lordship even more. Under the direction of their separate leaders, clan-based troops became the foundation of the Lordship's armed capability. Often deployed to protect the Lordship's territory, attack rival clans, or assist allies in wars with the English monarchy or Scottish Crown, these forces were

Along with the military organisation of the Lordship, the navy infrastructure guaranteed control over important sea lanes and commercial routes. Maintaining the Lordship's autonomy and economic growth depended on this maritime supremacy.

Relationship with the Scottish Crown

Operating semi-autonomously, the Lordship of the Isles sometimes ran apart from the Scottish Crown. But the relationship between the Lords and the Crown was multifarious and dynamic, marked by times of cooperation, bargaining, and confrontation.

Usually, by acts of respect or treaties, the Lords acknowledged the notional authority of the Scottish Crown. For instance, the Lords helped the Scottish Crown in the Wars of Independence in exchange for political and geographical concessions during the rule of Robert the Bruce. But the Lords also opposed Crown efforts to directly rule the Isles, sparking regular conflicts.

The late fifteenth century saw one of the most important turning points in this relationship: King James IV's lordship was forfeited, ending Scotland's semi-autonomous character. This occasion underlined Scotland's rising centralisation of power and the Crown's determination to include the Western Isles in its territory.

Economic and Cultural Governance

Apart from political leaders, the Lords of the Isles were supporters of Gaelic culture and managers of a flourishing marine industry. They kept monastic establishments like Iona Abbey, backed bards and poets, and advanced the Gaelic language. Even while the Lordship negotiated the larger political terrain of mediaeval Scotland, these cultural projects strengthened its reputation as a stronghold of Gaelic legacy.

Economically, the Lords handled a complicated system of resource allocation and trade. With the Lords in charge of tribute collecting and commodity distribution, the economy of the Western Isles was mostly dependent on fishing, agriculture, and marine trade. Managing these economic operations, the Council of the Isles ensured that resources were distributed effectively to maintain the Lordship's armed force and population.

The Lordship left a legacy even though it finally gave way to the centralising powers of the Scottish Crown. Representing Gaelic identity and resilience against outside pressure, the Lords of the Isles symbolised the spirit of self-determination and cultural preservation.

Key Events in the Lordship's History: The Role in the Wars of Scottish Independence

The Lordship of the Isles played a significant role in pivotal events throughout Scottish history, particularly during the Wars of Scottish Independence (1296–1357). This period of prolonged conflict between Scotland and England reshaped the political landscape of the British Isles, and the Lords of the Isles emerged as key players, navigating the shifting alliances and power dynamics of the time.

Allegiances During the Wars

The Lords of the Isles were in a dangerous posture throughout the Wars of Scottish Independence. Semi-autonomous leaders of a large maritime area had to carefully manage their interactions with the Scottish Crown, the English monarchs, and the competing clans fighting for influence in the Isles. Their allegiances were thus often erratic, changing in reaction to shifting political and military environments.

Because of its control of the western seaboard and strong naval force, the Lordship's backing was essential to both Scotland and England. The Isles provided a strategic base for launching naval operations, invading coastal towns, and controlling maritime trade routes. Understanding this, the English monarchy and the Scottish Crown worked to win the Lords of the Isles' support.

Still, there was not always harmony between the Lordship and the Scottish Crown. Although Bruce's supporters, the Lords of the Isles, kept their autonomy and opposed Crown attempts to directly rule their lands, even if they were faithful to Bruce during pivotal events. This conflict would last the whole history of the Lordship and shape its contacts with the Scottish Crown in the next centuries.

Internal Clan Conflicts During the Wars

The Wars of Independence also stoked clan strife inside the Lordship. Clans, including the MacDonalds, MacLeods, and MacDougalls, often associated with opposing sides in the fight, fought for supremacy. Rivals of the MacDonalds, the Lord's reigning family, the MacDougalls, for instance, helped the English during the wars, sparking violent clashes and clan conflicts that upended the area.

The Battle of the Pass of Brander (1308), in which Robert the Bruce firmly defeated the MacDougalls, was among the most famous disputes of this age. Bruce's place in the west was confirmed by this triumph, which he attained with the help of the MacDonalds, therefore transforming the Lordship's relationship with the Scottish Crown. Driven into exile, the MacDougalls helped to reinforce MacDonald rule over the Isles.

The fractured and frequently turbulent character of Gaelic-Norse politics is highlighted by the alliances and conflicts among the clans inside the Lordship during the Wars of Independence. These internal forces would still impact the history of the Lordship, hence affecting its involvement in later wars and final fall.

The Decline of the Lordship

The downfall of the Lordship of the Isles in 1493 marked the end of an era for Gaelic Scotland. This event, often referred to as the forfeiture of the Lordship, was the culmination of centuries of political manoeuvring, clan rivalries, and the growing centralisation of power by the Scottish Crown.

Driven by both internal and external forces, the Lordship started to fall in the late fifteenth century. The Lords of the Isles faced growing challenges in maintaining the allegiance of subordinate clans. The Lordship was vulnerable to fragmentation even though its federated system of government had prospered. Rising rival clans like the MacLeods and Macleans were claiming their independence, therefore weakening the power of the MacDonald Lord in charge.

Externally, the Scottish Crown, under King James IV (1488–1513), aimed to unite its power over the Highlands and Islands. The semi-autonomous position of the Lordship was progressively perceived as a danger to the Crown's attempts to concentrate authority and acquire direct control over the western seaboard. The Lordhood's history of rebellion and its connections with England during past wars drove James IV to control it.

James IV robbed John MacDonald II, the last Lord of the Isles, of his titles and territory in 1493, hence delivering the fatal blow. John's failure to control internal clan conflicts and his alleged Crown treachery set off this forfeiture. The Scottish Crown essentially ended its semi-autonomous position when it declared the areas of the Lordship under royal control.

The Impact of the Forfeiture

The Highlands and Islands suffered considerable and long-lasting effects from the loss of the Lordship.

Centralisation of power: The Scottish Crown's attempts to concentrate power took a major turn when the Lordship was dissolved. The Crown diminished the autonomy of the Gaelic clans by bringing the western seaboard under direct royal administration, therefore establishing its authority over a territory long under operation beyond its jurisdiction.

Clan fragmentation: The loss of the Lordhood's uniting power resulted in more clan division across the Isles. Rival clans regularly fought over land and resources without the centralised leadership of the Lords of the Isles, which resulted in decades of instability and death.

Cultural decline: The forfeiture also helped Gaelic culture in the area to fade. The Lords of the Isles had supported Gaelic language, art, and customs, therefore undermining the cultural cohesiveness of the Highlands and Islands. Lowland standards and practices imposed by the Crown throughout time further undermined Gaelic identity.

Economic changes: Major economic changes resulted from the Lordship's domains' inclusion into the Crown territory. New land management and tax policies enforced by the Crown upset established Gaelic customs. The socio-economic framework of the area changed as well with the change in a maritime-based economy to one centred on land-based agriculture.

Strategic relevance: The Lordhood's maritime emphasis persisted even in decline. For the Scottish and English Crowns in the next centuries, the strategic relevance of the western seaboard remained a top priority. The facilities and networks the Lordship built made constant marine activity in the area possible.

Legacy of the Lordship

Though the Lordship of the Isles was legally disbanded in 1493, its influence persisted in the political and cultural identity of the Highlands and Islands. Though they lost their official title as Lords of the Isles, the MacDonald clan stayed powerful in the area, and their descendants still inspire the memory of Somerled and his successors as markers of Gaelic independence and resilience.

Celebrated as a major phase in Scottish history, the legacy of the Lordship of the Isles has been modern. Apart from their military and political prowess, the Lords of the Isles are revered for their contributions to Gaelic culture and for helping to define the distinct Western seaboard identity.

Although the Lordship's political power was lost when it was forfeited in 1493, its cultural and historical influence endures. The narrative of the Lords of the Isles still inspires contemplation on the complexity of mediaeval government, the tenacity of Gaelic customs, and the interaction between centralising power and autonomy in Scottish history.

Chapter 15

Somerled and the Gaelic Renaissance

The cultural scene of Scotland's western seaboard underwent a transformation during Somerled's rule. Following his direction, Highland and Island Gaelic culture saw an amazing comeback. Combining Norse and Gaelic customs that marked Somerled's time set the stage for a period of vibrant language, art, and identity, guaranteeing that the Gaelic legacy endured against outside forces.

Preservation of Gaelic Language and Traditions

Somerled was a steward of his people's cultural legacy as much as a warrior and strategist. Somerled became a champion of the Gaelic way of life at a period when Norman influence started to permeate Scotland and threatened to undermine indigenous customs. Emphasising the value of their language, storytelling, and family systems, he stressed how the clans should develop a shared identity.

Under his direction and that of his descendants, the Gaelic language, which is fundamental to the culture, was kept and advanced. Through oral traditions, bards kept their common past alive by reciting histories, genealogy, and epic stories, thus linking communities. Many of these early works reportedly commemorate Somerled himself as a leader who challenged outside control and restored dignity and harmony among his people.[1]

Revival of the Gaelic Language

Gaelic identity revolved mostly around its language. The Gaelic tongue was a vehicle for law, history, and communal ideals as much as a method of communication. Somerled understood the need to aggressively promote Gaelic as the pillar of his people's identity as Norman French started to spread across sections of Scotland, especially in Lowland areas.

Patronage of bards and storytellers: Somerled restored and raised the profile of bards, Gaelic writers, and oral historians who preserved language and tradition. Reciting genealogies, heroic epics, and histories at feasts, council meetings, and religious rites, the bards were indispensable to Gaelic culture.

1. 'Robert Burns', The Robert Burns Society of Charleston, 2024, www.burnscharleston.org/2024-scottish-performing-arts-classic. Accessed 17 Dec. 2024.

Like earlier Gaelic leaders, Somerled made the bards important to his court and government framework.

He guaranteed their livelihood and raised their place in society by assigning bards of honour, enabling them to maintain and spread the Gaelic language. Bards wrote and performed poems honouring Somerled's achievements, lineage, and deeds. These poems were a means for cultural preservation as well as amusement, immortalising leaders and events.

Promotion of oral traditions: Oral storytelling was fundamental in the Gaelic culture in passing on information and ideas across generations. Within his territories, Somerled promoted this habit to create an environment where oral histories were preserved and respected. Clan meetings evolved into chances for the recitation of stories, binding the people to their leaders, territories, and ancestors.

By his actions, Somerled guaranteed the passing down of histories of the Gaelic clans as well as tales of his own successes. By stressing themes of kinship, bravery, and fortitude against outside forces, these oral traditions strengthened Gaelic identity.

Strengthening Gaelic Kinship Systems

One of the defining aspects of Gaelic society was its kinship. Unlike the Norman feudal model, Gaelic society was defined in great part by its kinship-based government. Leading by example, Somerled supported customs of kinship, reciprocity, and loyalty, which have long defined Gaelic society.

The clan structure: Somerled built his power on the *derbfhine*, the extended Gaelic family group. Unlike Norman feudal rulers, who gave land ownership and vassalage priority, Somerled governed as the *ceann-cinnidh* (head of kin) under a common structure of reciprocal responsibilities. Appealing to their common familial beliefs and cultural traditions, his leadership encouraged harmony among the Hebridean clans.

Gathering clan leaders for councils, Somerled's approach echoed a long-standing Gaelic custom whereby decisions were taken in groups. This method guaranteed that authority was dispersed in accordance with Gaelic conventions and safeguarded Gaelic government systems. Somerled strengthened kinship links to help the Gaelic clans feel cultural pride and solidarity, therefore strengthening their identity against outside influences.

Gaelic laws and customs: Somerled strengthened the application of Brehon law, the oral, traditionally based Gaelic judicial system. It emphasised arbitration, reparation, and reconciliation rather than strict hierarchies and punitive actions that Norman law imposed.

Somerled's dedication to Brehon law not only preserved a key component of the Gaelic legacy but also showed his respect for cultural norms serving the Gaelic people for centuries. Maintaining these legal customs helped Somerled preserve the Gaelic way of life and guarantee that his people kept control over their own affairs.

Integration of Christian Faith with Gaelic Culture

While adjusting to the rising impact of Christianity, Somerled's ecclesiastical policies were crucial in maintaining Gaelic customs. Somerled combined the two rather than letting the faith define Gaelic customs, therefore producing a synthesis that honoured both.

Support for Gaelic monasteries: Particularly on the Isle of Iona, a site of both religious and cultural significance, Somerled patronised monastic institutions following Gaelic-Christian traditions. Somerled made sure that Gaelic religious traditions were preserved and that the language was used in liturgical settings going forward by helping these establishments.

As centres of scholarship, monasteries like Iona taught the Gaelic language, copied manuscripts, and recorded histories among their monks. These establishments evolved into safe havens for Gaelic culture at a period when Norman influence threatened to alter regional customs. Somerled's respect for Iona highlighted his responsibility to safeguard faith and culture. His encouragement helped the island to remain a lighthouse of Gaelic identity and religious continuity.

Gaelic-Christian art and iconography: Stone carvers and artists under Somerled combined Christian ideas with Gaelic creative customs. This fusion produced unique creations reflecting the cultural and religious legacy of the Gaelic people – high crosses and gravestones, among other things. To honour Gaelic identity, the carvings sometimes featured complex knotwork, warrior images, and symbols of faith, forming a visual language.

Somerled's support of these creative projects not only enhanced holy areas but also strengthened the cultural values of his people, thus safeguarding them for the next generations.

Strategic Alliances to Protect Gaelic Identity

Safeguarding Gaelic customs also depended much on Somerled's political approach. Under his direction, the western clans came together to form a barrier against outside powers trying to impose Norman systems on areas speaking Gaelic.

Unification of the Hebrides: Somerled's attempts to unite authority in the Hebrides were not driven just by geographical control. Through connections with influential Gaelic figures, he presented a united front that let Gaelic culture grow. This unity guarded the area from the impact of Norman feudalism, which had started to change the political and cultural scene of mainland Scotland.

Desperate to recover Gaelic power over the Isles, Somerled's operations against the Norse overlords were driven in part by the desire to drive away alien influence. This helped him reestablish the autonomy of the Gaelic clans and protect their traditional customs. Common cultural values formed the foundation of his alliances and strengthened the ties of kinship and loyalty among the clans.

Resistance to Normanisation: Somerled's opposition to the Norman invaders in Scotland was as much a political as a cultural statement. He maintained the Gaelic way of life for his people by stopping the development of feudal systems and alien traditions. His leadership proved that strong, culturally conscious leadership could enable Gaelic traditions to flourish, thus providing a substitute for Norman authority.

Legacy and Influence on His Descendants

Deliberate efforts by Somerled to protect the Gaelic language and customs produced a legacy his successors carried on. Building on the groundwork he laid, especially Clan Donald, the Lords of the Isles became even more ardent supporters of Gaelic culture.

Supported by the patronage of leaders who descended from Somerled, Gaelic poets, musicians, and artists flourished under the Lords of the Isles. Established by Somerled's successors, the Council of the Isles preserved the traditional principles of kinship and reciprocity by reflecting the Gaelic practice of communal government. Monasteries, including Iona, stayed hubs of knowledge and cultural preservation, carrying on the activities Somerled had sponsored during his rule.[2]

According to Somerled's vision, Gaelic customs saw a rebirth rather than a decline that would define the character of the Highlands and Islands for centuries. Through the actions Somerled took to maintain Gaelic customs, their survival throughout a period of great transformation was guaranteed, hence preserving a legacy that defines the cultural legacy of Scotland's Highlands and Islands even now.

Although Somerled's leadership helped to preserve Gaelic culture, his descendants brought this cultural rebirth to full bloom. Supporting customs honouring their origin, authority, and the resilience of their people, the Lords of the Isles – especially Clan Donald – became the main sponsors of Gaelic poetry, music, and art. Through their sponsorship, the descendants of Somerled guaranteed the flourishing of Gaelic culture, therefore leaving a legacy that is still felt today.

Gaelic Poetry: The Voice of the Clans

Renowned supporters of Gaelic poets, the Lords of the Isles made sure their legacy was preserved in song. Often called *filidh* or bards, these writers were instrumental in safeguarding the history and culture of the Gaelic realm. Through their works, the

---

2. John Marsden. *Somerled: And the Emergence of Gaelic Scotland.* Tuckwell Press, 2000.

Somerled ancestors became heroes and cultural icons, and their story was handed down through the years.

The Role of the Bards

The *filidh* were political analysts, historians, and genealogists – more than just performers. The bards received great compensation for their work and occupied honourable roles in the courts of the Lord of the Isles. Poets under the MacDonalds produced compositions honouring their relationship to Somerled, praising the Lord's lineage, and saluting their military successes.

The way bardic poetry served to support the legitimacy of the Lords of the Isles was among its most significant features. Poets underlined the Lord's right to reign and their responsibility as defenders of Gaelic tradition by following their pedigree back to Somerled.

Notable Examples of Gaelic Poetry:

The Praise Poems of the MacDonalds

Early in the 16th century, the Book of the Dean of Lismore was assembled and included various praise songs honouring the MacDonald lords. These pieces honour the Lords' bravery, kindness, and connection to their Gaelic background. These pieces, produced following the formal end of the Lordship of the Isles, capture the ongoing influence of the MacDonald legacy. One poem, for instance, celebrates John of Islay, the first Lord of the Isles:

The blood of kings flows in his veins,
The son of Somerled, ruler of waves.
His halls resound with feasts and song,
The clans find strength where they belong.

Celebrating their leaders as cultural guardians as well as leaders, this kind of poetry strengthened the cultural identity of the Gaelic clans.

Poetry of Muireadhach Albanach Ó Dálaigh

Prominent thirteenth-century Gaelic poet Muireadhach Albanach Ó Dálaigh produced compositions honouring leaders throughout the Gaelic realm. He apparently wrote songs for the MacDonalds and other Somerled descendants. Keystones of Gaelic society, his poems mixed vivid imagery with ideas of kinship and chivalry.

One surviving poem details Somerled's ancestry:

Born of the sea and shaped by stone,
Sons of the west, in power alone.
Guardians of the sacred land,
Their strength, a shield, their will, a hand.

Such works celebrated the MacDonalds as inheritors of Somerled's vision, binding their leadership to the cultural and spiritual heritage of the Isles.

Laments and Elegies
To pay tribute to dead leaders, the bards often wrote *caoineadh* – or laments. One well-known instance is the eerie piece Lament for the Lord of the Isles, which laments the death of a MacDonald chieftain.

He sleeps where sea and stone abide,
The heart of the Isles, silent in pride.
No more his voice, no more his sail,
Yet still his spirit rides the gale.

These laments were not only tributes but also powerful expressions of collective grief and cultural identity, reminding the clans of their shared history and loss.

Music: The Soundtrack of the Gaelic Renaissance

Like poetry, music was integral in Gaelic society, and under the Lords of the Isles, it attained unprecedented levels of complexity and expressiveness. The descendants of Somerled were well-known for supporting musicians, including pipers and harpers, who produced works honouring their cultural background and leadership.

The Gaelic Harp (Clàrsach)

The instrument of choice at the Lords of the Isles' courts was the clàrsach, sometimes known as the Gaelic harp. Harpers presented music that raised the dignity of their clients at feasts, celebrations, and councils. With harpers writing both joyous and elegiac compositions, the clàrsach tradition flourished under the MacDonalds.

One well-known example is the Lament for Ranald MacDonald, a harp tune purportedly performed upon the death of a MacDonald lord. The sombre and eerie work caught the respect of the Lords and their responsibility for defending the Isles.

Bagpipe Music: The Birth of Piobaireachd

Highland bagpipe became a main instrument of Gaelic culture during the period of the Lords of the Isles. Emphasising long, expressive melodies, the *piobaireachd*, sometimes known as 'great music,' became a distinctive kind of bagpipe composition. Many of these works were produced to pay tribute to the Lord of the Isles, his successes, and defeats.

One well-known example is 'MacDonald's Salute', a *piobaireachd* presumably written to honour Clan Donald's military successes. Its structure captures the majesty and martial might of the Lord, and its broad notes inspire pride and wonder.

Another notable piece is 'The Lament for the Children', which is attributed to the aftermath of a tragic conflict involving the MacDonalds. Though mournful, this composition reflects the emotional depth of Gaelic music and its role in preserving the memory of pivotal events.

Art: Stone Carvings and Visual Legacy

The Somerled ancestors also supported visual art, especially stone carvings and monuments, combining Christian themes with Gaelic traditions. These pieces strengthened the cultural character of the Isles and honoured the Lords and their forebears.

West Highland Carvings

Among the most important artistic works from the period of the Lords of the Isles are the West Highland burial slabs and high crosses. Found all around the Hebrides and Argyll, these sculptures show complex designs reflecting both Norse and Gaelic inspirations.

- The MacMillan Cross, located in Kintyre, is an excellent example of this artistry. Commissioned to honour a Gaelic lord, it features interlaced patterns, warrior imagery, and Christian iconography, reflecting the dual spiritual and martial identity of the MacDonald lineage.
- The Keills Cross and gravestones at Iona similarly blend religious symbolism with depictions of Gaelic warriors, reinforcing the connection between faith, leadership, and cultural pride.

The Council of Finlaggan

On the Isle of Islay, the administrative capital of the Lords of the Isles, Finlaggan developed into a nexus of both political activity and cultural patronage. Ornamental masonry, pottery, and relics reflecting the richness and sophistication of the MacDonald court have come from excavations at Finlaggan.

Intricate knotwork and images of warriors, ships, and animals abound in ornamental carvings on stone slabs at Finlaggan, thus representing the marine might and Gaelic identity of the Lords. Reiterating their responsibility as defenders of Gaelic culture, these graphic depictions acted as a potent reminder of the Lords' relationship to both their land and the sea.

Particularly in the Highlands and Islands, the cultural rebirth fostered by Somerled and continued by his descendants had a lasting impression on Scottish identity. More than just safeguarding the legacy of the Western seaboard, this blooming of Gaelic traditions – poetry, music, and art – shaped the very essence of Scotland, giving voice to a people whose values, history, and sense of location defined their identity.

The Highlands as the Heart of Gaelic Identity

Particularly, the Lords of the Isles, Somerled's descendants, produced a cultural heritage that came to define the Scottish Highlands and the Hebrides. The Gaelic customs supported by the Lords gave the clans continuity and fortitude at a time of transition and strife.

Poetry and Oral Traditions

The bardic heritage guaranteed that history, values, and identity would be maintained across generations. Celebrating the exploits of Gaelic leaders and narrating clan hardships, the bards created a shared story for the Highlands that went beyond clan rivalry. Along with preserving Somerled's memory and those of his ancestors, this storytelling custom produced a distinctive Highland identity that prized loyalty, honour, and kinship. This cultural inheritance moulded Scotland's literary customs even hundreds of years later. Inspired by the bardic works sponsored by the Lord of the Isles, poets such as Alasdair Mac Mhaighstir Alasdair in the eighteenth century highlighted the ongoing impact of this legacy on Gaelic society.

Music as a Unifying Force

Highland society came to define the music that blossomed under Somerled's descendants. Celebrated clan histories, the bagpipe, harp, and piobaireachd tunes exalted their leaders and lamented their losses. The distinctive cultural expression this music provided for the Highlands distinguishes it from the rest of Scotland.

These musical traditions evolved throughout time into markers of Scottish pride. Particularly, the bagpipes changed from a local instrument into a worldwide emblem of Scottish identity. The rich legacy of Highland music that still exists today sprang from the laments and marches written for the Lords of the Isles.

Visual Art and Symbols of Power

Commissioned under the Lordship of the Isles, the West Highland stone sculptures permanently changed the Highlands and the Hebrides. Often covered with warrior images, Christian iconography, and complex knotwork, these monuments supported the martial and spiritual legacy of Gaelic heroes. These carvings persisted as markers of Gaelic resilience and artistic ability long after the Lordship fell. Inspired by Somerled's descendants, succeeding generations saw the Highlands as a place where history and customs were etched into the very ground.

Cultural Resilience Amid Change

Under Somerled and his heirs, the cultural blooming became a barrier against outside influences trying to either absorb or stifle Gaelic customs. The Highlands and Islands kept their unique character, but Norman, English, and Lowland Scottish influences were changing the governmental and social systems of mediaeval Scotland.

The Lordship of the Isles was built upon mastery of the waves. Here, a fleet of high-prowed birlinns battles a fierce Atlantic gale, demonstrating the exceptional seamanship that allowed the Lords of the Isles to control a maritime empire stretching from the Isle of Man to the Outer Hebrides.

Warfare in the Isles was a brutal, year-round reality. This scene captures a desperate clash on the snow-swept rocks of the Kintyre coast. Clad in heavy wool and furs, warriors of the Lordship fight with axe and shield to defend their ancestral lands against rival encroachers.

Control of the landscape relied on a network of fortified raths (often called ringforts) and timber castles. This tactical assault depicts the frantic moment of a siege, as ladders are raised against a timber-palisaded fort. It illustrates the high-stakes struggle for territorial dominance in the rugged West Highland interior.

Archaeological excavation at Dunyvaig Castle on Islay, a key stronghold associated with the later Lords of the Isles. The site reflects the strategic importance of controlling sea routes in the Hebrides and the maritime nature of power in the region. The author is pictured participating in the excavation.

The power of the Isles lay in the ability to mobilise hundreds of men at a moment's notice. This vast landing shows a fleet beached in a secluded bay as a disciplined invasion force assembles on the sands—a striking display of the military might.

Warriors of the western seaboard gather in prayer before conflict, guided by a Gaelic cleric whose role was to offer blessing, counsel, and spiritual strength rather than take up arms. In the era of Somerled, faith was not separate from warfare, but woven into it—shaping leadership, loyalty, and the resolve of those who fought.

Dunyvaig Castle in the landscape of southern Islay, positioned to command access to vital coastal waters. Its role as a naval stronghold underlines the seaborne character of the Lordship.

Lagavulin Distillery with Dunyvaig Castle visible beyond—a striking contrast between Islay's medieval power centre and its modern global identity. The continuity of activity in this area reflects the enduring importance of this coastline.

Finlaggan, on Islay, the principal seat of the Lords of the Isles. It was here that authority was exercised, councils were held, and governance carried out across a maritime kingdom spanning the western seaboard.

Finlaggan, Eilean Mór from the north. (Rob Farrow / *Finlaggan in Loch Finlaggan* / CC BY-SA 2.0)

This monolith, known as the Finlaggan Standing Stone, stands as a silent sentinel overlooking the ancestral seat of the MacDonalds. While the stone itself likely dates to the Bronze Age, its continued prominence in the landscape during the medieval period is deeply significant to the story of the Lordship of the Isles. For the Lords of the Isles, such ancient monuments were more than just relics; they were markers of a sacred and ancient landscape that helped legitimise their rule. Positioned on the ridge overlooking the loch, this stone would have been a constant visual reference for those attending the great installations and councils on Eilean na Comhairle. In a world where lineage and land were everything, the Standing Stone stood as an enduring symbol of the deep-rooted authority and the timeless nature of the 'Cradle of Clan Donald'. (Sandy Gerrard / *Standing stone at Finlagga*n / CC BY-SA 2.0)

An aerial perspective of power. Viewed from above, the strategic layout of Loch Finlaggan reveals why it was chosen as the 'cradle of Clan Donald'. The two islands, Eilean Mòr and Eilean na Comhairle (the Council Island), formed a unique, water-guarded administrative hub. Unlike the towering stone fortresses of the south, the Lordship was governed from this open, accessible site, symbolising a rule based on naval supremacy and the consensus of the Council of the Isles. From this small loch in Islay, the Lords of the Isles commanded a maritime principality that once rivalled the kingdoms of Scotland and England. (Gunther Tschuch / *Finlaggan Aerial* / CC BY-SA 4.0)

Another aerial perspective of Eilean Mòr. (Gunther Tschuch / *Finlaggan Pan* / CC BY-SA 4.0)

The Finlaggan Cross and the Heart of the Lordship. The finely carved Finlaggan Cross stands as a powerful testament to the spiritual and cultural sophistication of the Lordship of the Isles. Such high-status stone carvings were not merely decorative; they were symbols of the MacDonalds' patronage and their deep-rooted connection to the Celtic Church. This cross-head, with its intricate foliage and traditional designs, reflects the unique artistic 'School of Finlaggan' that flourished under the Lords' protection. (Otter / CC BY-SA 3.0)

Iona Abbey, founded by St Columba, one of the most significant religious centres in the Gaelic world. Its influence extended across the regions later shaped by Somerled and his descendants.

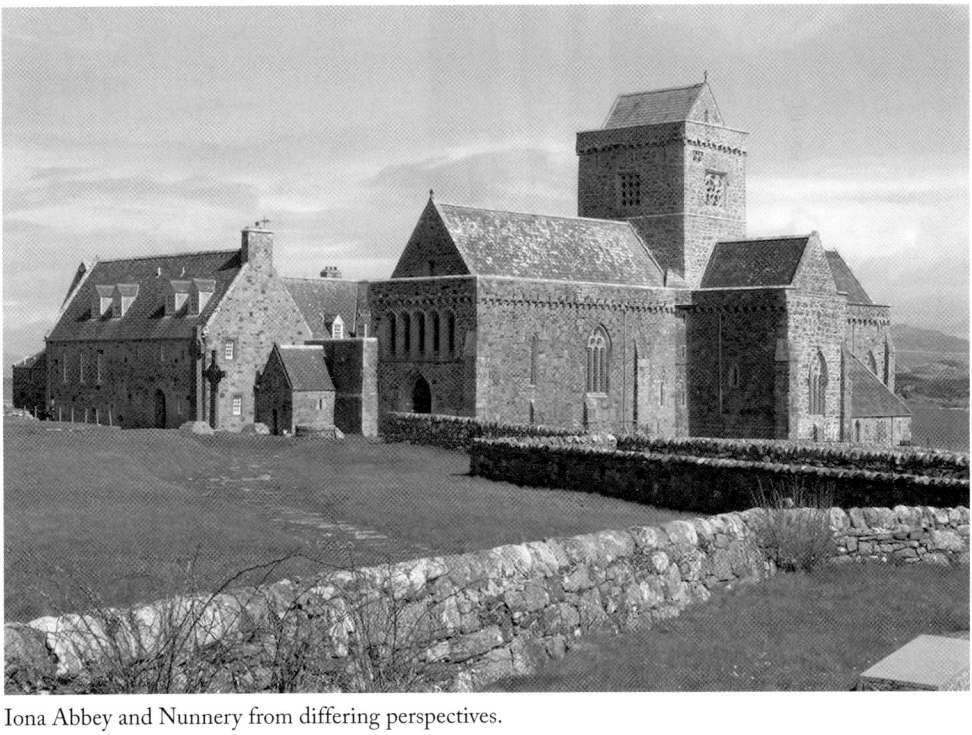

Iona Abbey and Nunnery from differing perspectives.

The Kildalton Cross on Islay, one of the finest surviving early medieval high crosses in Scotland. It reflects the long-established Christian culture of the region that continued through the era of Somerled and the Lords of the Isles.

Archers were used in the warfare of the western seaboard, providing support at range, often working alongside advancing warriors. While large, tightly ordered formations were less common, more disciplined groups and warbands could and did form up when required, particularly in more direct engagements.

Warbands of the western seaboard were often made up of a mix of men, with varying levels of equipment and experience. Some were better armed and protected, while others fought with more basic gear, reflecting the realities of local resources and status. Archers, spearmen, swordmen, and axemen could be found fighting side by side.

This haunting ruin of Skipness Chapel stands as a monument to the sea kingdom of the Lords of the Isles. Built by the descendants of Somerled near their stronghold of Skipness Castle, this seaside sanctuary guarded the strategic waters of Kintyre from 1325 until 1493. Today, its weathered walls and medieval grave slabs remain a powerful testament to a lost Celtic empire that once ruled the western waves.

Lochranza Castle on the Isle of Arran. While not a central site of the Lordship, it lies within the broader maritime zone shaped by competing powers in the western seaways during and after the period of Somerled.

A manuscript page from the *Annals of Ulster*, an important medieval chronicle recording events across Ireland and the wider Gaelic world, including the period in which Somerled rose to prominence.

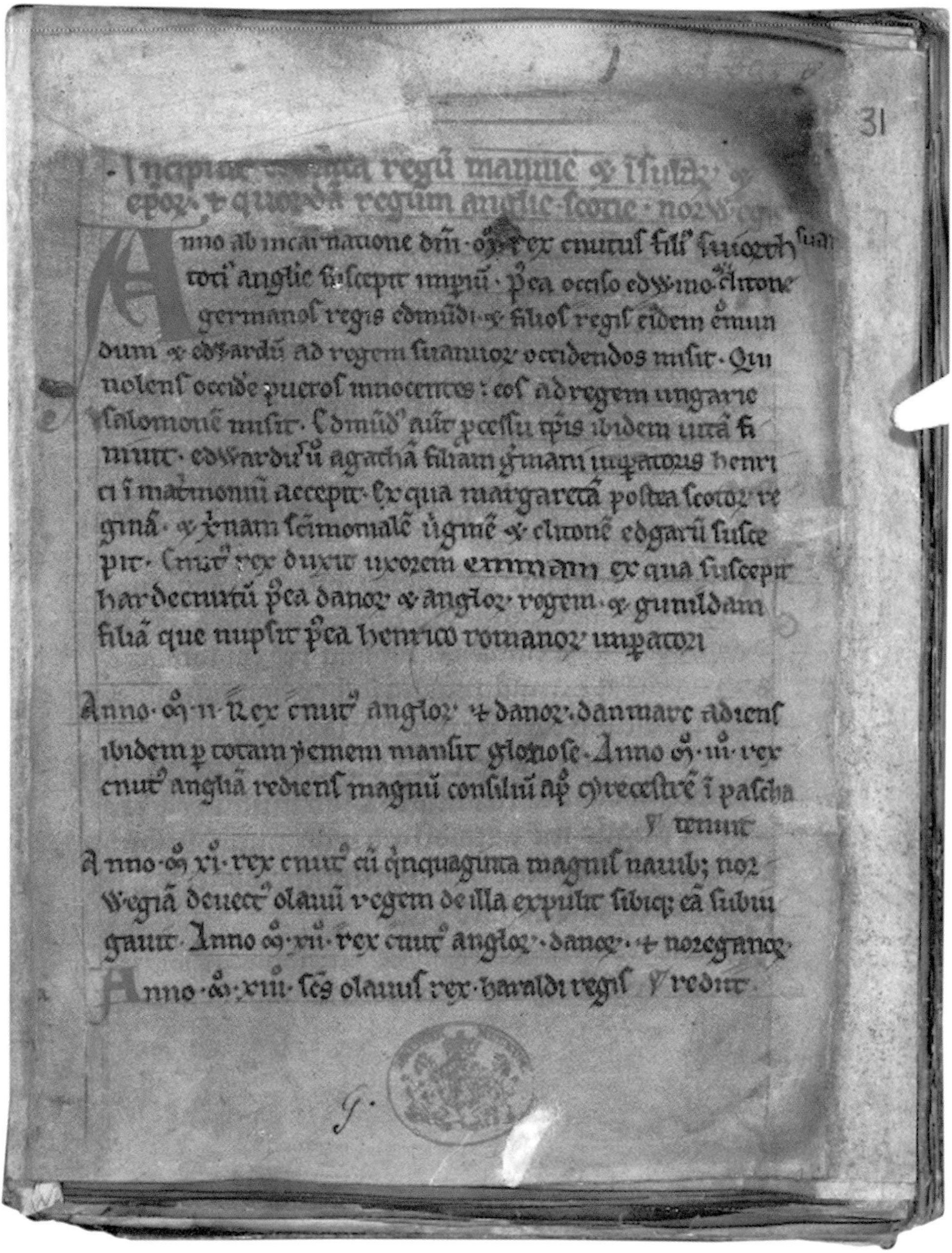

A manuscript page from the *Chronicles of Mann*, a key narrative source for the history of the Kingdom of the Isles, providing insight into the political world from which the later Lordship emerged.

Heraldic arms associated with Clan MacDonald, the dynasty that traced its origins to Somerled and later ruled the Lordship of the Isles.

A modern depiction of Somerled, commemorating the figure whose legacy shaped the political and cultural landscape of the western seaboard.

Kilchiaran Bay on Islay, part of the Atlantic coastline that defined the maritime world of the Hebrides. Such landscapes formed the natural setting for the seaborne power exercised by Somerled and his successors.

Uiskentuie Strand, Islay. This wide Atlantic-facing shore reflects the scale and exposure of the western seaways that connected the territories of the Lordship.

Support of Gaelic culture by the Lords of the Isles helped it to flourish in the face of outside challenges. A potent tool of cultural resistance, the preservation of the Gaelic language, music, and art gave the clans pride and unity. This cultural basis stayed even when political control changed when the Lordship of the Isles was lost in 1493, guaranteeing that Gaelic customs would survive.

The Legacy of National Identity

Somerled's descendants made cultural contributions outside of the Highlands and the Hebrides. They evolved throughout time into a fundamental component of Scottish national identity.

Romanticisation of the Highlands

The Highlands were idealised as the centre of Scottish cultural legacy by the eighteenth and nineteenth centuries. Celebrated as markers of a proud, warrior people who reflected the spirit of Scotland, the poetry, music, and customs favoured by the Lords of the Isles were writers like Sir Walter Scott brought the tales and customs of the Gaelic realm to a larger audience by mostly depending on Highland topics.

Although this romanticisation of Highland culture sometimes simplified or romanticised it, it, nonetheless, strengthened the ongoing impact of Somerled's ancestors on forming Scotland's image both domestically and internationally.

Gaelic as a Symbol of Scottish Identity

Preserved and advanced by Somerled and his descendants, the Gaelic language became a focal point for cultural pride. Though its use dropped in succeeding ages, the history of the Lords of the Isles inspires efforts to bring the language back and defend it. Eminent in education, media, and the arts, the Gaelic language is still fundamental in Scottish identity today.

Highland Traditions in the Modern Era

Scotland's cultural scene still bears traces of the music, artwork, and narrative traditions that sprang from the Lords of the Isles. Rooted in Gaelic customs, Highland games, piper music, and clan meetings are now honoured all around as markers of Scottish history.

Festivals of Gaelic music and literature, the yearly Royal National Mòd, have their roots in the cultural rebirth started by Somerled's descendants. These customs are living reminders of the Gaelic identity that the Lords of the Isles battled to protect.

An Enduring Influence

Scottish identity was permanently changed by the cultural blooming that started with Somerled and grew under his heirs. By supporting artists, musicians, writers, and craftspeople, the Lords of the Isles not only maintained Gaelic customs but also raised them to a level of continuing significance.

This rebirth in the Highlands and Islands produced a shared identity anchored in language, kinship, and artistic sensibility. The cultural basis of the Lordship of the Isles persisted even after its political fall; it became a pillar of Scotland's national legacy.

The bagpipes echoing across the glens, the poems honouring Gaelic pride, and the stone carvings silently attesting to a golden age of Gaelic culture reflect today the heritage of Somerled's descendants. Their impact reminds Scotland – and the world – of the resilience, inventiveness, and vitality of the Gaelic people over time.

Although Somerled's descendants might have used sword and sail to exercise authority, their greatest legacy is in the blossoming of a society that still inspires and defines the core of Scotland.

Chapter 16

Warfare and Diplomacy in Somerled's Realm

Rising in the twelfth century, Somerled's narrative is one of strength and cunning. He changed authority in the Hebrides and western Scotland in a period of Norse and Gaelic strife. His diplomatic and military acumen brought together scattered Gaelic tribes and questioned Norse rule.

Somerled raised a new benchmark for leadership in a divided area by combining tactical innovation, elite warriors, and strategic relationships. This chapter investigates his strategies by beginning with the tools and training of his Norse-Gaelic fighters. Forming the backbone of his army, their tools and skills combined Norse workmanship with Gaelic inventiveness.

We then examine his military plans, concentrating on naval tactics like those applied at the Battle of Epiphany. At last, we go over his diplomatic initiatives, particularly how he developed alliances to support his cause.

The Norse-Gaelic Warrior: Equipment

The tools of the Norse-Gaelic fighters under Somerled show a distinctive blend of Norse workmanship with Gaelic utility. Their gear, armour, and weapons were made for adaptability, so they would be useful in land and marine warfare. These warriors carried weapons of combat that represented their heritage and skill, with archaeological evidence illuminating their sophisticated technology and creativity.

Weapons

Swords

Warriors carried single-edged or double-edged swords, often made of excellent steel and embellished with complex hilt decorations. The blade forms, stressing balance for slicing and thrusting, clearly show Norse influence.

Often with runic or Gaelic motifs, swords were status symbols signifying the warrior's devotion and personal identity. These lightweight yet robust weapons were designed for close combat situations common in naval operations and clan clashes.

Example:

- Langseax: Designed as a tool as well as a weapon, this short, single-sided blade was small and lightweight, making daily chores and close-quarters fighting practical.

- Ulfberht swords: Renowned for their exceptional craftsmanship and the quality of the steel, these double-edged swords featured emblems and engravings that reflected the diverse ancestry of Gaelic fighters.
- *laidheamh* (claymore): Designed for slashing strikes, the claymore was noted for its great reach. In an open fight, this long sword was ideal for breaching opposing ranks.

Axes

Among the available axes were small one-handed variants suited for rapid strikes and more powerful two-handed axes capable of breaking shields and cleaving armour. Axes were flexible weapons for battle and useful tools made of strong wooden handles and reinforced iron heads. During boarding operations in naval wars, warriors frequently used axes because of their cutting force in limited spaces.

Example:

- Dane axe: A long-handled axe with a broad blade that could destroy thick armour or shields in melee fighting.
- Bearded axe: A smaller, one-handed axe with a hooked blade, often used for snagging shields or weapons.

Spears and Javelins

Spears were both melee weapons and throwing weapons, or javelins. Built with iron ends and hardwood shafts, they were light yet lethal, best for thrusting from behind shield walls or from ship decks. In naval operations, spears were especially successful since it let fighters strike from a distance during ship-to-ship clashes.

Example:

- *Gae Bulg:* While largely symbolic, this barbed spear referenced in Gaelic lore underscores the cultural importance of spears in Gaelic combat.
- Throwing spears: Lightweight and adaptable, throwing spears were utilised for close-quarters thrusting and ranged strikes.

Bows

- Self-bows: Close-quarters thrusting as well as ranged blows made use of lightweight, flexible throwing spears.
- Recurve bows: More advanced in design, these bows offered superior power and accuracy and were suitable for precision strikes against armoured opponents.

Defensive Gear

Shields

Warriors carried wooden shields strengthened with iron bosses in the middle. Rich painted decorations highlighted clan insignia or personal emblems, and leather bindings improved longevity.

Along with protection, shields were employed for offensive manoeuvres, including shield pounding and to create protective formations during ground skirmishes.

Example:

- Targe: A circular shield covered in elaborate clan insignia or designs and strengthened with iron bosses.
- Kite shields: Mostly inspired by Norse designs, tear-shaped shields offering complete-body protection.

Helmets

Iron helmets were defined by simple conical shapes to more complex Norse-inspired models with cheek and nose guards. Crucial in both naval and land-based combat, helmets provided protection against head hits and flying missiles.

Example:

- Spangenhelm: A segmented helmet with a nose guard that balances protection and movement.
- Conical helmets: Useful designs that avoided strikes and were light enough for long wear.

Mail Armor and Padding

Reserved for higher-ranking fighters, chainmail proved great defence against slashing strikes. Padded gambesons absorbed impact and offered flexibility, perfect for fighters demanding agility in shipboard warfare, worn under mail or as stand-alone armour.

Example:

- Chainmail hauberk: Excellent slosh resistance comes from a tunic composed of interlocking iron rings.
- Gambeson: A padded garment with flexibility and impact absorption worn either beneath chainmail or alone.

Naval Elements

During maritime operations, warriors often changed their weapons for efficiency; they used shorter swords and lighter shields to fit limited areas on ships. Warriors fought on birlinns, equipped with a mix of oars and sails for speed and manoeuvrability, and the design allowed for fast boarding and evasive strategies.

Example:

- Boarding hooks: Essential tools for grappling enemy ships during naval battles.
- Seax (short blades): These were small and adaptable, vital for close-quarters fighting aboard ships.
- Birlinns: Inspired by Norse longships, small galleys with oars and sails have unparalleled agility in coastal waters.
- Iron rivets and wooden hulls: These characteristics guaranteed the birlinns' lightweight yet strong enough nature to resist the demands of war.

The Norse-Gaelic Warrior: Training

Reflecting the challenges of their twin roles as land and naval fighters, Somerled's warriors received thorough and varied training. Men were instructed early on to master weaponry, develop physical endurance, and operate as cohesive groups. Training courses stressed coordination, strategy, adaptability, and not merely personal talent.

The armoury of Somerled's warriors reflects the cultural synthesis of Norse and Gaelic cultural expression, where craftsmanship and practicality combined with the need for symbolism to provide effective tools of war with a strong sense of identity. They were intended to be a statement of personal and clan pride as much as a tool for battle. The armoury comprised deadly axes, flexible swords, and spears, each painstakingly made to meet the many needs of land and sea battles. This part examines the designs, purposes, and cultural value of the several weapons these fighters carried.

Spear and Sword Techniques

Warriors practised thrusting, parrying, and slashing techniques with both spears and swords, often under the guidance of experienced mentors. Training emphasised precision, enabling warriors to deliver fatal strikes efficiently.

Example:

- *Glasadh*: A technique focusing on parrying and counter-striking, ideal for defending against multiple opponents.
- *Lann Slisneach*: Wide, slashing strikes designed to penetrate shield walls and overwhelm adversaries.

Archery and Javelin Throwing

Archery training focused on accuracy and speed, which are critical for weakening enemy forces before close combat. Javelin throwing required warriors to develop strength and aim, allowing them to incapacitate opponents from a distance.

Example:

- *Fuadach*: A precise throwing technique practiced against moving targets, critical for ranged engagements.
- *Creachanna*: Drills focusing on thrusting and blocking to maintain formation in shield walls.
- *Dartadh*: Long-range shooting exercises to improve accuracy and composure under pressure.
- Swift-firing drills: Rapid-fire techniques for situations requiring high-volume attacks.

Shield Use

Warriors practiced defensive manoeuvres, such as forming shield walls and using shields to deflect arrows and strikes. Offensive techniques also included using shields for bashing opponents or pushing back enemy lines.

Example Techniques:

- *Luchd*-shields: Warriors used the shield to absorb blows while simultaneously thrusting with their sword or spear to strike back at the opponent.
- *Bheatha Bàs*: A technique where the shield was used as an offensive weapon, bashing into an opponent's face or midsection to destabilise them or break through their defences.
- *Cosc na Faileas*: A manoeuvre that involved pushing the shield forward to drive enemies back or create openings for allies to attack, especially useful when forming the shield wall.

Axe Combat

Axes were among the staples of Somerled's arsenal, combining pure power and practical versatility for devastating effect. Warriors utilised these weapons because they would deliver crushing blows in any form of land or sea battle. The range of axe designs, from the dexterous bearded axe to the fearsome Dane axe, offered strategic flexibility in battle, allowing warriors to be versatile in situations.

Example:

- *Cromadh Bas*: Hooking and destabilising techniques with the bearded axe to exploit enemy weaknesses.
- *Briseadh*: Overhead strikes designed to penetrate even the toughest defences.

Physical Fitness

With his forces well-conditioned for the demands of both land and sea warfare, Somerled's warrior training was fundamentally based on physical fitness. The Highlands were difficult terrain, and living on board a ship was not simple; hence, these soldiers needed to be physically strong. These fighters sculpted their bodies to withstand extended conflicts, carry big equipment, and move over challenging terrain with considerable ease using rigorous drills and other conventional strength-building activities.

Endurance Training

Warriors engaged in long-distance running, swimming, and rowing to build stamina, vital for prolonged battles and maritime expeditions. Regular drills simulated the physical demands of carrying weapons and armour over varied terrain.

Example:

- *Sliabh* climbing: Ascending hills and mountains with weighted gear to develop stamina and leg strength.
- *Fad Troid*: Prolonged combat simulations designed to replicate the exhaustion of real battles.

Strength Building

Lifting big stones and participating in wrestling competitions were part of strength training to develop the core muscles required for hand-to-hand fighting.

Example:

- *Clach Neart*: The Highland tradition of lifting heavy stones to build upper body and core strength.
- *Tarraingt an Ghiolcaigh*: Pulling weighted sleds to mimic the demands of naval operations.

Agility and Reflexes

Mock fights and obstacle courses sharpened fighters' agility so they could move quickly to evade enemy assaults. Reflex training sharpened reaction times by dodging missiles and reacting to surprise attacks.

Example:

- *Léim Corr*: Leap-and-dodge drills to improve quick footwork and evasive manoeuvres.
- *Turas Bàta*: Combat training on unstable ship decks to develop balance and coordination.

Naval Training

Ship Handling

Warriors learned to manoeuvre birlinns, coordinate with oarsmen, and adapt to shifting tides and wind conditions. Training included boarding manoeuvres, where warriors practised jumping between vessels under simulated battle conditions.

Combat on Deck

Warriors rehearsed fighting in confined spaces, adapting their techniques to the unique challenges of shipboard combat. Drills focused on maintaining balance and effectively using shorter weapons in tight quarters.

Coordination and Communication

Emphasising collaboration, naval training had soldiers practise coordinated rowing and swift response to commands. Effective communication was critical for executing complex manoeuvres during battles.

Rowing and Manoeuvring

For Somerled's fighters, rowing was a basic ability essential for both maintaining physical stamina and agility in combat as well as for birlinns manoeuvring. These little yet strong ships depended just on the oarsmen's strength and tactical ability. Trained to row in perfect synchrony, warriors modified their speed in response to tides, winds, and tactical requirements.

Boarding Actions

Often, naval battles resulted in boarding operations whereby soldiers would leap from one ship to another. Usually under fire, training for this vital talent concentrated on enhancing the warriors' capacity to rapidly and effectively board enemy warships. Techniques like *Léim Na Luinge* (ship-to-ship leaps) and *Cliseadh Luinge* (close-quarters combat onboard ships) ready soldiers for the tumult and ferocity of these conflicts.

Maritime Navigation

Successful navigation of the Hebrides' dangerous seas was as dependent on military prowess as anything else. Using the sky and coastal features as guides, warriors taught in *Treòrachadh Rionnag* – star navigation – found their way during nighttime raids. Understanding *Gaoithe Smachd* (wind patterns) was another key part of their training, enabling them to exploit favourable conditions in naval warfare.

Mock Battles and Clan Gatherings

Regular mock bouts let fighters evaluate their abilities against one another, hence encouraging a spirit of rivalry and friendship.

Example:

- *Cath Mór*: Clan-wide battle simulations to practise leadership and cohesive formations.
- *Dorn Mòr*: Individual duels to sharpen personal combat skills and build confidence.
- Clan gatherings: These gatherings gave warriors chances to practise together, enhancing inter-clan connections and preparing them for major wars.
- *Samhain* drills: Training sessions held during festivals to combine cultural bonding with physical preparation.
- *Ceangal Cogaidh*: Pre-war customs meant to unite the fighters and raise spirits.

More than just fighters, Somerled's warriors were highly skilled experts armed with advanced gear and refined skills. Products of a special cultural mix, their swords, axes, spears, and naval weapons combined the versatility of Gaelic design with the inventiveness of Norse workmanship. Their rigorous physical and tactical training guaranteed their efficacy over a broad spectrum of combat situations and helped them prepare for the complexity of both land and marine warfare.

Negotiations with the Kings of Scotland

Careful management of Somerled's relationship with the Scottish Crown guaranteed his rule's existence and autonomy. Somerled found a compromise that let him keep control over his territory while avoiding royal punitive action during a time when the monarchy was strengthening its hold over areas once under the authority of local leaders.

Paying Tributes and Asserting Autonomy

Local leaders customarily paid tributes to the monarch to show allegiance, but for Somerled, it also served as a tool for preserving the impression of freedom. He made sure these tributes reflected an awareness of the Crown's notional power rather than compliance, therefore limiting their extent.

Emphasising the local ruler's supremacy over their immediate realm, Somerled drew on the Gaelic idea of *cenn na cathrach* (head of the seat), acknowledging the king's distant, general jurisdiction. This subtle reading allowed Somerled to rule his territory free from outside intervention.

Diplomatic Recognition of Authority

Somerled maintained actual freedom by paying ceremonial respect to the king, therefore avoiding direct military confrontations. This strategy guaranteed that, even while he followed his aspirations inside the Hebrides, he was seen as an ally and a faithful servant.

Somerled positioned himself as a major regional actor vital to the security of Scotland's western coast by proving his capacity to ward off outside dangers, most importantly Norse raids.

Leveraging Strategic Value

The Scottish Crown depended critically on Somerled's control of important sea channels. Along with supporting trade, these paths protected the western seaboard from Norse incursions. Somerled acquired political clout by presenting his monarch with his control of these channels as a service.

Somerled most certainly obtained tacit acceptance of his reign over the Hebrides in return for his loyalty, therefore guaranteeing that the aspirations of the Scottish Crown did not compromise his power.

Forging Alliances with Gaelic Chiefs

Central to Somerled's political success was his ability to bring disparate Gaelic clans together into a coherent power. He accomplished this by means of well-crafted alliances, the use of family ties, financial incentives, and mutual defence contracts. Marriages between his family members and powerful Gaelic chieftains reinforced bonds and lessened conflict among competing clans.

Mutual Defence Agreements

Somerled saw how important it was for Gaelic clans to work together to offset outside challenges, particularly Scottish Crown incursions and encroachment. In response to Norse raids, he provided military support and security, forging a network of allied clans united by shared objectives.

Somerled's capacity to arbitrate conflicts and project himself as a leader of equals rather than a conqueror guaranteed the allegiance of his friends. His philosophy stressed mutual benefit and reciprocity above servitude.

Economic Partnerships

Through his control of important trade routes, Somerled was able to provide allied chiefs with financial incentives, including access to common resources and safe passage for traders. This strengthened his allies' allegiance and, therefore, increased their wealth.

Agreements to distribute agricultural surpluses, cattle, and fishing rights further enhanced his connections and fostered clan interdependence under his direction.

Balancing Norse and Gaelic Interests

Somerled lived in a melting pot of Norse and Gaelic ideas. His diplomatic approaches revealed a keen awareness of this cultural dichotomy, which helped him heal divisions and unite a political entity.

Engaging with Norse Leaders

Through his marriage to Ragnhild and his activities in the Isles, Somerled became known as a qualified candidate for leadership among Norse-Gaelic people. This hybrid identity allowed him to appeal to both Gaelic and Norse groups.

Somerled concentrated on strengthening local support while fighting Norse control in the Isles, cautiously avoiding starting full-scale battles with more potent Norse kingdoms.

Promoting Gaelic Unity

Emphasising common language, rituals, and kinship ties to bind his Gaelic friends, Somerled positioned himself as a champion of Gaelic traditions. He built a network of devoted supporters prepared to mobilise against outside threats by encouraging a shared identity among the Gaelic clans.

Conflict Resolution and Mediation

Somerled's standing as a mediator confirmed his power even further. His political sense and leadership were evident in his ability to settle conflicts among competing groups without turning to force.

Negotiating Peace

Frequently serving as a neutral party in inter-clan strife, Somerled used his clout to help negotiate peace. This improved his reputation as a stabilising agent and guaranteed the clans engaged would remain loyal.

Through diplomatic meetings and councils, Somerled promoted honest communication among competing groups, fostering collaboration and confidence.

Incorporating Rival Factions

Rather than subjugating his rivals, Somerled often incorporated them into his network through favourable terms of alliance. This inclusive approach minimised resistance and expanded his influence. By emphasising mutual benefits, Somerled turned potential enemies into valuable partners, strengthening his position without the need for prolonged conflict.

Somerled's Enduring Legacy in Scottish Conflicts

Scotland's history was impacted by Somerled's military tactics and diplomatic acumen, which in turn affected his successors and the power dynamics of the country. His strategies affected the ties among the Scottish Crown, Norse kings, and Gaelic tribes. This part examines how his diplomatic and military style shaped later wars and strengthened the Gaelic government and culture.

Influence on Military Tactics

Somerled's military philosophy, especially his focus on naval supremacy, mobility, and agility, set a standard for the next military operations in Scotland.

Gaelic warfare was typified by Somerled's use of birlinns to regulate marine paths and execute naval raids. These adaptable galleys let him rule the oceans, therefore guaranteeing control over trade and military activity in the Hebrides. Using birlinns to keep their hold on the principal seaways of the area, his descendants – including the Lords of the Isles – kept up this custom.

Birlinns' speed and agility helped Gaelic leaders to outmanoeuvre more massive, slower troops, hence influencing the evolution of hit-and-run strategies. Cementing birlinns as a pillar of Gaelic military strategy, these strategies were successful in opposing both Norse invaders and Scottish Crown forces trying to exert control over the western seaboard.

The way Somerled combined naval and land operations set a benchmark for combined-arms combat in the area. His armies could launch amphibious assaults, attack enemy strongholds, and guard important strategic areas along the coast thanks to this double capability.

Later, Gaelic clans adopted the guerrilla warfare strategies Somerled's troops used – surprise attacks, ambushes, and strategic use of terrain – to fight outside armies. Particularly in battles involving the Scottish and English Crowns, these techniques became defining characteristics of Highland warfare.

Impact on Diplomatic Strategies

The diplomatic policies of Somerled, which stressed alliances, diplomacy, and cultural cohesiveness, had a big impact on how later Gaelic leaders dealt with friends as well as enemies. One pillar of his legacy is his deliberate use of marriage to create alliances with both Gaelic and Norse groups. Adopted by his descendants, this habit proved crucial in preserving stability and increasing impact without resorting to continuous conflict.

Building on Somerled's success in bringing opposing clans together, future Gaelic leaders were motivated to use coalition-based government. This approach guaranteed mutual defence, encouraged economic collaboration, and helped once-rival groups come to a common goal. Moreover, Somerled's approach to the Scottish Crown, which respected local autonomy while nevertheless accepting its power, created a model for the Lords of the Isles. Using their strategic relevance to maintain influence with the monarchy, this approach helped Gaelic leaders preserve their independence.

In their interactions with the Scottish Crown, Somerled's descendants continued using similar strategies, providing military support or tribute in return for respect for their sovereignty over the Hebrides. Their pragmatic diplomatic style helped them negotiate the convoluted political terrain of mediaeval Scotland and maintain great authority.

The Rise of the Lords of the Isles

The legacy of Somerled emerged in the founding of the Lordship of the Isles by his descendants, mostly Clan Donald. This semi-autonomous political body embodied the blend of military strength and diplomatic strategy that characterised Somerled's leadership.

Inheriting Somerled's focus on naval might, the Lords of the Isles established their authority over the western seaboard with a fleet of birlinns. Their maritime superiority helped them maintain their dominion for ages and fight Scottish Crown invasions.

Like Somerled, the Lords gently negotiated their relationship with the Scottish Crown, showing respect when called for and expressing their autonomy. Often supporting the Crown's adversaries to safeguard their interests, this diplomatic approach allowed them to function as power brokers in Scottish politics.

The Lords of the Isles continued Somerled's quest to create a unique identity for the Hebrides by supporting the Gaelic language, culture, and customs. This cultural cohesiveness reinforced their political unity and opposition to assimilation by Lowland Scotland.

Influence on the Wars of Scottish Independence

Somerled's legacy continued throughout the Wars of Scottish Independence (1296–1357), during which his descendants were instrumental.

Descended from Somerled, the Lords of the Isles were important allies of Robert the Bruce on his mission to guarantee Scotland's independence. Bruce's triumph at the Battle of Bannockburn (1314), when they gave vital support, was greatly aided by their naval might and dominance of the western seaboard.

The guerrilla-style fighting developed by Somerled's troops shaped the strategies Scottish commanders used during the independence struggle. These strategies were especially successful in the difficult Highland terrain, where smaller, mobile forces might outmanoeuvre bigger English armies.

For years, military and diplomatic strategies developed by Somerled impacted the approach of Gaelic clans toward combat and government. The complex web of links among Gaelic clans reflected Somerled's focus on alliances as a tool for consolidating power. Even if antagonism continued, the foundation of Gaelic politics remained its capacity to create strategic alliances.

The autonomy kept by Somerled's successors motivated opposition to the Scottish Crown's centralising initiatives. This opposition resulted in the Lordship of the Isles being forfeited in 1493, a turning moment in the Crown's attempts to include the Highlands and Islands into its territory.

For centuries, Somerled's military and diplomatic approaches shaped the political and cultural path of Scotland. His naval strategies shaped the next wars and his method of juggling loyalty with autonomy set a benchmark for leaders. The ascent of the Lords of the Isles shows the continuing impact of his vision. Apart from conflict, his legacy marks Scotland's history by reflecting the resilience and solidarity of Gaelic culture.

Chapter 17

The Economy of a Maritime Kingdom

Traders steer their ships into the harbour, glistening like gold in the morning sun on the waves. A concoction of smells from dried fish, newly made fresh oatcakes, and sweet honey fills the sea. As fisherman bring forth their herring and cod, traders wrangle over the barrels of salted fish heading to markets on the other side of the Irish Sea, Somerled's ports, Dunstaffnage, and Finlaggan, hum with activity.

Stalls of driftwood along the dockside, offering anything from hand-carved wooden bowls and complex jewellery set with Celtic knots to delicate woollen fabrics dyed with woad. Traders from Ireland, Norway, and the Scottish mainland mix with residents to share news and stories as much as commodities. Driving cattle through the packed streets, Gaelic farmers mix their lowing with the cries of traders and the clatter of cash.

Artists are pounding out iron tools and weapons, which clang rhythmically close to the edge of the market. Small textile sacks for the preservation of fish and meat sell salt collected and prepared from the seaside pans. The market day is not merely an economic event but a time of celebration as people from Somerled's realm come to trade, connect, and sustain their livelihoods.

The Foundations of Prosperity: Resources and Industries

From a scattered collection of islands, Somerled's strategic control over commerce, encouragement of a variety of economic enterprises, and integration into larger trade networks of his ports turned the Hebrides into a vibrant marine hub. This metamorphosis combined Norse inventiveness with Gaelic resilience to create a monarchy capable of challenging more expansive, centralised powers such as the Scottish Crown and the Norse realm.

Fishing: The Lifeblood of the Hebridean Economy

Thanks to the rich waters of the Hebrides, fishing was the pillar of the society. Herring, cod, and mackerel abound in the area from its rich fisheries, which were mainstays for trade as well as local food. Using *lín agus cliabh*, nets and creels made from flax or willow, fishing methods were advanced for the time. Longlines baited with hooks let one make notable catches of cod and other species for deeper waters.

With particular months devoted to herring runs or mackerel shoals, seasonal fishing cycles guaranteed sustained harvest.

Often grown locally, the catch was kept using salt and then stored in barrels for export. Salted fish became a primary export commodity, feeding populations in Ireland, Norway, and Scotland. Fish markets thrived in key ports like Dunstaffnage, where merchants from distant lands gathered to purchase this highly sought-after product. Fishing not only supported the local communities but also brought in a lot of revenue that supported other sectors of the economy.

Cattle Raising and Pastoral Economy

Cattle lay at the very heart of Gaelic life and economy in Somerled's kingdom. The harsh yet fertile grasslands of the Hebrides were perfectly suited to breeding robust breeds of cattle. Raised here, animals provided not only meat and dairy but also status symbols, indicators of riches, and a type of money.

Herds were pushed to trading hubs during market days when they were traded for items such as iron tools, textiles, and grain. The cattle business also produced by-products such as tallow, which was necessary for candles and lamps and hides needed for leather manufacturing. Valuable hides were shipped to Ireland and other locations, where they produced armour, belts, and shoes.

Cow ranching was cyclical, with seasonal grazing and careful breeding assured a consistent supply of cattle for home consumption and trade. Moreover, livestock were frequently given tribute by allied clans, hence strengthening political ties and economic relations within the realm.

Salt Production: The Strategic Commodity

Driven by its value in preserving meat and fish, salt manufacture was a major business in Somerled's domain. Carefully built to gather salt from seawater, coastal salt pans were found in places like the Isle of Mull. Using evaporation methods, workers let seawater gather in shallow pools set with stone. The sun and wind naturally dried the water, leaving behind refined, scraped, crystallised salt.

Salt was traded widely and utilised locally. It helped the fishing business by allowing catches to be kept for long trips to far-off markets. It is impossible to overestimate the strategic value of salt since it allowed Somerled's kingdom to control the fishing trade and preserve food security in hard winters or inadequate crops.

Timber Production and Shipbuilding

The kingdom's most significant industry derived its raw supplies from the forests of mainland Argyll. Cut down and transported to waterfront shipyards, tall, straight woods like oak and pine were turned into birlinns, the flexible galleys defining the

Hebridean navy, by expert workers. Their speed, agility, and durability – qualities valued in trade and warfare – made them essential.

Carpenters, blacksmiths, and rope makers worked on labour-intensive shipbuilding projects. The timber hulls were strengthened with iron rivets and nails, either imported from the mainland or produced locally. Not only did Somerled's navy seek ships, but traders and other clans also sought to purchase them for their use.

Timber was also an export commodity traded with regions lacking sufficient forest resources. The shipbuilding industry not only bolstered Somerled's naval power but also created employment and economic opportunities for many in his kingdom.

Textile Production and Wool Trade

Another significant economic activity in the Hebrides was textile and wool manufacturing. Sheep kept on the rocky slopes produced wool that, under expert hands, was sheared and spun into cloth. Women were crucial in this business, working with spinning wheels and looms to create premium fabrics.

Plants and lichens were used to create natural dyes, woad for blue and kermes for red, giving the textiles vivid hues. Important to the native inhabitants, woollen clothing offered protection from the hostile Hebridean environment. People appreciated the quality and longevity of the material, so excess fabrics were sold to Ireland and the mainland for Hebridean textile items.

Apart from a commercial activity, it was a kind of cultural expression since the methods and designs expressed the distinctiveness of the Gaelic people. Many people found work in this sector, therefore improving the state of the local communities.

Agriculture and Subsistence Farming

Although the Hebrides' rugged topography restricted major farming, agriculture remained a vital component of the economy. Barley and oats were the main crops grown on little plots and used to make bread, porridge, and ale. With hand tools and *cas-chrom*, or curved foot ploughs, these crops were grown utilising age-old techniques. Agricultural operations were set by seasonal cycles; harvest celebrations marked the end of labour-intensive times.

Apart from grains, vegetables, including leeks and cabbage, were grown, and herbs like thyme and sage were raised for both culinary and medicinal uses. Often exchanged locally, surplus goods gave rural towns a meagre but consistent revenue.

Maritime Trade and Connectivity

Trade was Somerled's economic lifeblood, connecting his kingdom to Ireland, the Scottish mainland, Norway, and further abroad. His ports were the heart of bustling commercial centres where salted fish, cattle, wool, and leather were traded for grain, iron, wine, and high-end products. Pots and precious metal wares came from the Irish, timber, furs, and amber from the Norwegians.

Somerled's kingdom's strategic location allowed it to operate as a link between the North Atlantic and the mainland, a key crossing point in regional and international trade networks. Trade's wealth also helped to develop a rich and vibrant civilisation, benefiting the whole people.

Artisanal Craft and Local Industry

Skilled artists were vital in the economy, creating tools, weapons, and jewellery. Blacksmiths made swords, axes, and agricultural equipment out of iron; potters made cooking and storage pots. Combining Gaelic and Norse creative traditions, jewellers fashioned complex decorations from glass beads, amber, and silver.

These goods were sold not only at home but also traded, bringing into the greater world the craftwork of the Hebrideans. Their manufacturing added yet another dimension to the economy and the kingdom, enhancing its diversity with exports and its culture by reputation.

Peat Extraction and Fuel Supply

Peat extraction was a vital commercial activity in an area with limited availability of firewood. From bogs, workers removed slabs of peat that they dried and substituted for fuel for cooking and heating. Peat was also traded locally so that those distant from bogs would have a ready supply of fuel.

Peat extraction required careful management to avoid overharvesting, and the practice reflected the resourcefulness of Somerled's people in adapting to their environment. This industry, while modest, was essential for the daily survival of the population.

Economic Integration and Political Strength

Somerled's economic policies were not isolated from his political ambitions. He guaranteed a consistent flow of riches, supporting his military campaigns and government by growing several sectors and connecting his kingdom to the international commerce networks. The wealth generated by these projects secured his position, guaranteed his friends' allegiance, and allowed him to project force outside of his borders.

Moreover, the Hebrides' cultural cohesiveness improved with the economic integration of his realm. Trade and industry's shared wealth helped the clans unite, allowing Somerled to maintain stability and fight against outside pressure.

A Lasting Economic Legacy

Long after Somerled's rule, the Hebrides' economic basis kept shaping them. Inspired by his initiatives, the Lords of the Isles carried on their work, creating one of the most prosperous and long-lasting Gaelic governments in Scottish memory. His kingdom benefitted from the trading networks he established and from its ability to provide flexibility to survive changes in political and cultural dynamics. Through such financial restraint, Somerled not only guaranteed the survival of his people but also their flourishing in a world of demand and dynamism.

Somerled's Trade Networks: Bridging the Hebrides to the World

Connecting the Hebrides to the world, Somerled's rule marked a turning point in the Hebrides' assimilation into the more general North Atlantic trading routes. Making use of his strategic location, Somerled turned the Hebrides into a hive of trade linking local markets with Ireland, the Scottish mainland, and even farther-off areas. Along with enhancing his kingdom's political authority and cultural interactions with other areas, these trade routes enhanced its riches.

Trade with Ireland: The Gaelic Connection

Thanks to its physical proximity and similar cultural legacy, Ireland was among Somerled's most important trading allies. Although trade between the Hebrides and Ireland existed before Somerled's rule, under his direction, these ties grew formalised and strengthened. Frequently sailing to Hebridean ports like Finlaggan, Irish businessmen traded goods and ideas with native businesses.

To Irish markets, the Hebrides exported livestock, wool, and salted fish. A mainstay of Irish diets, salted fish was in great demand, and a consistent source as the Hebrides had easy access to many fishing areas. The quality of the wool from the hardy sheep in the area was highly valued, and cattle, which are fundamental to both societies, were frequently sold either live or as processed hides.

Ireland gave food, pottery, and well-made metal objects in return. Grain was especially crucial as the Hebrides' rough topography made extensive farming difficult. Irish traders brought metal items and pottery that enhanced daily life in the Hebrides and mirrored the artistic and technical developments of Irish craftspeople.

This trade promoted close diplomatic relations between Somerled and Irish chieftains. Mutual economic dependence guaranteed that these ties were marked by collaboration; trade acted as a link between the two Gaelic-speaking areas. Common cultural activities like music, language, and narrative deepened this link even more.

The Scottish Mainland: A Link to Urban Growth

Particularly as the Scottish mainland saw urban expansion during the twelfth century, trade with the mainland became increasingly important in Somerled's economic plan.

Hebridean commodities arrived at Lowland markets via ports such as Oban and Ayr, which acted as gateways. Maintaining their own character while incorporating the Hebrides into the larger Scottish economy required these interactions.

From the Hebrides, traders transported leather, wool, and salted fish as well as goods to the continent. In Lowland Scotland, where demand for food, clothes, and raw materials was rising, these items fed the expanding towns and fortified estates. While Hebridean leather ended up in the manufacture of shoes, belts, and harnesses, salted fish was a mainstay for both urbanites and monastic groups.

The mainland returned food, iron tools, and luxury goods. Grain imports were essential for maintaining the Hebridean population, particularly in lean years. Luxury items, including beautiful linens and superb wine, attested to the growing riches of the Hebridean aristocracy under Somerled's leadership. More efficient iron equipment allowed the development of agricultural and shipbuilding businesses.

Maritime routes along the western seaboard gave Somerled control over this trade, and his kingdom's coffers filled up with goods moving safely and efficiently between the Hebrides and the mainland. This was not only a source of wealth but also increased his political power because the mainland leaders needed the resources of the Hebrides to sustain their economies.

Connections to Norway and the Norse World

Somerled, a leader with a dual Norse-Gaelic background, stayed close to Norway and other areas of the Norse realm. These ties reflected Somerled's pragmatic diplomatic and commerce philosophy as well as a legacy of earlier Norse rule in the Hebrides.

Frequent visitors to Hebridean ports, Norwegian traders brought amber, furs, and lumber. Given that the Hebrides' treeless isles depended on imports for construction and shipbuilding, timber was especially precious. Meanwhile, luxury goods like furs and amber gave the Hebridean elite's belongings more status.

The Hebrides returned salted fish, leather, and wool to Norway. A mainstay of the Norse diet, salted fish was an especially valuable export that guaranteed a consistent income flow into Somerled's realm. His fleet of birlinns guaranteed safe passage for traders and safeguarded trade routes against piracy, thus facilitating these trades.

Trade with Norway likewise had political and cultural ramifications. It strengthened Somerled's credibility among Norse-Gaelic people and helped him present himself as a middleman between Norse and Gaelic interests. By strengthening commercial links with Norway, Somerled made sure his kingdom stayed connected to the larger North Atlantic economy.

Long-Distance Trade: Beyond the Isles

Trade networks under Somerled linked the Hebrides to far-off markets in Flanders, northern Germany, and even the Mediterranean, transcending the nearby area. The Norse trade networks, which stretched great distances and carried items from all throughout Europe to the North Atlantic, helped to create these ties.

In continental marketplaces, where they served to expand urban populations and supported businesses like leatherworking, wool, cattle hides, and Hebridean salted fish, these were extremely valuable. In return, the Hebrides imported exotic spices, glass beads, silver jewellery, and exquisite fabrics. Along with enhancing the Hebrides' material culture, these luxury goods represented the wealth and cosmopolitanism of Somerled's court.

The Hebrides' inclusion in these long-distance trading systems brought attention to Somerled's strategic value. Somerled ensured his kingdom was a critical link in the chain of trade from northern Europe to the globe by underlining important marine routes. This function reinforced the Hebrides' prominence in the mediaeval economy, providing riches and respect.

The Strategic Role of Ports

The beating core of Somerled's commerce systems was his ports. Strategically placed along the western seaboard, these ports helped ideas, people, and things to flow. Merchants from Ireland, Scotland, Norway, and beyond gathered at these vibrant hubs of trade to trade.

These ports were markers of Somerled's power and vision as much as commercial hubs. Market taxes and docking fees provided a consistent source of income that was spent on the infrastructure and defence of the kingdom. By enforcing rules and preserving order, port officials ensured that trade might grow free from disturbance.

The ports were also cultural melting pots combining Irish, Norse, and Gaelic inspirations. The items traded, the languages spoken in the markets, and the evolving common customs over time all mirrored this cultural interaction. Somerled strengthened the cultural and economic resilience of his country by supporting active and inclusive trade centres.

The Prosperity and Might of Somerled's State

Somerled's economic measures were more than just the policies that sustained his state; they comprised the foundations on which he grounded his political strength and prosperity for his land. Through strategically traded control, promotion of varied economic engagements, and consolidation of his harbours with trade networks of further lands, Somerled repositioned the Hebrides to become a booming maritime business venture that had managed to infuse Gaelic perseverance with the sagacity of Norsemen.

He was able to create a prosperous economy by developing the sea resources of his kingdom. Fishing and cattle raising provided the basic food for his people, and salt making was always there as a surplus product that could be sold in trade. All this was possible because he strengthened these industries with an efficient infrastructure, like markets and coastal salt pans. This economic independence made his kingdom strong against the weaknesses of famine, isolation, and exploitation.

Somerled's ports were strategically located on the most vital maritime routes. More than being the centres of commerce, they became instruments of political and military control. By managing access to the ports, Somerled was not only able to enrich his treasury through docking fees and market taxes but also to use his position as a gatekeeper of trade. For those merchants desiring safe passage or access to markets of wealth, he could provide them and, in doing so, ensured that all around him was subjugated under his rule. This economic activity also attracted settlers, traders, and artisans who eventually fostered a cosmopolitan atmosphere, blending in their Gaelic, Norse, and Irish cultures.

Under Somerled's control, trade networks reached well beyond the Hebrides. He integrated his kingdom into the wider mediaeval economy by exporting salted fish, cattle, and wool to Ireland, the Scottish mainland, and even into continental Europe. These networks brought wealth, prestige, and access to luxury goods, which enhanced the prestige of the Hebridean elite. Most importantly, it was through trade that diplomatic relations were secured, which enhanced the political influence of Somerled. The economic cooperation with Ireland and Norway allowed Somerled to retain stability in his territory and ward off threats by external powers.

The economic gains were rechannelled back into military machinery, making his power even more solid. It was through this money that the birlinns were funded and kept on the waters since they formed the core of Somerled's naval power. With a powerful fleet at his disposal, Somerled was able to secure maritime routes, dissuade piracy, and project power across the region. Beyond securing lifelines to the kingdom's economy, his domination of these routes heightened his political bargaining power in Scotland as well as with Norse overlords.

Just as crucial was Somerled's attitude toward the division of riches in his domain. He fostered unity and loyalty by sharing the benefits of commerce and tribute with allied clans, therefore strengthening his rule. This created an interdependent network of clans whose prosperity lay in the success of the Hebrides and tied them up with Somerled's leadership. It also strengthened Gaelic traditions of kinship and reciprocity, retaining the cultural integrity of the area while it adjusted to new economic circumstances.

Somerled's economic strategies guaranteed not only his kingdom's short-term wealth but also long-term success in line with the Lord of the Isles tradition. Under his successors, the economic model he developed in strategic partnerships, local resource management, and marine trade kept blossoming. This produced riches and stability that could enable the Hebrides to hang on to at least some degree of autonomy as the Scottish Crown travelled over the ages toward more centralisation.

Somerled's vision for his economy was ultimately not separable from his vision for his kingdom. He assured the Hebrides would survive and flourish as a political and cultural pillar by emphasising economic resilience and building relationships with the larger world. His legacy as a leader is one of flexibility, insight, and relentless dedication to the welfare of his people, thus transforming the history of Scotland and the North Atlantic.

Chapter 18

Somerled's Court and Administration

Rising over the craggy Hebridean terrain, the sun sent a golden beam across Somerled's territory. Nestled on a rocky ledge with a view of the turbulent sea, the wooden hall stood strong against the elements, and its worn-out walls were evidence of ongoing workmanship. While the thatched roof of woven heather showed traces of many storms, thick oak beams imported from Argyll supported the construction. Rising upward, smoke from the centre hearth mixed with the salty breeze carried the subtle hum of life from the busy town below.

Inside, the hall exuded intent. Long tables stretched throughout the area, their surfaces worn with years, and the weight of choices taken evident. The walls were covered with shields carrying the emblems of allied clans, each silently reminding us of the alliances keeping the kingdom together. A steady undercurrent of activity as courtiers, chieftains, and advisers debated the day's events, combined with a rhythmic crackle from the hearth.

Sitting at the front of the hall was Somerled, his presence powerful but not obtrusive. Designed with complex sea and sky themes, his high-backed chair raised him above the assembly. Wearing a cloak of deep blues and greens secured with a silver brooch fashioned like a leaping fish, he looked about the room with the piercing eye of a leader who missed no detail. His face was one of calculated serenity, a man skilled in the art of listening and decision-making.

To his right stood the seneschal, a thin man whose hands, soiled with ink, held a leather-bound ledger loaded with records and accounts. Somerled's keen eyes flew around the hall, organising conflicts to be settled, taxes to be paid, and petitions just waiting for review. On Somerled's left, a figure of quiet authority bearing the weight of the Brehon rules in their memory stood robed in plain, unadorned wool. Gallowglass captains nearby leaned against the walls, their chainmail catching the firelight, a subdued but continual reminder of the military force supporting the court's power.

The day started with a measured beat, the clang of a staff on the stone floor muffling the quiet buzz of speech. Rising from the assembled throng, a farmer had years of work on his worn-out face. He lowered himself before the dais, gripping his woollen cap firmly in his hands. His voice, sharpened by work and wind, told of a terrible conflict over shared grazing territory with a nearby clan.

As the lawgiver carefully reviewed decades of precedents, lips remained mute. When the farmer ended, the lawgiver spoke, offering a verdict anchored in justice and custom. Somerled nodded his agreement and offered a last word of advice to support the decision. Clearly relieved, the farmer bowed once more and then turned back into the throng.

Then, the morning moved toward issues of defence. The gallowglass commanders moved forward, their heavy feet resounding on the stone floor. Rising to deliver his report, the leader – a seasoned fighter with a scar down the line of his jaw – knelt momentarily. He described coast patrols, birlinns' preparation, and the sighting of a Norse fleet skirting the outlying isles.

Somerled listened carefully, then gave orders with a tone of unquestionable power. The captains nodded, their determined features set as they turned out of the hall. Petitioners kept moving ahead, each carrying complaints and needs. A blacksmith showed a just-created blade with promise on the edge. With hands rough from work, farmers asked permission to clear fresh areas for sowing; their words carried promise. Her voice firm despite the grief in her eyes, a widow begged for justice against a neighbour who had taken her livestock. Every matter was carefully considered, and the lawgiver consulted chieftains and advisers before rendering his decision.

The day's activity came to an end as the sun sank lower in the sky and sent sweeping shadows across the hall. Rising from his chair, Somerled greeted everyone assembled. He talked of solidarity, resilience, and the power discovered in custom and teamwork. For those who listened, his comments had a subdued intensity that really connected. As he concluded his remarks, faces revealed a mix of pride, will, and respect; a roar from the assembly swept the hall with a common goal.

When the hall finally emptied, the echoes of the day mixed with the crash of waves against the coast. The little fire in the hearth warmed the room with its embers. The day's work was finished for Somerled, but its consequences would flow throughout his realm like the tide, constantly, powerfully changing the fate of his people.

The Legal and Administrative Systems of Somerled's Realm

Drawing on the rich roots of Gaelic custom and adjusting to the practicalities of running a varied and sometimes divided maritime realm, Somerled's government was a careful mix of invention and legacy. His administrative and legal institutions were meant to guarantee order, fairness, and allegiance throughout the Hebrides and western Scotland. Reflecting his dual background, they combined aspects of the Norse and Gaelic worlds into a coherent framework that supported the stability of his authority and the demands of his people.

The Foundations of Justice: Brehon Law

Brehon law, the ancient Gaelic legal system that prioritised restitution and reconciliation above punitive actions, was fundamental in Somerled's legal framework. Deeply rooted in Gaelic society, this approach stressed group responsibility and communal participation. Unlike the strict hierarchies of Norman feudal law, Brehon law was based on oral tradition and depended on the expertise of educated judges, or brehons, who memorised great volumes of legal precedent.

Somerled maintained and enhanced the Brehon law such that it remained the pillar of justice in his domain. Respected brehons he assigned to monitor legal affairs in important areas were given the power to resolve conflicts and render decisions. These autonomous brehons ran under strict instruction, and their social position helped to protect their objectivity. They moved between villages, holding court in local halls or open-air events where the people might see events.

Under Brehon law, disagreements frequently centred on property, cattle, and kinship responsibilities. The way Somerled applied these rules highlighted the ideas of restorative justice. For instance, in cases of theft or harm, the guilty party had to pay the victim or their family, usually in labour, goods, or livestock. This strategy helped maintain peace in society and lower the possibility of the development of conflicts.

Codifying Laws and Addressing Local Needs

Though Brehon law established the basis of justice, Somerled also proposed policies to handle the difficulties of running a maritime nation. These encompassed rules on trade, maritime behaviour, and resource management that catered to his people's requirements.

Maritime Laws

Understanding the vital part the sea played in his kingdom's defence and economy, Somerled instituted thorough marine rules to control behaviour on the seas. These rules set standards for the division of spoils from naval operations, defined the obligations of ship captains, and created procedures for settling problems at sea. The treatment of shipwrecks, which frequently resulted in conflicts among tribes fighting for recovered valuables, was one especially divisive topic these rules addressed.

To guarantee equitable distribution, Somerled established strict policies emphasising the return of items to their original owners should they be able to be found. These policies not only lessened disputes but also helped the seafarers under his control feel equity and order, strengthening his power and the cohesiveness of his maritime realm.

Land and Resource Management

Shared resources like grazing areas, fishing waters, and peat bogs dominated Somerled's territory. He issued edicts controlling access to these resources to stop overuse and strife. Clan leaders had to keep thorough records of their territories, and local councils helped brehons decide boundary disagreements.

In areas where fishing was the main way of life, Somerled instituted seasonal limitations to guarantee sustainable output. These steps represented his forward-looking attitude to resource management and his dedication to the long-term welfare of his people.

Taxation and Tribute

To sustain his kingdom, Somerled formalised systems of taxation and tribute that were both practical and fair. Taxes were often paid in kind, with cattle, fish, and grain serving as the primary forms of currency. Wealthier clans contributed larger shares, while poorer communities were given leniency during difficult times.

Payments of tribute from allied clans strengthened the links of reciprocity and loyalty. Infrastructure, navy maintenance, and court operations were funded via these donations.

The Administration of Justice

Under Somerled's guidance, justice was a very participatory process, stressing community involvement and openness. Legal procedures were sometimes conducted in public places like village halls or open fields where every member of the society could see and help.

Dispute Resolution

Presiding over legal conflicts, the brehons listened to witnesses' and parties' evidence. Their strong awareness of precedent and oral tradition helped them make decisions that maintained justice and cultural values.

Sometimes, Somerled himself intervened in well-publicised instances, especially those involving inter-clan conflicts or strategic concerns. His decisions reflected his image as a fair and forceful leader and carried great weight.

Punishments and Restitution

Under the Brehon law, penalties were intended to bring peace rather than wreak revenge. Often, offenders had to compensate their victims in labour, goods, or animals. When a major offence like murder occurred, the brehon aimed to avoid blood feuds by negotiating a cumulative, or compensation, arrangement among the families engaged.

Another prevalent punishment was public humiliation, in which offenders had to make apologies before society. This strategy emphasised the need for responsibility and group welfare even more.

Appeals and Oversight

Somerled developed systems for appeals so that people can bring unresolved conflicts to the court for a decision. This structure guaranteed that everyone from different social levels could get justice.

Royal authorities' regular checks guaranteed local leaders followed the laws and regulations of the kingdom. These trips strengthened Somerled's leadership and stopped regional-level abuses of authority.

A Vision of Balanced Governance

Legal and administrative institutions developed by Somerled reflected his ideal of a united and rich kingdom. He developed a structure that promoted stability and resilience by combining the egalitarian ideas of Gaelic tradition with the organisational efficiency of Norse and Norman methods. His people were devoted to him because of his dedication to justice, fairness, and cultural preservation; he also guaranteed his legacy as a wise and forceful ruler.

Key Figures in Somerled's Government: Leadership and Loyalty

Somerled's capacity for good government was derived not only from his own leadership, but also from the talented and devoted people who underpinned his government. His governance was a complex network of functions designed to meet the needs of a maritime kingdom distinguished by cultural variety and ongoing outside pressure. Important players in preserving order, defending the realm, and guaranteeing its wealth were the seneschal and gallowglass mercenary captains.

The Seneschal: The Chief Administrator

Somerled's governance was based on the seneschal, a reliable officer who served as the kingdom's main administrator. The seneschal's responsibilities included financial control, coordination of regional government, and application of Somerled's ideas throughout the Hebrides.

Financial Stewardship

The seneschal oversaw the treasury of the kingdom to guarantee equitable and effective collection of taxes and tributes. Given Somerled's varied economy – from trading and specialised crafts to fishing and cattle raising – this function demanded a strong awareness of economic dynamics.

Often paid in kind, taxes were based on the riches of the kingdom – cattle, fish, and grains comprising the backbone. The thorough records of the seneschal guaranteed that these donations were used wisely, thereby supporting military operations, preserving the court, and financing building projects, including shipbuilding.

Coordination of Regional Governance

The seneschal served as a link between Somerled's court and regional officials, guaranteeing the consistent application of kingdom regulations. Clan chiefs answered to the seneschal, who then sent their worries and developments to Somerled during council sessions.

Given that the seneschal sometimes arbitrated conflicts between clans or counselled local leaders on issues of government, this position demanded diplomatic acumen.

Oversight of Legal and Administrative Systems

Working closely with brehons and other legal authorities, the seneschal guaranteed equitable application of justice. This covered keeping records of conflicts and their resolutions, supervising the execution of decisions, and planning court hearings.

Apart from legal concerns, the seneschal supervised administrative logistics, such as royal land management and market day planning, in important ports, including Finlaggan and Dunstaffnage.

The post of the seneschal demanded constant allegiance and extraordinary organisational skills. Often acting as Somerled's right-hand counsel, this person made sure the daily operations of the kingdom functioned without hiccups so the king could concentrate on military and strategic issues.

Gallowglass Mercenary Captains: The Enforcers of Security

The gallowglass mercenaries represented the kingdom's martial might, while the seneschal oversaw its administrative core. Gallowglasses were crucial in preserving peace, guarding the realm, and projecting Somerled's force.

Origins and Role of the Gallowglasses

Originally of Norse-Gaelic background, the gallowglasses were well-equipped mercenaries known for their discipline and fighting skills. Reflecting their varied cultural background and professional rank, their moniker, derived from the Gaelic *gallóglaigh*, meaning 'foreign warriors',

Equipped with long axes, wide swords, and chainmail, the gallowglasses were fierce on the battlefield. Their weighty armour and commanding weapons made them perfect for shock fighting, where they might breach enemy lines and overwhelm less experienced forces.

Gallowglasses were defensive as well as offensive under Somerled's command. In areas prone to upheaval, they enforced royal edicts, guarded important persons, and guarded critical territory.

Leadership and Structure

Under direction from a captain selected for their expertise, allegiance, and strategic sense, every band of gallowglasses. These captains guaranteed that their efforts complemented the more general goals of the kingdom by reporting directly to Somerled or his military advisers.

Training their fighters, upholding discipline, and arranging their deployment fell to the captains. Their close awareness of local terrain and opponent strategies helped them significantly organise and carry out military campaigns.

Dual Role as Diplomats and Enforcers

Apart from their military responsibilities, gallowglass captains sometimes served as middlemen between Somerled's court and provincial officials. Their presence acted as a reminder of the ruler's power, and their capacity to arbitrate conflicts strengthened their significance as peacekeepers and stabilisers.

When needed, the gallowglasses – whose martial reputation guaranteed compliance – were called upon to enforce royal directives. Their intervention in disputes or rebellions was often enough to resolve tensions without bloodshed, as few dared to challenge their might.

Other Key Figures in Somerled's Government

While the seneschal and gallowglass captains were central to Somerled's administration, other officials and advisers contributed to the kingdom's governance.

Lawgivers and Brehons

These legal professionals advised Somerled on issues of justice and significantly helped him to understand the Brehon law. Their great awareness of Gaelic history guaranteed that the legal system of the realm stayed just and culturally relevant.

Harbourmasters

Oversaw the heavy traffic at Somerled's ports, harbourmasters controlled commerce, paid docking fees, and guaranteed seamless goods movement. Reporting straight to the seneschal, they were an essential link in the economic system of the kingdom.

Religious Advisers

Held in great power in Somerled's court, clergy and monastic leaders oversaw ecclesiastical affairs and provided spiritual direction. Drawing on their moral power to promote reconciliation, they also acted as middlemen in conflicts.

Balancing Authority and Delegation

Somerled's approach to government depended on a careful mix between centralised power and assigned responsibilities. Surrounding oneself with talented and devoted people helped him to guarantee that his kingdom was not only well-run but also strong against adversity. From the seneschal to the gallowglass captains, every official performed a particular function in preserving the delicate balance of power, security, and wealth that marked Somerled's rule.

Through this network of reliable people, Somerled was able to spread his power over the Hebrides and western Scotland, uniting a varied and sometimes divided populace under one coherent leadership. Rooted in both pragmatic innovation and Gaelic tradition, this framework established a paradigm for efficient government that spoke to people long after his lifetime.

Balancing Cultural Influences in Somerled's Governance Style

The rule of Somerled is a masterful example of how to balance several cultural elements to produce a strong and unified nation. Under the direction of a Norse-Gaelic leader, the Hebrides evolved into a melting pot of customs where Somerled deftly combined the Norse and Gaelic legacies to create a distinctive government model. Drawing on these two rich cultural traditions guaranteed the stability of his country and helped his people to develop a shared identity.

A Dual Heritage as a Strength

Somerled's background put him up as a link between the indigenous Gaelic clans and the Norse colonists who had governed the Hebrides for ages. Instead of choosing one legacy over the other, he embraced both, leveraging his twin identities to create alliances, arbitrate conflicts, and justify his authority.

Norse Influence in Maritime Strategy and Trade

Using Norse nautical customs, Somerled's rule enhanced his naval might and helped his realm become part of the North Atlantic trade routes. The birlinn, the famous ship of his fleet, was built with Norse workmanship modified to fit the requirements of Gaelic seamen.

Somerled's economic policy reflected the Norse concentration on sea trade. Ports such as Finlaggan and Dunstaffnage developed into hive centres where Norse traders mixed with Gaelic traders to create economic interdependence, bridging cultural divisions.

His government used Norse administrative techniques, such as ordered trade rules and regulated taxation structures, to guarantee the effective management of his maritime economy.

Gaelic Traditions in Leadership and Law

Particularly in his attitude to leadership and judicial systems, Somerled greatly revered and defended Gaelic customs. Representing the Gaelic idea of kinship-based government, he presided over as a *ceann-cinnidh*, head of kin. Under his leadership, this strategy gave loyalty, reciprocity, and group decision-making top priority, which spoke to the clans.

Brehon law's ongoing application guaranteed that conflicts were settled by arbitration and payment instead of punishment. Retaining this structure helped Somerled preserve cultural continuity and support his legitimacy as a Gaelic leader.

Crucially important for the Gaelic government, clan councils, and assemblies allowed local leaders to express their worries and take part in decision-making. These meetings preserved Gaelic practices and provided venues for including Norse immigrants in the more general political system.

Symbolism and Identity: Bridging the Divide

Beyond pragmatic policy, Somerled's governing approach promoted a single identity that cut across cultural differences. His people were connected by a visual and ceremonial language he invented by combining Norse and Gaelic symbols.

Artistic Synthesis

His domain's creative traditions mirrored this cultural mix. Combining Norse knotwork and warrior themes with Gaelic Christian imagery, stone sculptures, high crosses, and burial markers became lifelong markers of the kingdom's composite identity.

Royal regalia, weapons, and common objects all included decorative motifs that similarly highlighted this synthesis, therefore supporting the belief that Norse and Gaelic influences were not antagonistic forces but rather complementary facets of a shared history.

Religious Integration

Somerled's rule overlapped the Hebrides' Christianisation of their Norse inhabitants. Along with making sure freshly converted Norsemen felt part of the religious fabric of his kingdom, he encouraged Gaelic monastic establishments such as Iona.

Under Somerled's sponsorship, churches and monasteries were hubs of both faith and cultural preservation, liturgical uses of the Gaelic language notwithstanding Norse architectural and artistic expression.

Ceremonial Practices

Under Somerled's direction, public events and celebrations sometimes mirrored this mixing of customs. Along with Norse-inspired ceremonies, seasonal Gaelic holidays, such as Samhain and Beltane, created common cultural events promoting unity.

Somerled himself presented this twin character in his public persona. While Norse societies praised him as a strong and just leader, Bardic poetry honoured him as a Gaelic hero. His capacity to negotiate and welcome these twin stories enhanced his reputation as a uniting man.

Balancing Power and Unity

Somerled's style of government revealed a knowledge that the stability of his domain depended on balancing power between several groups and thereby promoting unity.

Inclusive Leadership

Among Somerled's court were officials and advisers from Norse and Gaelic origins. This inclusiveness guaranteed that his policies represented the interests of every one of his people, therefore reducing the possibility of factionalism.

Somerled avoided the alienation sometimes accompanying centralised control by arming local leaders and honouring their customs. His government approach promoted loyalty and cooperation by harmonising the general power of the crown with the autonomy of regional clans.

Military Cohesion

With Norse-Gaelic men fighting side by side, Somerled's army was a microcosm of the cultural variety of his realm. His Gallowglasses descended from Norse immigrants, and his Gaelic clansmen united to demonstrate the pragmatic advantages of military battle cultural fusion.

Legacy of a Hybrid Kingdom

The Hebrides have a heritage from Somerled's skill to strike a mix between Norse and Gaelic inspirations. His approach to governing set a standard for the Lords of the Isles, who kept their autonomy while still negotiating the complexity of cultural dualism. For years, the mixed identity created under Somerled became a distinguishing feature of the Hebrides, influencing its politics, economy, and society.

His rule was evidence of the strength of inclusion, adaptation, and cultural synthesis; it also provided insightful leadership and unification teachings that are relevant even today.

Chapter 19

Women in Somerled's World

The hall of Finlaggan was alive with the low murmur of advisers discussing, the measured step of warriors standing watch, and the odd laughter from attendants gathered by the hearth. At the core of it all was Ragnhild, Somerled's wife, whose presence possessed the force of the sea beyond the stone walls of their stronghold. She was the epitome of two worlds – the haughty daughter of Norse monarchs and the loyal mother of a Gaelic lord – draped in a superbly woven cloak painted deep blue with silver thread in Norse knotwork.

By Olaf the Red, King of the Isles, Ragnhild was the daughter of the strong Norse kings who had long ruled over the western seaboard. Raised amid sailors and fighters, she was used to the weight of government and the careful dance of diplomacy. She brought that wisdom into her new house after seeing her father negotiate the turbulent waves of alliance and rivalry. She was married to Somerled. Their marriage cemented the blending of Norse and Gaelic dominance in the Isles by solidifying their bloodlines rather than only a joining of hands.

Ragnhild's influence in Somerled's court went well beyond what a consort would have had effect. She was not a woman happy to play a quiet role nor a token in the great game of politics. She sat at the centre of the affairs of the realm, her words weighty among warriors and chieftains both. Leading campaigns or forming new alliances, Somerled was away, ensuring that the kingdom ran in his absence and keeping the court stable. She watched over the everyday administration of their possessions, handled clan conflicts, and heard the complaints of noblemen. Her awareness of the complex network of alliances inside the Isles was claimed to be only matched by Somerled's own.

She also oversaw the court's domestic and financial operations, ensuring that food, trade, and diplomatic presents flowed as consistently as the tides from the management of its great resources. From the well-stocked granaries to the artists creating exquisite fabrics and handcrafted metalwork and preparing extravagant feasts marking the grand assemblies of nobles, the richness of the household reflected her meticulous leadership.

Still, Ragnhild's influence extended outside of Finlaggan's hallways. She was a supporter of storytellers and poets so that the heroic deeds of Gaelic warriors and the sagas of Norse forefathers would be told in equal measure. She fostered the customs of both societies, therefore strengthening the harmony that distinguished Somerled's rule. When conflicts developed between Norse and Gaelic groups, her touch often directed peace, and her voice calmed hardened hearts.

Despite her great pedigree and strong presence, she did not rule with conceit or force. Those who knew her described a lady who understood when to demand and when to submit, one with the wisdom of an elder and the shrewdness of a sea captain. Her impact was quiet, unquestionable authority rather than open dispute. Ragnhild was the current under Somerled's hand, wielding the sword, making sure every stroke landed exactly.

She was, in every respect, a queen in all but name; her legacy permeated Somerled's court like certain banners hanging from its walls. Though history would recall her husband as the warrior-king who determined the fate of the Isles, those who stood in the halls of Finlaggan knew that at moments, even he was steadied, and his power was equalled by the woman standing next to him.

The Women Who Shaped Somerled's Realm

Although Ragnhild was the queenly presence at Somerled's court, she was not the only woman whose influence formed the realm. Surrounding her was a tapestry of diplomacy, government, and survival spun by noblewomen – Somerled's daughters, the wives of his closest allies, and the matriarchs of strong clans – that was just as crucial as any battle fought with sword and ship. These women were not only passive characters confined to their halls or tokens of power. These were the hands keeping alliances, the brains guiding their homes, and the voices influencing Isles politics.

Somerled's Daughters: The Carriers of Legacy

The daughters of Somerled were more than just the children of a powerful lord. They were instruments of diplomacy, the flesh-and-blood bonds that linked rival clans and ensured the stability of the realm. Marriages among the Gaelic and Norse aristocracy were rarely matters of love; they were calculated, strategic unions designed to fortify power and secure peace. Somerled, a man whose ambition extended beyond the battlefield, understood this better than most. Though history has left few names behind, his daughters played an essential role in the careful balance he maintained between Gaelic and Norse rulers.

One such marriage was to the MacLeods, a clan with deep Norse roots that controlled key strongholds in the Isles. A daughter of Somerled wed into their family, ensuring that they remained loyal to his rule rather than seeking alliances with distant Norwegian kings. Another was given in marriage to a powerful chieftain in Ulster, strengthening ties across the Irish Sea and securing safe harbours for Somerled's fleets. These women forged a living map of alliances through their unions, each marriage binding disparate factions into a unified force.

But marriage alone was not the extent of their influence. As wives, these women often served as the chief advisers to their husbands, their voices carrying weight in matters of diplomacy, trade, and governance. Many would go on to become the mothers of future rulers, ensuring that their father's legacy continued through the next generation. The sons they bore would claim their right to rule not only by blood but by the alliances their mothers had crafted, their inheritances built upon the quiet negotiations conducted within the halls of stone-built strongholds and timber-walled keeps.

The Wives of Somerled's Allies: Diplomats, Stewards, and Warriors

Beyond Somerled's daughters, the upkeep of power was much aided by the wives of his most reliable friends. Often nurtured in the homes of Norse jarls or the courts of Gaelic lords, they were women of aristocratic birth who learnt the skill of government early on. Their responsibilities went much beyond running their homes; they were stewards of riches, managers of alliances, and, during times of conflict, even defenders of their territory.

A noblewoman in the tough, sometimes explosive environment of the western seaboard had to be more than just a token headpiece. Many of these women governed in the absence of their husbands, supervising rent collecting, resolving conflicts among their people, and making sure warriors were prepared and provisioned for combat. Some even travelled to the front lines personally. Stories of noblewomen guiding their men through difficult times, protecting their homes from marauding groups while their husbands were abroad serving in far-off countries, abound. Understanding the frailty of power, these women used it with the same accuracy that their husbands used their swords.

Among them was the wife of a major ally from Kintyre, a woman of Gaelic background whose astute administration of her clan's lands guaranteed their allegiance to Somerled even under trying circumstances. She was renowned not only for her knowledge but also for her capacity to inspire respect among her people, guaranteeing that traders, farmers, and fighters all considered her an authority in her own right.

Another was the wife of a Norse chieftain who had promised fealty to Somerled. From a family of Viking fighters, she embraced the customs of her Gaelic neighbours but kept her people's fierce autonomy. She reportedly had her kids trained to use axes as soon as they were strong enough to lift them, and she wore a short sword at her belt. She did not withdraw into grief after her husband died in a struggle with competing clans; instead, she seized command of his fighters and led them in a battle to exact revenge before finalising a new marriage partnership that would fortify the position of her clan.

These women knew that survival in Somerled's world was taken, negotiated, and defended, not granted. Their capacity to negotiate the perilous waters of power guaranteed that the kingdom stayed together even in uncertain or wartorn times.

The Power of Women Beyond the Court

While the noblewomen of Somerled's realm held sway in matters of politics and governance, their influence extended beyond the halls of power. Preserving the customs binding the Gaelic and Norse cultures together, the female poets, healers, and seers of the Isles carried the wisdom of generations.

Highly esteemed members of Gaelic society, poets, or *filidh*, immortalised the acts of kings and fighters in their songs. Among these writers were women; their works had as much power as those of their male colleagues. They changed popular opinion, transforming conflicts into stories and guaranteeing that Somerled's dominion would live long after he died.

Also important in society were healers. Whether they were farmers hurt in the fields or warriors returning from war, women taught in the use of herbs and salves, and restoring draughts tended to the injured. Every generation carried on their medical expertise, combining the pragmatic with the spiritual.

In Gaelic tradition, seers and wise women, known as *banfháidh*, held a particular position. Their visions, their interpretations of omens, and their capacity to counsel leaders were sought through uncertain times. Before starting significant wars, even a man of tremendous ambition and military skill – even Somerled – was known to consult the wise ladies of the Isles.

A Legacy of Strength and Influence

Women were the cornerstone upon which his authority was based, the hands that brokered peace, the voices guiding tribes, and the spirits guaranteeing the survival of their people. From Ragnhild, the queenly strategist, to the warrior wives of his friends and the poets who would always remember his deeds, these women determined the fate of the Isles as definitely as any chieftain or monarch.

Though history usually notes the names of warriors and warlords, the real power of Somerled's kingdom was found in the women who kept it together, who made sure the relationships established in blood and combat lasted through generations. Their impact went beyond the court's boundaries and into the heart of the kingdom itself, silently shaping its power.

The Legal Status of Women in Norse-Gaelic Society

The junction of Gaelic and Norse traditions impacted women's legal standing in Somerled's society since it gave them more rights than in many other mediaeval European communities. These legal rights were especially obvious in issues of property ownership, inheritance, marriage, and justice. Though they were different, Gaelic Brehon law and Norse law, such as the Grágás codes of Iceland, shared fundamental ideas that let women own property, arbitrate legal issues, and function as major players in family discussions.

Property Rights and Inheritance

Women in Norse-Gaelic society benefitted most from their right to own and inherit land. If a daughter had no surviving brothers, Norse law let her inherit property;

this custom continued in the Hebridean villages. Though focused on male kinship inheritance, Gaelic Brehon law let women own land either as part of their *céile* (marriage agreement) or as part of a dowry.

Practically speaking, when their husbands were away at sea or in battle, noblewomen frequently looked after the land belonging to their families. If widowed, especially if she had sons who were not yet of age to inherit, a woman may keep power over family property. Their autonomy allowed them to handle rentals, distribute inheritance, and file legal claims on disputed land.

Example: Aud the Deep-Minded

The biography of Aud the Deep-Minded, a ninth-century Norse noblewoman who inherited her husband's lands and guided her family to Iceland, where she divided the land among her followers, offers a pattern for female proprietors in the Norse realm. Aud lived before Somerled's period, although her narrative captures the long-standing Norse custom of women wielding power over homes and territory. Noblewomen of Somerled's society most certainly followed similar customs while their husbands were involved in political or military matters.

Marriage Laws and Divorce Rights

Many mediaeval European countries saw marriage as essentially a legally enforceable contract with little redress for women. Nonetheless, under some circumstances, Norse and Gaelic customs both acknowledged a woman's right to divorce. For instance, Gaelic Brehon law allowed a woman to break from a marriage if her husband mistreated her, neglected her, refused to support her, or suffered from a major infirmity. Norse law similarly permitted divorce should a woman show cruelty or neglect.

Unlike their Norman and Anglo-Saxon colleagues, women also kept their property in case of a divorce. In England and France, a woman's belongings usually became her husband's, but in Norse-Gaelic society, she was entitled to recover her dowry and any riches she had brought into the marriage.

Example: Aife's Divorce Case

An Irish legal source from the twelfth century notes the instance of Aife, daughter of Diarmaid, who proved her husband had neglected to support her and thus effectively split from him. This case illustrates the legal defence accessible to women in Gaelic law, which carried into Somerled's domains.

Women in Legal Disputes

Women actively participated in legal conflicts even though they did not usually operate as brehons, judges, or lawgivers. They might forward issues involving personal grievances, inheritance, and property. Sometimes, they served as clan mediators, especially if their marriage gave them influential contacts that helped to resolve disputes.

Brehon law mandated recompense (including fines) for personal injury and let women seek reparation either on behalf of their family or personally. This legislative framework guaranteed that women actively participated in preserving justice in their local areas.

Example: The Widow's Appeal
A Gaelic legal record notes an unidentified widow who successfully sued a brehon judge following attempts by her late husband's clan to grab her cattle. She claimed her right to keep her property, and the court decided in her favour, underlining once more how a widow's possessions could not be removed without proper legal procedure.

The Social Status of Women in Norse-Gaelic Society

Although the legal system gave women a structure for protection and autonomy, their social status was mostly determined by their position inside the family and the larger society. Women in Somerled's society were spouses, mothers, traders, healers, religious patrons, and even unofficial political consultants.

Marriage and Clan Alliances

For aristocratic women, marriage was the most significant social institution since it was the main way clans could form alliances. A noblewoman's marriage can help to unite territorial claims or bring peace between warring tribes. However, unlike in Norman and Anglo-Saxon communities, women in Norse-Gaelic culture frequently had input in their marriage plans.

Through their marriages, women were expected to maintain the honour of their families, but as wives of chieftains, they also acquired great authority. Rising from being a highborn woman who controlled everyday events on her estate and even counselled her husband on matters of government, she might become a formidable presence in her household.

Example: The Marriage of Ragnhild and Somerled
Somerled's wife, Ragnhild, was instrumental in bolstering her husband's claim to the Isles. Being the daughter of Olaf Godredsson, King of the Isles, her marriage to Somerled gave him credibility among Norse immigrants to the area. This shows how important marriage was for political strategy rather than as a personal concern.

Women in Trade and Craftsmanship

Lower-status women engaged more actively in economic life than noblewomen, who were limited to running estates and maintaining alliances. In Norse civilisation, women held market booths, oversaw fisheries, and laboured as traders and weavers. Women engaged in textile manufacture, brewing, and food preservation by salting and smoking continued to occupy these positions in Norse-Gaelic colonies.

Maritime trade included women as well. Some women controlled merchant businesses, especially in coastal towns where trading with Ireland, Scotland, and Norway was vital to economic life, even though they were unlikely to captain ships.

Example: Hebridean Wool Traders
The *Annals of Ulster* mention Gaelic women involved in the wool trade, exporting high-quality cloth to Ireland and beyond. Given that Hebridean sheep produced durable wool, it is likely that many women managed weaving enterprises that sustained their households.

Religious and Cultural Influence

Women in Somerled's world also possessed authority through religious patronage and cultural preservation. Noblewomen's family history was preserved in great part by monastic patronage; some of them established abbeys or churches. Crucially for preserving Gaelic cultural identity, they also participated heavily in oral storytelling and poetry.

Women, often the custodians of history and genealogy, passed on tales of historic wars and forebears. This was especially crucial in Gaelic society, where lineage controlled political legitimacy.

Example: Monastic Patronage by Noblewomen
Somerled's daughters most certainly participated in monastery endowments, as was typical of Gaelic nobility of the day, even if there are no surviving records of their founding religious sites.

Women and Warfare

Although direct participation in fighting was unusual, women occasionally helped defend their homes during attacks. They also managed fortifications and guaranteed food supply for soldiers, therefore helping with the logistical elements of combat. Women occasionally also worked as peacemakers, arranging truces between competing groups.

Example: The Defence of Dunstaffnage
Later, Scottish customs involved women in the Hebrides guarding castles while their husbands were away on battle. Although the details of these tales are still unknown, they show that noblewomen oversaw keeping their homes orderly even in times of difficulty.

Shaped by the blending of Norse and Gaelic customs, women in Somerled's culture occupied a unique role in mediaeval society. Women in the Norse-Gaelic realm enjoyed more legal rights and social mobility than those in Capetian France, Norman England, and the Holy Roman Empire. Still, they were limited by marital ties, kinship systems, and social mores. This study investigates important areas where the roles of women in Somerled's domain differed from or reflected those in other mediaeval European communities.

The legal position was one of the most obvious distinctions between women in Somerled's environment and those in much of mediaeval Europe. Compared to their Norman, Anglo-Saxon, and feudal equivalents, Norse and Gaelic traditions gave women more liberty in matters of property, inheritance, and marriage. The inheritance rules in mediaeval France and Norman England were quite severe for women.

Inheritance rules were controlled by primogeniture, the custom whereby all lands and titles were passed to the eldest son. Only if they had no surviving brothers did women inherit the land; even then, they were frequently expected to marry to keep control. Their husbands or male guardians typically administered their property. By contrast, in Somerled's world, women – especially noblewomen – had far greater access to land ownership.

A habit carried on in the Norse-Gaelic Hebrides, Norse women could inherit land and run estates. Though it gave male heirs preference, Gaelic Brehon law let women keep their dowries and hold property after marriage. Often managing land and fortune until their sons came of age, widows had great autonomy.

Another area where Norse-Gaelic women exercised more agency than women in other mediaeval Europe was marriage. In Capetian France and the Holy Roman Empire, women had little influence over their marital destiny, and weddings were sometimes set aside just for political and financial advantage.

Under church law, marriage was seen as an indissoluble sacrament, so divorce was almost impossible. Women in Norman England enjoyed somewhat more freedom but still needed permission from their male guardians to get married; annulments were quite rare. In Somerled's culture, nevertheless, marriage contracts sometimes contained clauses safeguarding the bride's rights. Both Norse and Gaelic customs allowed women to divorce under guidelines. Should a husband mistreat a woman, neglect her, or engage in adultery, she might lawfully split from him and keep her dowry. Under feudal systems, this degree of liberty was almost unheard of.

Mediaeval Iceland's Grágás law codes show how Norse women could initiate a divorce by just stating their intention in front of witnesses. This custom probably continued into Norse-Gaelic colonies, giving women more power over their marriage than most of their European counterparts.

While women in Somerled's realm participated more in economic and cultural life, mediaeval European women remained mostly limited to the home. Noblewomen in feudal England and France were mostly in charge of running estates in their husbands' absence, but peasant women had little economic freedom.

Most were linked to the land and labour of their husbands, working in fields, weaving, and rearing cattle with no legal status. In Norse-Gaelic civilisation, however, women were often involved in trade, especially in the marine business. Some ran ships and worked in textile manufacturing, fishing, and food preservation for export.

The predominance of Norse trading routes guaranteed women's acknowledged participation in economic life. Playing a significant part in the wool trade, women in the Hebrides spun premium fabrics exported to Ireland and beyond. In feudal Europe, on the other hand, guilds generally limited female involvement in textile manufacture.

In every mediaeval society, women made an impact by supporting religious activity and cultural preservation. In the Norse-Gaelic civilisation, women participated more actively, but in feudal Europe, this influence was largely limited to noble or monastery environments. Although their functions were mainly limited to religious life, noblewomen supported monasteries in mediaeval England and France.

Though they had limited political influence outside of the Church, women who became abbesses possessed authority inside the establishment. Noblewomen of Somerled's society supported monasteries, but they also participated in law, oral narrative, and genealogy.

They kept family histories, made sure their kids received Gaelic education, and occasionally even acted as clan mediators. Noblewomen in Ireland and Scotland sometimes helped to fund the building of abbeys and churches. Like other Gaelic noblewomen, Somerled's daughters most certainly participated in monastic patronage to ensure their family's heritage, even if no direct record of them doing so exists.

Except as occasional leaders under dire circumstances, women in mediaeval Europe were hardly active in combat. Norse-Gaelic women, however, were more actively involved in both logistical military assistance and home defence. Noblewomen sometimes commanded castles during sieges in Norman England and feudal France, although their tasks were typically limited to defence and diplomacy.

In Somerled's universe, noblewomen were often in charge of supervising fortifications, arming troops, and even engaging in strategic planning. Although they did not engage in combat, their contribution to keeping defences was greatly acknowledged. Later, Scottish customs remember tales of noblewomen defending their castles against raids. Though specifics are few, these stories imply that women in the Norse-Gaelic society were required to actively protect their homes during periods of war.

While Somerled's society was nonetheless patriarchal, women in the Norse-Gaelic Hebrides enjoyed more privileges and social mobility than their European counterparts. They might inherit land, run companies, institute divorces, and have sway in court cases. Their active participation in trade, storytelling, religious patronage, and defence distinguishes them from women in Norman and Capetian society, where they were sometimes assigned passive duties.

This harmony between Norse autonomy and Gaelic kinship systems produced a special culture in which women, despite social expectations, had a great impact in both home and public life. This mix of legal rights, financial involvement, and cultural agency set apart the position of women in Somerled's world from that of more inflexible feudal Europe.

Chapter 20
Somerled and the Viking World

When the Hebrides first saw the longships approaching, they knew what was ahead. With their carved dragon heads and billowing sails, the elegant wooden boats cut across the waters with an eerie quiet more sinister than the approaching storm behind them. These were not the basic fishing boats used by neighbourhood vendors. These were Norse ships, messengers of fire, steel, and sorrow.

As the first cries of caution rang around the coast, the village went silent. Hoping to lose themselves in the deep forests and tough hills, some residents quit what they were doing and grabbed their children and any belongings they could carry before fleeing inland. Others grabbed weapons – rusty knives, hunting bows, farming tools – knowing they had little chance of escaping the intruders. Better than the alternative was a desperate stand.

Attacks began the instant the Norsemen set foot on the coast. Moving with terrible speed, they seemed to be practising a routine they had done many times before. Homes were set ablaze, cattle herded toward the longships, and storehouses opened. Those who objected were quickly killed, their bodies left among the burning wreckage. Men, women, and children, all among the stronger prisoners, were tied and marched toward the waiting ships headed for the slave markets of Dublin or the service of Norse nobles elsewhere in the Isles.

This was simply another day of plunder for the invaders. It served as yet another reminder of who owned these territories for the locals.

Nearly two centuries of Norse hegemony over most of the western seaboard transformed the Kingdom of the Isles into a major outpost of their maritime empire. From the Isle of Man to the Outer Hebrides, the kingdom comprised a mix of Viking warlords and Gaelic leaders, some of whom had collaborated with the Norse while others had been subjugated. The attacks were not only acts of greed – they were a means of exercising control, a tool for preserving authority, eliminating opposition, and underlining the message that these territories belonged to the Norse.

Still, things were beginning to evolve. Previously scattered Gaelic clans were starting to rebel. Not satisfied with battle just on land, some had studied the strategies of the Norse and started assembling their own fleet. Others realised that survival depended on unity and sought coalitions. A new kind of opposition was developing, one that sought to oppose Norse control completely rather than only defend against it.

At the core of this change was a man who, more than anybody else, could grasp both sides of the dispute. Though raised in Gaels' customs, he had Norse blood running through him. Though he had seen the Viking invasions' terrible efficiency, he had also seen their shortcomings. Somerled was perhaps so deadly since he was neither totally Norse nor totally Gaelic. For years, he had watched, learned, and prepared. Now, he was ready to act.

Somerled's Norse Heritage: Influence Beyond Lineage

Somerled did not live apart from the Norse world. His own blood bore their tradition, a legacy derived from Viking colonists who had settled the western seaboard. Although Gillebride, his father, descended from a noble Gaelic dynasty, Somerled also had links to the Norse kings who had ruled the Isles for centuries through his lineage. This made him a product of two worlds – Norse and Gaelic – a mix that would define not only his approach to leadership but also his identity.

Somerled would have been exposed to the impact of both civilisations early on. Master mariners, the Norse were driven by their capacity to strike where they pleased and withdraw just as rapidly as they could go across the sea. Their longships made them almost unbeatable, and their naval might helped them to dominate the Kingdom of the Isles.

Conversely, the Gaels were close to the ground; their authority derived from kinship, livestock abundance, and a system of clan alliances rather than naval might. Whereas the Gaels governed by bloodline, custom, and alliances, the Norse dominated the oceans.

Growing up between these two cultures, Somerled observed how each used authority in unique ways. While the Gaelic lords kept control via loyalty, marital alliances, and clan ties, he secured Norse rule by military strength, trade, and maritime excellence. He would apply both to his benefit when his turn came to lead.

Somerled understood many Gaelic leaders who opposed the Norse, unlike many others who did it just out of resentment at their reign. He embraced what was practical and cut off what was not, not rejecting their ways entirely. His leadership approach embodied this harmony – pragmatic, flexible, and anchored in both Gaelic and Norse traditions. He changed his strategy, knowing that battling the Norse with Gaelic techniques by itself would not be sufficient; he made sure his forces could match them in land warfare as well as at sea.

The Influence of Norse Naval Power

Using naval force was one of the most obvious ways his Norse background moulded him. Depending on their quick, agile boats able to negotiate both open oceans and narrow coastal waters, the Norse had long depended on their longships. With unparalleled speed, these ships let them raid, trade, and rule the islands. Somerled developed his own fleet so he could combat Norse kings on their own terms, therefore transcending mere opposition to this naval superiority. Unlike previous

Gaelic chiefs, he was not only opposing the Norse but also learning from them and adjusting in line with their strategic orientation.

Somerled changed the way his troops fought by constructing a fleet of galleys fashioned like Viking longships. He could now strike where he liked, control important water lanes, and protect his territory against Norse attacks, thus transcending the constraints of land conflicts alone. This gave him a tactical advantage that many Gaelic rulers before him had lacked.

A New Kind of Leadership

His rule likewise mirrored this mix of customs. Like the Gaelic lords, he ensured allegiance by marital alliances, personal bonds, and the defence of his people, therefore strengthening his rule through kindred ties. Like the Norse leaders who had made the Isles a hive of trade, he likewise understood the value of trade, prosperity, and resource management. Rather than objecting to change, Somerled adjusted to produce a new type of government combining the best of both traditions.

His approach to leadership was also strategic and pragmatic. True power, he realised, derived from political stability, economic strength, and alliances across time rather than from battle by itself. While numerous Gaelic leaders had spent years battling the Norse with little success, Somerled took a different tack. Not only was he aiming to drive them out, but he was also replacing them, not as a warrior but as a king capable of commanding both Gaelic and Norse allegiance.

Preparing for War

Still, government and diplomacy alone would not be sufficient. The Norse lords of the Isles would not give up their authority readily; they had ruled too long. Somerled recognised this. Years of alliance building, position securing, and opponent learning had gone toward him. Now, though, the time had come for him to prove his mettle on the front lines.

Somerled was no longer simply a man observing from the sidelines. He was a leader prepared to challenge the mightiest monarchy in the Western Isles, thus preparing for war.

Political Strategy and Alliances

Somerled realised that the sword does not grant power by itself. Strength in war counted, but without allies, without ensuring loyalty and stability, no king could hope to hold onto what they acquired.

The Kingdom of the Isles was not a united Norse kingdom at this time. It was a precarious network of rival warlords, local chieftains, and aspirational kings, all fighting for domination. With changing allegiances and internal strife endangering stability, Norse control in the Isles was always shifting. Somerled saw this volatility as a chance. Rather than trying to wage a battle he could not win alone, he would combine his own network of alliances to challenge Norse control from within.

Marriage to Ragnhild – A Calculated Move

Marrying Ragnhild, daughter of Olaf the Red, the King of Mann and the Isles, was among his most significant political actions. This was not only a marriage of two people; it was a declaration of intent. Somerled positioned himself as both a challenge and a legitimate heir to the Norse-owned lands by marrying into the reigning Norse family of the Isles. He was not merely another Gaelic chief opposing Norse control but a man with a true claim to authority inside their world.

This marriage helped him in two key ways:

Legitimacy among Norse-Gaelic rulers: Many Norse-Gaelic lords, who could have written him off as a foreigner, suddenly had to admit his claim. Ragnhild was a direct descendant of the Norse royal line. Hence, her children would inherit both Gaelic and Norse power, and it would be impossible to discredit Somerled totally.

A strategic opening to undermine his rivals: The Kingdom of the Isles was not presenting a united front; competing groups battled for dominance, and alliances changed regularly. Married into the ruling family, Somerled learnt about their inner conflicts, flaws, and power struggles. He realised he could fight them from inside – not just as an enemy but also as a contender for the throne – if he played his hand right.

Still, his aspirations did not stop inside the Norse world. Securing his links to the Isles, he was also assembling a coalition of Gaelic lords, many of whom had suffered for decades under Norse attacks.

Uniting the Gaelic Clans

Somerled recognised that solitary opposition had never effectively driven out the Norse from any Gaelic ruler. The Norse could play the clans against one another as they had been overly split and consumed in their own conflicts. But Somerled possessed something many before him lacked: a vision outside of local strife.

Instead of relying solely on traditional Gaelic bonds of loyalty, he offered something more:

- **A common enemy and a shared purpose**: Gaelic chiefs who had fought alone against the Norse were now presented with an opportunity to stand together. Somerled positioned himself as the leader who could unify them against a common threat.
- **Military and economic stability**: He was not just gathering warriors for a fight – he was promising a lasting shift in power, one that could restore Gaelic rule over their ancestral lands.

- **A leader who understood both Norse and Gaelic worlds:** Keeping the allegiance of the Gaelic clans, he could bargain, plan, and outmanoeuvre his Norse competitors using their own strategies.

Somerled reinforced his claim to the western seaboard through deft diplomacy, a mix of military pressure, negotiated concessions, and well-timed allegiances. He was a leader creating a completely new power structure, not only a Gaelic noble opposing Viking control.

Rising Suspicion Among Norse Rulers

The Norse rulers, however, were not blind to his growing influence. At first, some saw him as a useful ally, a Gaelic noble who could be managed and controlled. Others recognised the danger he posed – a man who was not only gaining power but doing so using their own tactics.

His fusion of Norse and Gaelic leadership styles made him difficult to predict. He was not an outsider to Norse rule, but he was not fully one of them either. As his authority grew, divisions emerged within the Norse leadership over how to deal with him.

His marriage to Ragnhild was originally considered a bridge, a means of guaranteeing harmony across groups. But as Somerled's authority kept rising, what had formerly appeared to be a political partnership started to seem like a direct challenge. Once viewed as a diplomatic gesture, his marriage now caused mistrust.

Stress mounted, with Norse warlords starting to see him as a direct threat rather than a possible ally. His fleet was growing, his Gaelic base was widening, and his aspirations were impossible to overlook. If Somerled had a claim to the Isles, how long before he tried to take them by force?

The Limits of Diplomacy: Preparing for War

Somerled was aware that diplomacy had its limits. He had built alliances, strengthened his claim, and secured the loyalty of powerful clans. But sooner or later, words and marriages would not be enough. Now was the moment to grab weapons and directly challenge the Norse.

Somerled had set the foundation by the time he was ready to act. Among the Gaelic clans anxious to rebel against Norse rule, he had formed alliances, enhanced his legitimacy by marriage, and developed a sizeable following. But politics and diplomacy could only go so far; he would have to use force to attack the leaders of the Kingdom of Man and the Isles.

Somerled did not act carelessly. He knew the Norse were still powerful, particularly at sea. For decades, the longship fleets of the Kingdom of Man had dominated the western seaboard, enabling them to attack quickly and seize key trade routes. Somerled would have to match their waterpower if he were going to challenge them.

Thus, Somerled embraced Norse maritime tactics instead of depending solely on traditional Gaelic land-based warfare, assembling a fleet of galleys fashioned like Viking longships. These swift, agile boats could engage in coastal attacks as well as open-sea conflicts. His army not only engaged in defensive engagements against them but also brought the fight to them, employing their own strategies against Norse raids.

Somerled's military operations were deliberate and planned rather than based just on force. He employed coordinated strikes, quick navy movements, and surprise invasions to undermine Norse strongholds. Understanding the importance of psychological warfare, he also conveyed a message to the Norse kings, indicating their power was no longer absolute by winning decisive wars.

The toughest obstacle Somerled faced was the King of Man and the Isles, Godred Olafsson. Son of Olaf the Red, Godred was a strong king with strong links to Norway. Godred was a particularly fierce opponent as he had the support of the Norwegian Crown, unlike past Norse warlords who had mainly concentrated on local disputes.

There was no instant hostility between Somerled and Godred. Using his marriage to Ragnhild to bolster his claim, Somerled initially sought to establish himself as a legitimate leader inside the Norse-Gaelic society. However, it was evident that a conflict was unavoidable as hostilities increased and his support among the Gaelic tribes expanded.

Somerled and his army attacked Godred's fleet decisively from the sea in 1156. Both sides suffered great losses in the intense struggle. However, the crucial element turned out to be Somerled's strategic preparation and the ability of his Gaelic-Norse fighters. The Kingdom of the Isles was split by the end of the war, Somerled having driven Godred into an agreement whereby the Western Isles would separate.

Somerled was unfinished, though. Two years later, in 1158, he started a final campaign aiming at totally driving Godred out. This time, there would be no compromise. By seizing the Isle of Man, Somerled's armies virtually destroyed Norse rule over the western coast. By the end of the campaign, he was the monarch of the Isles rather than merely a Gaelic chieftain opposing Viking control.

The triumphs of Somerled went beyond mere territory acquisition. They signalled a turning point in the conflict between Norse and Gaelic control in Scotland. Somerled had shown the Norse that they could be challenged and vanquished, whereas they had long dominated the western seaboard.

But was his intention to simply carve out his own separate government or to totally erase Norse influence? That issue would define his leadership going forward.

Somerled's Role in the Decline of Norse Influence in Scotland

While Somerled's triumphs over the Kingdom of Man and the Isles changed western Scotland's political scene, his goals were never entirely free from Norse influence. Unlike many Gaelic leaders who considered the Norse as invaders to be driven, Somerled realised their presence had become firmly ingrained in the area. His aim was not only exile but also domination; he intended to supplant Norse rule with his own and guarantee the Western Isles' independence under his direction.

With his victory in 1158, Somerled had essentially toppled Norse rule in the Isles. He became the most influential person on the western seaboard as the Norwegian-backed kings had lost their strongest grip over the area. Instead of eradicating Norse habits and influence, he kept combining Norse and Gaelic traditions to guarantee that both people would welcome his authority.

Was It a Permanent Decline in Norse Rule?

Though it signified a major change in power, Somerled's achievement did not indicate that Norse influence would vanish completely. Though the Kingdom of the Isles had been undermined, the Norwegians still controlled several areas of territory. Later years would see the Norwegian Crown try to retake sovereignty over the Isles, sparking more strife between Scottish and Norse leaders.

Still, Somerled's deeds prepared the ground for the Isles' ultimate Scottish annexation. His victories weakened the Norse grip, and in the subsequent century, Scottish kings – most notably Alexander III – capitalised on this instability to ultimately end Norse rule in Scotland with the Treaty of Perth in 1266. Somerled was dead by then, but his campaigns set the stage for what was to come.

Somerled's Legacy

The legacy of Somerled is one of resilience and transition. He was a leader who knew diplomacy as well as military might, and he applied both to help the Isles define their future rather than only being a fighter. Among the most powerful people in Scottish mediaeval history was his capacity to unify Gaelic clans, embrace Norse strategies, and question an established kingdom.

Later, the Clan Donald (MacDonalds), his descendants, and the Clan MacDougall would go on to become among the most influential aristocratic families in Scotland. Most of his vision was carried by the Lords of the Isles, who governed for centuries following his death – a mix of Gaelic freedom and Norse naval might.

Somerled's tale is still seen as one of a man who crossed two cultures, combining the best of each and creating something fresh even now. His ascent signalled the end of Norse rule in Scotland, not by annihilation but by calculated adaptation and leadership.

Though the Norse attacks had formerly defined life in the Western Isles, by the time Somerled was finished, it was he, not the Vikings, who defined the future of the area.

Chapter 21

The Clan System Under Somerled

Men from all over the Western Isles, some from close villages and others making the long trip from far-off coastlines, crowded the vast hall. Along the wooden benches sat warriors, chieftains, and elders whose cloaks were moist from the evening mist; their swords rested at their sides. The smell of roasted meat, ale, and burning peat permeated the air, reminding us that this was a gathering of kin and friends rather than merely a council.

Somerled sat at the head of the long table, listening as his soldiers spoke. His power derived not just from strength in combat but also from his capacity to unite the clans, resolve conflicts, and inspire allegiance, thus transcending the Norse sense of king or simple Gaelic warlord. One cannot reign just from the top. He required his people to be united, his chieftains' support, and the faith of his warriors.

Such clan meetings were as old as the earth itself. Leaders made decisions in these meetings, soldiers promised their devotion, and rivalries, at least for the time, were pushed aside in favour of the public good.

The assembly most likely happened in one of Somerled's strongholds, maybe Finlaggan on Islay, which would thereafter become Clan Donald's seat. The centre of government was the great hall, where alliances were developed, conflicts were resolved, and choices determining the course of the future were made.

A long hearth burned steadily in the middle of the hall, flickering light on the faces of everyone gathered. The fire was a symbol of unification, reminding everyone there that despite their differences, they were joined together by a common fate, not just a source of warmth.

Customs and Acts of Loyalty

Tradition had to be followed even before any important issues were dealt with. These meetings covered more ground than politics and government. Rooted in ceremonial and custom, they strengthened the ties, keeping the clans together. Loyalty was not something one assumed; it had to be confirmed, said out, and seen by others. Whether chieftain or warrior, every man in the hall had a part to contribute to the clan system's stability. These rites were not meaningless gestures; they were what kept alliances intact, stopped betrayals, and reminded all present of their shared obligations.

Somerled sat at the head of the hall, and the air got serious. The whispers subsided, and everyone's focus turned to the event that would formally mark the allegiance of those gathered. These ceremonies were not done lightly. Stories, presents, and oaths had long been the tools used by Gaelic society to uphold its customs, therefore guaranteeing that every leader possessed real respect rather than mere compliance. These ceremonies would take place as they had for centuries in the flickering torchlight, tying men together with language, honour, and shared history.

Oaths of Loyalty

Every warrior and chieftain was supposed to present before Somerled their fealty. This was more than just business politeness. It was a public statement of allegiance made in front of family and fellow fighters. A man's word was his bond; breaking such a vow would bring shame not only to him but to his whole tribe. These oaths confirmed Somerled's power and made sure every man there identified him as the legitimate leader.

Some sipped a sombre drink from a common cup to solidify their union. Drinking from the same vessel as one's leader was a gesture of trust, representing that one participated in both the riches and the responsibilities of leadership.

Others spoke their promise while waving a sword or holy relic aloft. Sharp and relentless, a blade fitted soldiers as it reminded them that their allegiance had to be equally unflinching. Some went further, pressing their palms together after making small cuts in them, letting their blood mix – a covenant that cannot be undone.

This ceremony was a reaffirmation of the allegiance people who had fought beside Somerled had already shown on the battlefield. For others, particularly those from clans who had just lately promised their allegiance, it was a pivotal event. To kneel before Somerled and swear fealty meant they acknowledged his vision as their own, his leadership as legitimate, and his rule as fair.

The Giving of Gifts

Still, loyalty was more than words. It had to be rewarded. Somerled realised that a leader trying to keep his men's respect had to earn it rather than just demand it. Gifts were presented as a token of gratitude and respect, a concrete acknowledgement of the allegiance these men had exhibited. A warrior who had shown himself in combat could be given a skilfully made sword, one whose blade had been created by expert hands and meant to be of use in the next battles. Silver, animals, or land – symbols of wealth that elevated their position inside their clans – were given to chieftains.

These presents were more than just symbolic offerings of kindness. They strengthened the ties between Somerled and his followers, therefore serving a political function. A chieftain who got a large gift would be expected to be loyal in response. A warrior carrying a sword given by his leader would fight even harder to protect the man who had given it. These interactions fostered commitment and guaranteed that devotion was not ephemeral but rather permanently ingrained in common prosperity and wealth.

At the same time, the chieftains presented their own tributes. These were not payments demanded by Somerled but offerings made willingly, signifying their respect for his leadership. Some brought cattle, a crucial source of wealth in the Gaelic world. Others offered goods from trade – furs, fabrics, or finely worked jewellery. The act of giving and receiving reinforced the balance of power. Somerled was not a tyrant extracting wealth from his people; he was a ruler whose leadership benefitted all who swore allegiance to him.

Feasting and Storytelling

Once the oaths were taken and the gifts were given, the hall turned to festivity. Feasting was a vital component of these events, not only as a celebration but also as a means of deepening the ties among the men seated side by side. Food – roasted meats, delicious bread, and strong ale – was set on long tables free from control. As warriors and chieftains put aside their disagreements for the evening, swapping tales and strengthening their camaraderie, laughter and chatter permeated the air.

Still, the feast celebrated more than just food and drink. It was a time for history to be told, for the stories of the past to be handed to a fresh generation. Bards stood in the firelight, their voices above the noise of the gathering, reciting tales of earlier battles, of great commanders who had come before, of victories that had moulded the territory they now controlled.

These tales brought back for the men their shared past and the knowledge that they belonged to something more than themselves. They were not merely people or tribes striving for their own survival but part of a long series of warriors and kings who had moulded the fate of the Isles.

For Somerled, this event held equal significance with the oaths and the gifts. A leader governed not merely with power but also with the narratives passed about him. His warriors listened as the bards spun tales of bravery and honour, their faith in their leader deepening. These gatherings were not just about maintaining order; they were about forging a legacy.

The Council: Decisions and Disputes

Once the formalities were done, the real purpose of the gathering began. The feasting and ceremonies had reaffirmed bonds of loyalty, but leadership was not measured in words alone. Somerled's authority was really tested in these times when tough decisions had to be made, conflicts settled, and futures moulded. A leader's strength was not only in warfare but also in his capacity to demand respect, arbitrate disputes, and ensure that the aspirations of several clans did not compromise the unity he had created.

As the discussion moved from joy to government, the flickering fire created long shadows across the hall. Here was the arena where authority was used – not with swords but with intelligence and negotiation. Though they were warriors, the men in this room were chieftains with their own territory, interests, and goals. Somerled understood well how sensitive that situation could be, and maintaining their unity behind a common purpose called for both diplomacy and power.

Hierarchy and Leadership

Somerled headed the council, but he did not rule alone. Unlike the Norsemen, who sometimes enforced their will without question, Gaelic leadership was based more on respect and influence than on absolute authority. Every clan in the room spoke; Somerled was smart enough to pay attention.

The clans' standings varied. Some had been faithful to him from the start, their commitment strong through doubt and battle. Others had just lately promised their allegiance, either by victory or persuasion. The difficulty was juggling these several groups to guarantee that neither rivalry nor resentment would compromise the unity he had so laboriously created.

Those who had fought for him expected land, power, and influence; those who had lost had to find a place in the new system. This configuration called for more than simply promises. It needed the precise allocation of authority to make sure no one clan was powerful enough to oppose him, yet none felt neglected or discounted.

Settling Conflicts

There were always going to be conflicts. Conflicts would develop regardless of the strength of the alliances or how skilfully Somerled had combined the islands. The causes of countless conflicts among the tribes were land, trade, and honour; if allowed unbridled, they might cause bloody wars that would destroy all he had created. These meetings offered a disciplined approach to addressing these issues before they went beyond fixing.

Somerled watched while complaints were raised. A chieftain could charge another with invading his territory. A fighter might ask for recompense for an insult that had gone unpunished. Seeking justice in front of their leader, a clan could exact revenge for past wrongs. Every problem was given much thought, and Somerled's choices were supposed to be just but firm. Neither could he afford to seem weak nor let bitterness persist.

Unlike previous Gaelic leaders who came before him, he realised that negotiations were insufficient. The Gaelic tradition often leans toward protracted debates where conflicts might linger for years while various factions fought for their reasons, but Somerled had also seen how the Norse treated leadership with unambiguous, forceful judgements devoid of any margin for doubt. He blended these two approaches, ensuring that justice was not merely done but that it was done swiftly.

Those who challenged his rulings knew that his patience had limits. Strength and decisiveness were just as necessary in council as they were on the battlefield.

Planning for the Future

Beyond conflict resolution, the most pressing matters of the night revolved around planning for the future. Leadership was not just about managing the present. It shaped what was to come. Somerled recognised that, for now, his authority was safe, but dangers still lay ahead. Though their impact persisted in some areas, the Norse had not been totally driven from the Isles. The Scottish monarchy also observed his ascent with great interest and recognised that fresh difficulties would inevitably arise sooner or later.

Discussions turned to military strategy. Which clans would stand with him in the next campaign? Who would provide warriors? Who would supply ships? If a conflict were to arise – whether against external enemies or from within – the alliances formed here would determine the strength of his forces.

Trade was another key topic. The Western Isles were strategically located on major sea paths, so regulating these waterways meant regulating trade. The council discussed how best to ensure that the Isles stayed rich and that ships could travel unhindered, preserving stability in the area. Just as important for Somerled's leadership as military might were keeping alliances with traders, securing important ports, and guaranteeing safe passage for merchants.

By the time the fire burned out and the last words were said, the gathering had done its job. Oaths had been taken, conflicts resolved, and the future explored.

Somerled had once more shown that his influence extended beyond combat to include his capacity to inspire the respect and allegiance of people who came under his direction. These councils served purposes beyond mere gathering places. They guaranteed that his leadership was based on power, stability, and discipline, therefore laying the basis of his authority.

Under his influence, new families were rising to power, forging a new political landscape that would endure long after his time. Among them, one name would rise above all others – Clan Donald, a dynasty that would shape the history of Scotland for centuries to come.

The Emergence of New Clans: Focus on Clan Donald and Its Branches

Somerled's rule redefined leadership in the Isles. Unlike earlier Gaelic leaders, whose authority was sometimes scattered among several chieftains, he set up a system in which power could be consolidated and passed down via bloodlines in a fashion that matched even the Norse kings. Especially among his successors, this change prepared the way for the birth of fresh clans.

Clan Donald was the most important of these; its name would originate from Domhnall (Donald), Somerled's grandson, whose power would ultimately span the Highlands and Isles. The MacDonalds would later become Lords of the Isles, possessing a degree of authority occasionally equivalent to that of the Scottish monarchy itself. However, Somerled laid the groundwork before this great dynasty could flourish, therefore determining the circumstances that allowed Clan Donald and other noble families to flourish.

The way Somerled's family was arranged mirrored the mix of Gaelic and Norse customs that defined his leadership. His sons were given power over several areas, therefore supporting his control and guaranteeing that his legacy would not wane with his death. Each new clan emerging from Somerled's direct line branched off from this distribution of power. Although his own authority had been concentrated, his successors would disperse to create new ruling families with his legacy felt all around.

The Origins of Clan Donald and Its Influence

One of Somerled's sons, Reginald (Raghnall), inherited most of his father's influence in the Isles, hence launching Clan Donald. Reginald's descendants, particularly his son Domhnall (Donald), would set the family name. The MacDonalds grew to be major players in the western seaboard throughout time, finally assuming the title of Lords of the Isles, which bestowed upon them authority over large areas ranging from the Hebrides to portions of mainland Scotland.

As Somerled himself had done, Clan Donald was distinctive among the rising noble houses in that its chiefs maintained both Gaelic and Norse elements. Though they governed with the kinship-based devotion of Gaelic society, they also appreciated trade and naval might – qualities passed on from their Norse background. Their great resilience came from their capacity to cross two cultures, which let them flourish even as Scotland's political scene shifted all around them.

Operating with its own laws, fleet, and allies, the Lordship of the Isles became a semi-independent monarchy under the MacDonalds. Their might occasionally was sufficient to confront the Scottish monarchy itself. Though they would eventually be absorbed into the kingdom of Scotland in later centuries, their rise was a direct result of Somerled's legacy and the political structure he had established.

The Branches of Somerled's Lineage

Although Clan Donald was the most well-known, several of Somerled's descendents created several strong families that were important in Scottish history. Other branches of his family would become the MacDougalls, MacRorys, and MacAlisters, each with territory and authority.

Originally ruling Argyll, the MacDougalls – derived from Somerled's son Dugall – would subsequently turn adversaries of Clan Donald as the two lineages fought for supremacy over the western seaboard.

From his son Ruaridh (Roderick), the MacRorys dominated portions of the Hebrides and mainland Scotland, therefore preserving the balance of power in the Isles. Another offshoot of Somerled's ancestry, the MacAlisters would thereafter develop as a separate clan with sway over Kintyre and beyond.

These differences strengthened Somerled's legacy rather than lessening it; rather, they guaranteed that his influence would endure across several noble houses, therefore transforming the political scene of Scotland for the next generations. His sons and grandchildren inherited the basis of power he had developed, not only land.

A Legacy That Endured

By the time his tenure came to an end, Somerled's vision had already started to blossom. Under his direction, the clan structure had changed to produce a network of aristocratic families defining the Western Isles' future. His ancestors made sure his impact went much beyond his own lifetime, even as he united the area under his direction.

With centuries of influence over the Western Isles, Clan Donald would go on to become among the most influential aristocratic houses in Scotland. Their assertion to the Lordship of the Isles preserved Somerled's dream – that the Gaelic realm could stay autonomous, strong, and wild even while the Scottish monarchy worked to subjugate it.

These clans emerged not just according to natural succession patterns. They were the direct outcome of the governmental system Somerled had developed, one that let bloodlines pass power while nevertheless preserving the unity of the area. He had started a change of Gaelic leadership that would leave a long legacy for Scotland.

The demand for a more ordered system of governance rose along with the impact of Clan Donald and its branches. Somerled had not only embraced the old customs; he had also changed them to produce a model his generations would polish throughout time. His use of military organisation, land distribution, and clan hierarchy helped to define the destiny of the islands and create a more unified clan structure.

His rule was about longevity, and in the rise of the MacDonalds and their rival clans, his vision was realised. But how exactly did Somerled modify the existing system to ensure his influence would endure? The answer lay in his approach to governance, his strategic restructuring of land and leadership, and the way he balanced tradition with innovation – elements that would come to define the very fabric of the Highland clan system in the years to come.

Somerled's Use and Modification of the Clan Structure

Somerled's impact did not stop when fresh clans emerged. By combining Gaelic customs with the Norse government to produce a more flexible and long-lasting system, his rule radically changed the way power was arranged in the Western Isles. Somerled brought a more deliberate and orderly approach to leadership that let his authority span beyond his own life and prepared the foundation for the strong clan systems that would rule Scotland for centuries.

One of his strongest suits was his capacity to rule entirely Gaelic clans as well as Norse-Gaelic hybrids. While Gaelic customs were anchored in the country, the Norse had brought with them their own systems of administration, trade, and warfare. The Western Isles had long been a site of cultural fusion.

Many Gaelic rulers before Somerled had either resisted Norse influence entirely or had been forced to submit to it. Somerled, however, did neither. Rather, he embraced the advantages of both systems, knowing that real power came from flexibility.

In governing Gaelic clans, he followed the customs of clan alliances, kinship, and loyalty. These chieftains were supposed to follow their family traditions, and loyalty was maintained through personal ties, marriage, and common successes.

When dealing with Norse-Gaelic clans, he included aspects of Norse governance – centralised authority, naval power, and economic control over trade routes – ensuring that these groups saw him as a ruler who knew their way of life rather than as just another Gaelic warlord. This harmony helped him bring both groups under one control, therefore restoring stability that had been lacking for decades.

Among the main adjustments he made were regarding clan duties and property ownership. In old Gaelic society, no one person had total power; land was sometimes shared jointly by extensive clan groups. Though rooted in custom, this structure sometimes caused internal conflicts about territory and succession.

Drawing from both Gaelic and Norse inspirations, Somerled presented a more centralised type of government whereby land was kept under the authority of a governing lord, not as absolute possession but rather in a more ordered arrangement. This guaranteed that regions could be passed down via bloodlines, more readily defended, and controlled, hence minimising the internal strife that had hitherto undermined Gaelic control.

In terms of military structure, allegiance, and government, Somerled's leadership set out from that of other Gaelic kings. Somerled realised that control of the water was equally as vital as control of the land, while conventional Gaelic warlords mostly depended on land-based forces and small-scale raiding strategies. He made significant investments in naval might to guarantee that his armies could strike where least anticipated, travel quickly between islands, and safeguard important areas from Norse counterattacks. Since the western seaboard was a major trading route between Ireland, Scotland, and Scandinavia, this naval might not only gave him military dominance but also financial dominance.

Loyalty under Somerled was safeguarded by a well-balanced system of land distribution, military service, and shared economic rewards, not by personal ties or conventional clan groupings alone.

Furthermore, his government approach was more ordered than the informal power systems of past Gaelic leaders. Somerled created a clearer hierarchy of rule, while the ancient clan system mostly depended on oral agreements and unwritten regulations. He positioned his sons and close friends as regional leaders so that power was distributed in a way that maintained his authority without undermining his general control.

Like the Norse jarls who ruled areas under the authority of a central king, these leaders were required to uphold order, supervise trade, and support military expeditions.

By means of these changes, Somerled transformed the clan system into something more ecologically viable. His leadership guaranteed that military might, economic control, and strategic government combined rather than only passed down through kinship alone. Particularly Clan Donald, his heirs would take these values on, honing and adjusting them to keep their rule long after his death.

But Somerled's impact transcended his lifetime's governance to include how his influence shaped the destiny of the Scottish Highlands and Western Isles. His changes to the clan system would outlive him and help shape the Scottish government's long-term development as well as the ascent of strong Highland clans. Examining how his decisions affected the long-term evolution of the clan system in Scotland, a change that would continue to define the area for centuries, helps one to grasp the whole influence of his rule.

Long-Term Impact on the Clan System in Scotland

Somerled's dominance permanently changed the Highland clan structure and transformed the Western Isles. He built a framework that held true long after his death. The strong clans that would define the area for centuries had their roots in his changes in property ownership, military organisation, and leadership succession.

Changing the mechanism of succession was among his most important accomplishments. Traditionally, Gaelic leadership followed tanistry, in which case election among male relatives decided succession and often resulted in internal strife. Somerled introduced a more structured hereditary system by assigning his sons to oversee specific territories, thereby ensuring greater stability. Later, Highland clans, especially the MacDonalds, whose claim to the Lordship of the Isles was based on this premise, were swayed by this strategy.

Many features of Somerled's system endured even if the Scottish monarchy later sought to discredit the authority of his descendants. Direct heirs to his rule, the Lords of the Isles, ran almost independently for generations, preserving a strong naval presence and a balance between Gaelic and Norse cultures. Highland government – land under the jurisdiction of a chief, military organisation based on clan warriors, and loyalty kept through kinship – remained fundamentally in place even when the monarchy finally asserted itself.

The way Somerled led set standards for future alliances and disputes. Later, Highland chiefs, as they negotiated power conflicts with both the Scottish monarchy and competing clans, found inspiration in his ability to unify several factions while retaining strict personal rule. Highland clans kept their autonomy for decades, thanks in large part to his focus on strategic land allocation and naval supremacy.

The Scottish royalty effectively undermined the Lords of the Isles by the late fifteenth century, therefore bringing the Isles under centralised control. Still, Somerled left behind a legacy. The clan-based power structure he formed remained the backbone of Highland society, with many of his reforms shaping the military and political organisation of the region well into the modern era.

Somerled was more than a warrior. He was a strategist and a builder of systems. His modifications to the clan structure ensured that his lineage would shape Scottish history for generations. Though time brought fresh leaders and a changing political terrain, his influence was permanent. He had reinvented leadership in the Highlands, demonstrating that the strength of the clans resided not in conquering alone but in loyalty, endurance, and the enduring traditions that kept them together, transcending mere power struggle.

Chapter 22

Somerled's Spiritual World

The hall was still apart from the sound of the fire and the monk guiding the prayers. Men stood silently; some had their heads lowered, others just observed. Burning peat combined with the saline air that usually hovered over the Isles smelled like something else. This was a night for something equally vital – a time to honour the power of faith in their environment – not for feasting or war councils.

Somerled stood among them, not as a priest or a monk but as a leader who saw the part faith played in his people's daily lives. Though he was not a man suited for outward displays of loyalty, he understood that religion kept the Isles together as much as any alliance or war triumph could do. His reign included the monks, the prayers, the blessings as much as the fighters beneath his flag.

Like the Isles themselves, this event had a blend of customs. Leading the assembly in Christian prayers, the monks spoke in the ancient Gaelic speech, calling for the saints and asking for their direction. Among the men here, some had followed the Norse gods, and although many had embraced Christianity, vestiges of ancient ideas persisted.

A few merely stood in silence, observing but not interacting; others mumbled their own silent words to the ghosts of their ancestors; still others crossed themselves.

Gifts had been arranged on one side of the hall, following long-standing Christian and Norse rituals. Offers for the Church included bread and alcohol, rich cloth for the monks, and silver. It was a reminder that faith and power regularly coexisted, as well as a gesture of loyalty. The monks depended on the defence of men like Somerled, and in exchange, their prayers and blessings gave his authority divine favour.

A warrior advanced, kneeling as a monk anointed his forehead with oil, a blessing before the battle. Before launching a raid or a campaign, men would often ask the Church for protection. Many thought that a priest's benediction would protect them from injury or at least grant an honourable death should they fall.

Faith in the Isles was not distinct from daily life; it was rather a normal aspect of existence. It was in the rhythm of the sea, in the seasonal turning, in the blessings before war, in the gifts offered at holy locations.

Somerled knew this well. He may not have been a deeply religious man in the way monks were, but he understood the power of faith. A leader who enjoyed the favour of the Church had more than just fighters at his rear; he had something more, something that gave his reign weight outside of the battlefield.

Looking beyond this hall and into the larger religious scene of the Isles helps one grasp Somerled's place in this universe. The Church was evolving, fresh ideas were emerging, and ancient Celtic customs were under pressure. Somerled had to negotiate carefully in this changing universe of faith, juggling the past with the future and discovering his own place within it.

The Religious Landscape of the Isles and Influence of Iona

Deep foundations of faith in the Western Isles go far beyond Somerled's lifetime. Arriving centuries earlier, Christianity was delivered by monks seeking to disseminate their lessons in areas where the ancient gods still lingered. But in this region of the earth, faith was not a straightforward issue. The Isles were a junction of Gaelic and Norse culture, of old customs and fresh influences, of monks and warriors. Somerled lived in a time when religion was evolving and, like everything else in his environment, it was moulded by the tides of events.

Iona Abbey stood at the core of Christianity in the area. Established by Saint Columba in the sixth century, Iona has long been a hub of study and faith. The monks of Iona were instrumental in disseminating Celtic Christianity, a faith unique from Roman Church practices that had blossomed in Scotland and Ireland. Once among the most significant religious places in all of Britain, the abbey was where monks preserved knowledge by painstakingly copying manuscripts, and rulers sought favours.

But Iona was not the only spiritual influence in the area by Somerled's time. The Church itself was evolving, and fresh religious groups, such as the Benedictines and Cistercians, were starting to have an impact. These monastic communities closely matched the expanding framework of the Catholic Church in Europe, so they followed a tougher discipline than the ancient Celtic monasteries.

These changes generated conflict between the younger religious movements and the conventional monastic communities of the Isles. While some saw the changes as a means of restoring order and more unity in the Church, others worried they would compromise the autonomy of the Celtic Christian heritage that had long defined the area. Simultaneously, the Norse influence in the Isles had not totally vanished. Many Viking immigrants had become Christians, but their faith was frequently entwined with more ancient customs.

Some Norse-Gaelic communities honoured both saints and ancestral gods, but they nevertheless combined Christianity with ancient pagan rituals. Even among individuals who had adopted Christianity entirely, the faith sometimes evolved to represent the Norse warrior culture. Christian crosses stood next to rune stones in certain areas, and churches were erected on former holy sites for the old gods.

Somerled ruled midway through this spiritual metamorphosis. He had to manage a world in which faith was political rather than only personal belief. By helping the Church, he might increase his legitimacy and thereby his support base. He had to be careful, though, not to alienate the colonists and fighters who still had bits of their

Norse background. This man knew balance – between Gaelic and Norse, between battle and diplomacy, and, in this case, between old and new faiths.

Outside the Isles, religious movements in Scotland and Ireland were also changing. Seeking more influence over the autonomous religious communities in the West, the Scottish Crown progressively aligned with the Roman Church and supported the new monastic orders. Ireland was profoundly impacted by its monastic customs; however, academics and monks still shaped religious doctrine. Somerled's choices in endorsing particular religious leaders or organisations would not only impact his authority but also position him within the larger conflict between reform and tradition.

Somerled faced decisions in this changing theological terrain. Would he stick to the ancient monastic customs of Iona, therefore bolstering the faith that had moulded the Isles over the ages? Alternatively, would he support the more recent religious groups, matching his own increasing power with that of the larger Church? His deeds would not only establish his own legacy but also help to determine the direction of faith in the Hebrides.

Examining his personal beliefs and his relationship with religious leaders helps one to more precisely grasp his stance. In this spiritual universe, how did Somerled see himself? Was he really convinced of the power of the Church, or was he just a king who exploited Catholicism as a weapon? His interactions with the priests, abbots, and monks of his day would provide a better picture of the part religion played in his governance.

Somerled's Personal Faith and Relationship with Religious Leaders

The Church might be a challenge, an institution with its own influence apart from that of any warlord or king, or an ally, a legitimising force bolstering Somerled's claim to rule. His ties to monastic communities and religious leaders went beyond personal belief to include the pragmatic reality of the Western Isles administration.

His support of monastic groups suggests that he was aware of the Church's need to preserve peace. While some leaders considered monasteries only places of prayer, Somerled most likely understood them as centres of knowledge, government, and financial might.

The monks controlled the nearby populace, kept information, and cared for the land. Supporting them entailed attesting to political allegiance in addition to divine favour. Records point to Somerled's possible involvement in the rebirth of Iona Abbey, thus guaranteeing its ongoing function as a major religious centre despite developments elsewhere in the Church.

But did he regard religion as a weapon of control or as a very personal conviction? Though his behaviour reveals a respect for faith that transcends simple political manoeuvring, there is little to indicate that he was especially devout. He ensured that monks and abbots would have a position in his court, respected holy customs, and supplied for religious establishments. His interaction with the Church was probably a combination of a pragmatic approach and personal dedication, warranting the loyalty of the clergy as well as the people.

Securing alliances would have depended much on Somerled's relationships with monks, abbots, and religious authorities. Somerled kept power via a network of clan chiefs, soldiers, and churchmen rather than kings who reigned with the support of a big, centralised government.

Monastic leaders were landowners, scribes, and trusted advisers rather than only spiritual leaders. Did Somerled seek their advice? Nearly always. Did he bolster his authority with them? Certainly. By aligning himself with eminent religious leaders, he presented himself not just as a warlord but also as a defender of the faith – a leader whose authority was approved by the Church.

Another distinctive feature of his attitude to faith was his capacity to strike a balance between Gaelic Christian traditions and Norse inspirations. Somerled had to oversee people from both origins since the Isles were a site where Norse and Gaelic cultures merged. Given that many of his fighters still possessed traces of Norse ancestry, it is improbable that he completely renounced such customs. Rather, he might have promoted a type of Christianity that embraced regional customs so his people might follow their faith in a way that felt familiar rather than mandated.

Furthermore, there is proof that he helped establishments and sites of worship. Many of the leaders of his day gave property, sponsored the building of churches, or travelled to demonstrate their devotion.

Though specifics of Somerled's contributions are unknown, his relationship to Iona and other monastic sites points to his active participation in fostering religious life in the Isles. His patronage would have guaranteed that these holy establishments stayed strong, therefore supporting his own legitimacy in the view of his adherents.

Somerled's attitude to faith was nuanced. Neither was he a monk nor a king using divine right to exercise power. Rather, he was a leader who saw faith's ability to unite people. Whether by sincere belief, political strategy, or a combination of both, he made sure religion stayed a constant in his administration. By doing so, he also helped define the religious destiny of the Hebrides, therefore impacting the way faith and government would be entwined for generations.

Still, his impact did not stop during his own lifetime. Long after his death, the religious buildings he sponsored, the monastic communities he safeguarded, and the balance he maintained between old customs and modern changes would still influence the Isles. Just as important as his military successes, his legacy in religion guaranteed that the Hebrides' spiritual world developed under the imprint of his leadership.

Somerled's Influence on the Religious Development of the Hebrides

The Western Isles' religious life underwent long-lasting change during Somerled's rule. Although he was not a churchman personally, his leadership helped define the spiritual character of the area such that Christianity remained at the core of both politics and daily life. His impact went beyond his lifetime; it shaped the way religion operated in the Hebrides and beyond into the next centuries.

His management of the several theological influences in the Isles was among the most remarkable features of his leadership. Long a gathering ground for customs, the area included the earlier Celtic monastic systems, Gaelic Christianity from Iona, and the residual influence of Norse ideas.

Unlike some leaders who aimed to establish a single religious authority, Somerled seemed to allow for a more mixed approach that reflected the variety of the people he governed. Although he did not entirely eradicate the Norse cultural impact that still survived in some areas, his patronage of monastery centres like Iona most certainly strengthened Christianity in the Isles.

The patronage of Somerled helped religious houses in the Isles to flourish and get protection. Somerled's support helped preserve the distinct character of the ancient Celtic monastic traditions at a period when new religious orders, including the Benedictines and Cistercians, were proliferating over Scotland and Ireland. By doing this, he maintained a unique religious culture on the western shore that was free from the Romanised buildings that were developing elsewhere in Britain.

Somerled's successors inherited his governmental power as well as his religious influence following his death. The Abbey of Saddell in Kintyre that adhered to the more recent Cistercian traditions, is one of the monastic institutions that his son Reginald is credited with formally creating. This implies that although Somerled might have favoured the more traditional monastic practices, his successors welcomed some of the more general religious reforms in progress throughout Europe at the time. Still, the Lords of the Isles, who descended from Somerled, kept close relations with the Church, leveraging faith to support their rule over the area.

Somerled's leadership helped the Hebrides create a spiritual character unique to mainland Scotland and Ireland. The Western Isles maintained a more localised and autonomous attitude to faith as the rest of Scotland came under the sway of a more ordered Church hierarchy.

Iona's customs endured, Norse components stayed in cultural memory, and the influence of the Lord of the Isles allowed Gaelic monasticism and its links to Irish Christianity to flourish. This special blend of elements gave the area a long-lasting religious identity with traces of both Somerled's leadership and the several customs he had overseen.

The Hebrides' theological evolution was heavily influenced by Somerled. His rule guaranteed that Christianity stayed strong in the area and still allowed for a mix of old and modern customs. His encouragement of monastic groups helped sustain the faith in a period of transition; his descendants carried his religious policies forward, adjusting them to the changing terrain of the Church.

Somerled's authority helped the Isles to preserve a distinctive mix of Gaelic Christianity, Norse heritage, and independent religious practice long after his time.

Although his military victories and political leadership are most recognised, his influence on the Hebrides' spiritual realm was equally important. His approach to spirituality matched his practical, flexible leadership style – one that was firmly anchored in the ground and the people he governed.

Through him, the religious identity of the Isles followed a different course from that of the rest of Scotland, so guaranteeing that his impact would be felt not only in conflicts and alliances but also in the very spirit of the nation for the next centuries.

Chapter 23

The Bards of Somerled's Court

Smoke floated sloppily from the hall's big hearth, its warmth pushing back the frost that seeped in through the stone walls. Between the occasional clink of drinking horns on wooden tables, there was a faint murmur of chatter as the torchlight flickered.

The night was dark and restless. Outside, waves slammed the coast. Inside, though, the men had gathered not for feast or warfare but for something just as vital – to remember.

The bard moved forward, and silence descended on the hall. He carried no weapon and wore no armour, but nobody questioned his presence. He was not obliged to ask for quiet. Men who had battled and bled for their homeland already knew what was next. Bards were guardians of memory, the voices bringing the past into the present, not just performers. Before he spoke, the bard plucked a few notes from his harp, letting the sound settle. His voice rose and fell like the waves outside the walls. He brought Somerled to life rather than merely recounting his story.

He described his ascent, of the winds carrying his fleet over the sea, of the battles waged with steel and guile. He related how the Norse had undervalued him, how the tribes had banded behind him, and how his simple presence had reversed the flow of conflict. The words created a picture so vivid it was as though the warriors in the hall could see it – the collision of blades, the spray of saltwater, the instant Somerled stood unshaken as his opponents dropped around him.

Still, the story went beyond war. The bard spoke of his knowledge, his fairness, and his authority that gave the Isles stability and power. A great leader was judged on his legacy rather than just his accomplishments.

Some of the elder fighters tightened their hands on their mugs, personally revisiting the events. The younger men leaned in, their imaginations filling in the scenes of war, of swords striking shields, of a leader fighting not just for himself but for those who followed him.

The hall seemed to hold its breath as the bard's voice grew higher. He related a difficult triumph – a time when all appeared lost – where Somerled boldly changed the tide. Then, the bard's voice softened, moving from the chaos of combat to the weight of leadership just as the suspense peaked. The way a ruler was remembered added more to his strength than his victories in combat.

The last stanza of the poem hung in the air – a wish that his bloodline would rule long after he was gone, a benediction for Somerled's reign. Nobody moved for a second. Then, as if on cue, the hall erupted. Warriors beat their fists on the table; some nodded in understanding while others raised their drinking horns in salute.

Somerled sat observing at the head of the hall, his face unreadable. He spoke nothing since bards knew their own value. Still, there was power in what had lately been uttered. Men could be commanded by a leader, but a bard could command time. Their words transformed successes into legends rather than merely stating them.

The poem lingered in the air, its melodies transmitted beyond these walls, even as the hall gradually returned to its normal rhythm – talk, drink, the odd burst of laughter. Somerled had been carved into memory rather than only lauded tonight. And long after he passed away, it would be the bards ensuring his name lived.

The Role of Bards in Norse-Gaelic Society

A warrior's might was determined by the ability of his sword, while a bard's power resided in his words. Back then, bards served purposes beyond mere entertainment. Acting as diplomats, historians, and storytellers, they helped to shape public perceptions of leaders and guarantee that significant events were never overlooked. Their words carried historical weight, transforming kings into mythologies and victories into stories.

Often receiving the protection and patronage of noble courts, bards were held in a revered position in Gaelic life. A well-trained bard was a status figure, occasionally rated almost as high as a chieftain, not a roaming entertainer singing for coin. Their remarks might inspire devotion, deepen friendships, and even forewarn of betrayal. A king honoured in verse cemented his place in history, thus transcending mere appreciation.

Training and Status of Bards

Learning to be a bard was no easy feat. Their instruction was rigorous and protracted, spanning years of study in the arts of poetry, music, and oral history. Many attended bardic schools, where they polished their harp or lyre, memorised vast epics, and studied the rules of lyric creation. Unlike fighters ready for combat, bards learned to honour the past and shape the present.

A bard's standing determined his level of ability. Known in Gaelic tradition as *filí*, the most revered bards could create complex praise songs for chieftains and kings, their words so weighty that an insult from a bard was thought to be a curse.

Rannaire, or lesser poets, might serve lower-ranking lords and create songs to entertain, but without the political clout of the *filí*.

Though their words sometimes held well-chosen embellishments, bards were expected to speak honestly. A smart bard understood how to strike a balance between fact and compliments such that his patron's reputation was improved without explicit dishonesty.

The best of them could create spontaneous poetry, reacting to events as they happened to guarantee that history was captured live.

Bards vs. Norse Skalds: A Cultural Comparison

Although Gaelic bards enjoyed a tremendous reputation, they were hardly the only poets of the day. In a similar vein, the Norse skalds, serving Viking warlords and kings, helped preserve history and elevate leaders. Still, these two traditions differed fundamentally in several important ways.

- Gaelic bards created highly stylised pieces following rigorous guidelines, concentrating on poetic structure and formal praise and transforming their words. Often, these songs were meant to be performed with musical accompaniment on the harp.
- Using kennings – metaphorical sentences that poetically characterised objects – for example, calling the sea a 'whale-road' or a sword 'wound-lightning' – Norse skalds depended more on sophisticated imagery and alliteration. Often more mysterious, their poetry was aimed at those who knew its complex interpretations.
- While Norse skalds could be more mobile, travelling from one warlord's court to another, Gaelic bards typically belonged to noble homes for a lifetime. This meant that bards of Gaelic kings such as Somerled had long-standing ties to guarantee that their history was preserved by reliable poets.

Though these customs varied, there was also influence and interaction between them, particularly in the Norse-Gaelic realm of the Western Isles. While Norsemen residing in Gaelic areas would have encountered Irish and Scottish bardic traditions, some bards most certainly borrowed parts of Skaldic poetry.

The Influence of Bards on Power and Politics

Depending on clan loyalty, Somerled would have realised the value of words in preserving his authority. A leader honoured in poetry would have his reputation carried well beyond his borders, ensuring his position among allies and frightening his rivals.

Furthermore, bards were well-known for their capacity to offer warnings. Not all their songs were compliments; some were masked cautions to leaders about conceit, treachery, or mistakes that might bring about their doom. A bard who warned of peril in his songs and provided an omen before battle was often seen as equally important as a warrior.

In the land of Somerled, where alliances were tested and power was always changing, bards were a ruler's voice, historians, and a barrier against being forgotten. Their impact guaranteed that even long after a leader passed away, his name and actions would still be mentioned in halls and around fires, carried forth in the songs that survived him.

As he constructed his dominion, Somerled's bards were vital not only in commemorating his successes but also in ensuring his position in the memory of the Isles. But what exactly did they sing about? What tales were told in their songs, and how much of them were myth rather than history? To understand this, we must study the surviving poetry and songs – that is, those recorded long after Somerled's time.

Poems and Songs About Somerled

One stanza at a time, the bards who stood in Somerled's halls created his legacy rather than only entertaining. Their songs guaranteed that his conquests, wisdom, and authority would not fade from memory even outside his own countries. They dubbed him a warrior-king, a leader of the Isles unlike any other. But what proportion of what they sang was myth, and what was truth?

Common Themes in Bardic Poetry About Somerled

The poetry composed in Somerled's time followed common themes found in the Gaelic bardic tradition. These songs changed the way a king was remembered, emphasising traits that made him deserving of allegiance and respect, hence transcending simple recounting of events.

- **Somerled the warrior-king**: Many of the pieces on him concentrated on his fighting prowess. He was presented as a leader who reclaimed the islands, rebelled against the Norsemen, and established a kingdom by tenacity and ingenuity. Bards talked of his fleet of ships slicing over the water, his sword killing adversaries, and his fighters gathering behind him with allegiance.
- **Protector of the Isles**: His defence of the Western Isles was another recurring theme. He was said to have given stability and unity to a broken country, one who drove out foreign control and guaranteed the clans had a leader powerful enough to keep them safe.
- **The wise and just ruler**: Although many bards concentrated on his triumphs, there were also songs stressing his wisdom and fairness as king. These poems detailed how Somerled balanced strength with justice, rewarded loyalty, and made sure those who followed him benefitted, transcending mere rule by fear.
- **A leader chosen by fate**: Some songs suggested Somerled was not simply any leader but one destined for greatness. Commonly used by bards to transcend simple mortal strength, these poems spun in aspects of prophecy or heavenly favour, depicting him as a king guided by forces outside human comprehension.

Historical Accuracy vs. Myth

Although bardic poetry drew on actual occurrences, it was never intended to be a perfect historical record. These songs were supposed to encourage, unite, and honour a leader, and occasionally, that meant distorting the truth.

- Exaggeration of victories: Many bardic stories would have highlighted Somerled's achievements, showing outnumbered victory, superhuman power, or foes fleeing just at his sight. This was not unique to Somerled – almost every Gaelic and Norse ruler was remembered in similarly grand terms.
- Silence on defeats: Bards were not in the business of tarnishing their patron's reputation. If Somerled had political failures or defeats, the oral tradition would have minimised or totally erased them.
- Mythic elements: Common in Gaelic narrative, some tales would have suggested that Somerled was fulfilling an old prophecy or having heavenly favour. Though this was not accepted literally, it would have strengthened the notion that his rule was more than simply ambition – it was fate.

Notwithstanding these embellishments, the central reality stayed: Somerled was a strong leader in transforming the Western Isles. He was more than just a warrior; he was a person who altered the path of history by outmanoeuvring Norse and Scottish forces, securing alliances, and creating a dynasty. The bards made sure his name was not lost, even if the finer points of his governance vanished with time.

Surviving Poems and Later References

Although no original bardic poetry from Somerled's era has survived, later works provide us with insights regarding his oral tradition's view.

- *The Book of the Dean of Lismore*: A sixteenth-century manuscript including Gaelic poems, some of which allude to the MacDonald clan (Somerled's descendants). Though penned long after his death, it captures the ongoing impact of bardic tradition on the standing of his family.
- Mediaeval chronicles: Though usually with their own prejudices, some Scottish and Norse histories record Somerled's campaigns. While Scottish chronicles stress his Gaelic background and resistance against foreign control, the Norse sources show him as a disruptive renegade.
- Oral tradition: Many Highland households carried tales of Somerled across generations orally. Some of his adventures are still part of local tradition, passed down in a way that combines fact and myth even now.

The influence of such songs endures even though no single poem from his own day has survived. They helped define how the next generations saw him, guaranteeing that he was remembered not simply as a warlord but as a king who had won his place in history by will, might, and wisdom.

Bardic Traditions and Somerled's Legacy

The bards sang his name long after Somerled had departed this life. Their songs guaranteed that his legacy developed rather than faded with time, passed from one generation to the next.

In a period when written records were rare, leaders lived on these oral traditions – their deeds were sung in halls, at events, and during times of war to inspire the next generations. Somerled may have ruled through strength, but it was the bards who secured his place in history.

The Power of Song in Shaping a Dynasty

Particularly, Clan Donald, Somerled's successors, saw the worth of these stories. Emphasising their link to the legendary king of the Isles, the MacDonalds, who claimed ancestry from him, utilised his tale to justify their own authority. The bards helped ensure that Somerled was regarded as the basis of a long-lasting Gaelic dynasty rather than only as a monarch of his day.

For the Lords of the Isles, who governed centuries later, these tunes evolved into a weapon of political power. Somerled's name kept alive reminded others that their right to rule sprang from heredity and destiny as much as from conquest. The more Somerled was revered, the stronger their own claim to power became.

Somerled's Image in Later Generations

The picture of Somerled changed with time to become something even more outstanding than the man himself. Highland clans later recalled him as a warrior-king who opposed foreign control, an idealised individual representing Gaelic might and autonomy. Somerled's narrative persisted even after the Lords of the Isles lost authority, coming to represent opposition to outside powers.

Scottish national identity also found room for his tale. As tensions between the Highlands and the Lowlands developed, stories of Somerled were occasionally used to underline the fighting spirit of the Gaelic people – a remembrance of a time when the clans stood strong and unified under a single leader.

The Continuation of Bardic Traditions

In Highland society, the custom of bardic storytelling endured robustly even as the world changed. Every generation of the Gaels carried on their oral history, and new bards arose in every one of them. They sang of Somerled as well as of his successors and the later Highland clan hardships. These songs were not only history; they were their identity, a link to the past that Highlanders carried with them even in difficult and changing times.

As Scotland modernised and the traditional clan system began to decline, bardic poetry persisted in different forms. Some of these stories were eventually written down in later manuscripts, preserving fragments of what had once been purely oral tradition. But even today, echoes of Somerled's legend remain in Highland folklore, his name still spoken in connection with the Western Isles and the enduring Gaelic heritage.

Somerled's Immortality Through Words

Somerled built his kingdom through strength, diplomacy, and vision, but the bards immortalised him. Without their songs, his victories might have been forgotten, his rule remembered only as a passing name in history. Because of them, he became something more – a figure whose memory outlived his time, a ruler whose story shaped the world long after his sword had been laid to rest.

Though the last lines of his songs were spoken centuries ago, the myth they created still lives. The tales of the bards, which were spread across the islands, preserved Somerled's name so that it would never be forgotten. His legacy extended beyond the territories he governed and the conflicts he prevailed in.

Chapter 24

Somerled's World in Words

Somerled governed over a territory whose languages blended as naturally as the waves. The Western Isles of Scotland were home to Gaelic speakers, Norse immigrants, and Latin-trained churchmen, each group employing language to convey their identity, trade, and power.

One must first grasp the words that moulded Somerled's universe before one may appreciate it. Gaelic, the speech of the native Scots and Irish, was the most often spoken language in Somerled's territory. It was the language of the average person, the fighters under his direction, and the bards singing of his triumphs.

In many respects, Gaelic connected the Isles, hence fostering clan and regionally consistent cultural continuity. It was the language of oral tradition, law, and storytelling, passed down through centuries without written records.

Norse was still extensively used concurrently in several areas of the western seaboard. For centuries, the Viking impact on the islands had been significant; many coastal towns still spoke Norse daily. For traders, seamen, and individuals who had once been under the authority of Norse warlords, it was their language.

Among Somerled's own fighters, especially those from mixed Norse-Gaelic backgrounds, some would have been naturally bilingual in both languages and would have moved between them.

Though significantly less popular, Latin had a status. Legal papers, monasteries, and the Church spoke this language. Recording history, treaties, and holy books in Latin, the monks of Iona and other religious centres guaranteed that significant agreements and documentation would be passed on for the next centuries.

Although ordinary people had little need for Latin, Somerled would have come across it in contact with church authorities and maybe in official treaties with Scottish and Irish kings.

How these languages interacted is a complicated matter. Norse and Gaelic remained distinct in other places, spoken by different groups living alongside but preserving their own customs. In others, especially in towns, words and phrases naturally blended. While some Gaelic idioms inspired Norse speakers, Norse loanwords found their way into Gaelic, particularly regarding sailing, battle, and trade. This interaction over time contributed to defining the distinct Norse-Gaelic character of the Western Isles.

In Somerled's universe, language was not only a means of communication but an instrument of power, diplomacy, and identity. His power and reputation were moulded by the way he governed these several languages. Beyond the spoken word, though, his impact also shaped the language itself by adding fresh vocabulary and guiding the communication of Islanders for the next generations.

Somerled's Impact on the Gaelic Language

Not only did Somerled's authority define the Western Isles' political scene, but it also changed its language. For centuries, Gaelic had been the main language of the area; however, under Somerled's direction, it kept changing and absorbing ideas from governmental systems, trade networks, and Norse colonists. His tenure corresponded with a period of linguistic mixing whereby the Gaelic spoken in the Isles diverged from that of mainland Scotland and Ireland.

Among the most important ways Somerled shaped Gaelic was by bringing Norse loanwords. Many Norse terms had already found their way into daily conversation, especially in fields relating to seafaring, combat, and governance, thanks in large part to his Norse background and the strong Viking presence in the Isles.

Particularly frequent were words for ships, navigation, and coastal life, as the Norse had dominated the oceans for centuries. Words originating from Norse that were ingrained in Gaelic during this era include:

- *Bàta* (from Old Norse *bâtr*), meaning boat
- *Sgìr* (from Old Norse *skíri*), meaning parish or district
- *Eilean* (from Old Norse *eyland*), meaning island
- *Birlinn* (a type of longship used by Somerled, adapted from the Norse *byrdingr*)

Beyond vocabulary, Somerled's leadership might have helped administrative Gaelic to be more standardised. His court would have needed a unified legal and political language over a population that included both Gaelic and Norse speakers.

Although formal Gaelic legal traditions had been firmly established for centuries, Norse conventions might have brought fresh words or changed existing phrases linked to military command, trade agreements, and government.

Combining Gaelic and Norse also had influences on grammar and pronunciation. Although exact alterations during Somerled's time are elusive, linguistic developments in succeeding centuries indicate that Gaelic spoken in the Isles preserved significant Norse phonetic influences, especially in place names and dialectal variations separating it from mainland Scottish Gaelic.

Somerled's impact guaranteed that the Gaelic of the Isles stayed unique and flexible, absorbing foreign influences while preserving its basic character.

The language of his people was dynamic, shaped by the movement of warriors, traders, and leaders like him who straddled two worlds and left a legacy not merely in stone and battle but in the very words people uttered.

This linguistic imprint is most clearly revealed by the names of places where the blending of Gaelic and Norse influence became a permanent element of the terrain. Examining the names of the territories Somerled governed – names that still reflect his world today – helps us appreciate his ongoing influence on the area.

The Significance of Place Names

The ground Somerled controlled was more than just land. Every valley, shoreline, and island on this historical map carried the weight of former leaders, conflicts, and colonies.

Rather than arbitrary names, these sites had names that reflected who had held authority, who had laid the foundation, and how civilisations had mixed over time. Gaelic and Norse place names clashed and blended during Somerled's leadership, indicating both continuity and change in the Isles.

Since Gaelic had long been the language of the Highlands and western seaboard, many sites within Somerled's territory still bear Gaelic names. These names, which linked the land to regional geography, mythology, and clan legacy, frequently used old Gaelic phrases to describe natural elements, including mountains, rivers, and islands. However, many place names had also been given Norse roots because of the lengthy era of Norse domination preceding Somerled's ascendancy, especially along the coasts where Viking colonies and trading ports had been founded.

During Somerled's rule, power was changing, and these developments were occasionally expressed in place names. Sometimes, as Somerled recaptured the area from Norsemen, Gaelic names would have substituted Norse ones, increasing his power and restoring Gaelic cultural identity. Other times, Norse names persisted, evidence of the mixed legacy of the area and the ongoing presence of Norse-speaking people under his control.

Kintyre perfectly illustrates this mixing; Somerled's impact is most evident there. Though nearby locations bore Norse influences, such as Islay (from the Old Norse *Íl ey*, meaning 'island of Íl) and Jura (from Old Norse *Dyrøy*, meaning 'deer island'), the name itself is Gaelic, meaning 'the headland'). These names persisted even after Somerled defeated the Norse, demonstrating that the Norse presence was never totally eradicated, even while Gaelic control had been restored.

Somerled's own name or lineage got etched in the local landscape in several areas. Although there is no clear 'Somerled's town' or 'Somerled's fortress' that stands today, his descendants – the MacDonalds – made sure his memory persisted in their territory. Oral histories in some areas still link Clan Donald to locales, while castles and towns connected with him often have their roots in his authority.

Place names across the Western Isles with both Gaelic and Norse components reflect the complicated character of Somerled's rule. Rather than forsake his Gaelic roots, he oversaw a hybrid culture that mirrored both traditions; he did not aim to totally eradicate Norse influence. The names of the land continue to be a reminder of this equilibrium, proof of the world he helped create, even centuries later.

But language expressed power and identity as much as it marked physical locations. Among what made Somerled such a great king was his capacity to negotiate these language and cultural changes. Therefore, to fully appreciate his impact, we must consider not just how he impacted language but also how language itself shaped his memory.

Language as a Reflection of Somerled's Rule

Somerled's rule was characterised by more than war and conquest; it was moulded by the words his people spoke about him, the languages in his court, and the words carrying his name.

Language marked power, identity, and legitimacy as much as a means for communication. Somerled ensured that language helped strengthen his power and unite his people in a society where leaders were recognised not just for their deeds but also for the patterns of their speech.

Language as a Political Tool

For Somerled, rule over a varied population entailed handling a careful mix of Gaelic and Norse influences. Although Gaelic was the most used language in the area, many of his subjects – especially in places long under Viking rule – still spoke Norse. Somerled most certainly adopted a bilingual approach, depending on the audience, instead of imposing a single language upon his people.

- In official government and among Gaelic-speaking clans, he would have depended on Gaelic, stressing his legitimacy as a native monarch rather than a foreign conqueror.
- In interactions with Norse traders, warriors, and former leaders, he probably spoke Norse, keeping ties to people who had before ruled the Isles.

With Church and monastic authorities, Latin would have been the language of written agreements and ecclesiastical diplomacy.

By letting Gaelic, Norse, and Latin coexist under his control, Somerled positioned himself as a king who united rather than eradicated cultures. This adaptability enabled him to keep control over an area long split by foreign pressures and internal strife.

Language as a Unifying Force

While political necessity required him to accomplish multiple languages, Somerled's rule strengthened Gaelic as the leading cultural language of the Isles. His defeat of Norse leaders in important areas helped Gaelic become the main language of government, law, and daily life once more.

This change guaranteed that, on the western seaboard, Gaelic rather than Norse stayed the language of identification and legacy across time. Still, hints of

Norse influence persisted not only in loanwords and place names but in the hybrid identity that developed among Somerled's people. The Norse-Gaelic world was one of adaptation rather than strict separation. Language became a reflection of this, blending words, traditions, and expressions that reflected the dual ancestry of the Isles.

How Later Generations Remembered Somerled Through Language

Somerled's name and deeds lived on not only through written records but also in the words passed down through generations, shaping his image far beyond the time in which he lived. Although no direct sayings or poetry from his time have remained whole, Gaelic oral traditions were vital in maintaining his legacy.

For centuries, bards and poets spoke of his triumphs, assuring that he was not only revered as a historical king but also raised to the rank of a legendary person. These songs and tales, which presented him as a strong warrior, a wise leader, and a symbol of Gaelic opposition against foreign control, impacted how the next generations saw him.

His heritage was carried on by his successors, imprinted in their honourable line. Among the strongest clans in Scottish history, the MacDonalds sustained Somerled's popularity, supporting his image as a fundamental individual in their family.

Beyond his family, his impact became a constant component of the cultural identity of the Scottish Highlands and the Isles. Respect for Somerled expressed the pride of Gaelic society not only regarding ancestry but also in its military customs and its resistance against outside dangers.

The oral traditions, folklore, and historical narrative of the Highlands show hints of his influence even today. Discussions about Scotland's mediaeval history still feature his name, and both historians and storytellers alike find great delight in his adventures.

Somerled's memory reveals the power of oral history in forming cultural memory by showing how a leader's actions may transcend time and become more than just events via the voices of those who followed him.

The Lasting Impact of Norse-Gaelic Fusion

Combining Norse and Gaelic in Somerled's day produced a distinctive language and cultural identity that endured for generations. Even after his rule ended, the language of the Isles retained elements of both traditions, reflected in:

- The survival of Norse place names, combined with Gaelic territorial designations.
- The use of Norse-derived words in maritime and warfare-related Gaelic vocabulary.
- The carrying on of bardic customs respecting both Norse and Gaelic forefathers.

Though Gaelic stayed predominant, the vestiges of Norse influence guaranteed the Isles maintained their own identity, shaped by the past of both cultures.

Somerled's Legacy in Words

Somerled transformed the words people used, the way they spoke, and the identity they carried on, therefore changing the land. His control enhanced Gaelic as the primary language of the Isles, but it did not eradicate the Norse presence that had defined the area for so long. Rather, he oversaw a mixed society in which language captured the reality of a people steeped in both Gaelic and Norse customs.

Even centuries after his death, the influence of his time lives on in the names of places, in the echoes of old Gaelic poetry, and in the identity of the Western Isles. His reign proved that language is more than just a means of communication – it reflects power, history, and the way a ruler is remembered long after his voice has faded.

Chapter 25

The Material Culture of Somerled's Kingdom

The great hall was the centre of power, where authority was not only exercised but also demonstrated in every direction. Warriors arrived there to show allegiance, leaders made decisions that moulded the Isles, and poets and bards ensured history was not lost. Designed to withstand the harsh Atlantic winds as well as time, these halls physically reflected the leaders under command.

The weight of heritage and the promise of future actions made the air inside its walls crackle. From the rafters, banners featuring clan insignia were hung, their vivid hues suggesting ancestry and loyalty. Gathering around the long, central hearth was the focal point. Here, the community's life was spun thread by thread amid the din of feasting and the resonance of spoken word.

Architecture: A Blending of Traditions

In Somerled's day, a high-status Norse-Gaelic household was a declaration of money, power, and cultural identity in addition to being a place of habitation. Its building combined the Norse longhouse form with Gaelic chieftain halls to depict the twin influences guiding the Isles. Often positioned strategically on raised land or close to harbours, these halls guaranteed both defence against the sea and access. Made from timber, wattle, and daub – or even stone in locations where supplies allowed – the walls were strong and robust. The roofs served as protection against the cold and wind, and they were either coated with turf or covered in straw.

Within the hall was a universe of voices, movement, and warmth. A huge fire burned nonstop, the household's lifeline, offering light, heat, and a cooking facility. Burning peat or driftwood sent smoke upward, escaping via a tiny hole in the ceiling to produce a foggy environment smelling of the sea, ground, and cooked meat.

The thick oak beams supporting the roof, often carved with symbols or patterns, reflected the ability of nearby craftsmen. While some showed Norse entwined creatures or runes, reflecting the shared creative traditions of the time, others exhibited typical Gaelic knotwork.

The hall lacked single-room architecture. Storage rooms, bedrooms, and workshops where blacksmiths, weavers, and craftspeople worked were housed in attached buildings, covered passageways, or enclosed courtyards. Though secondary, these extra areas were equally vital to the home since they guaranteed that items were constantly accessible for commerce or conflict and helped to meet the needs of the ruling elite.

The Interior: Wealth and Status on Display

Every element of the hall was deliberate, meant to communicate authority, hospitality, and status. Textiles and furs, which provided warmth and comfort, lined the long wooden tables where visitors, aristocrats, and fighters convened.

Drinking horns, polished to a silky sheen, complemented exquisitely wrought goblets of silver and bronze, so reflecting the position of those who ate there. The meal presented was not typical fare; roast meats, oatcakes, butter, and ale were plentiful, thus indicating the chieftain's affluence.

The high seat at the head of the chamber was often a big, throne-like chair upholstered with dyed wool or animal hides. Often displaying beast patterns or complex designs reflecting lineage and personal identity, the chairs of loyal warriors and noble guests were simpler but still exquisitely carved.

The walls whispered tales of previous glory and ongoing vigilance. Weapons and shields were shown as symbols of authority and readiness, not as kept objects. A Norse-style sword with its hilt wrapped in leather might hang near a Gaelic long spear in an unconscious acknowledgment of the shared martial traditions of the Isles. These items were not only decorations; they were reminders of the battles waged, the foes vanquished, and the need to always be ready for the next conflict.

Beyond weaponry, banners covering the walls showed genealogical history, past triumphs, and fables of warriors. The skill of narrative was not limited to bards; it permeated the very fabric of the house. Some rooms even included carved wooden panels featuring Norse and Gaelic designs, highlighting the best creations of nearby craftsmen.

Hierarchy and Ritual in the Hall

Entering this realm was a privilege that represented trust, partnership, or obedience. The seating arrangement was rigidly hierarchical; those closest to the chieftain were his most prized warriors, advisers, and family members. Lower-ranked fighters and craftsmen sat further down the table, and servants and messengers silently made sure the needs of the gathering were satisfied at the room's margins.

Feasting was not only a meal but a statement of allegiance and unity. The chieftain's hospitality strengthened his reputation, and the food and drink sharing fostered ties of obligation and thankfulness. Soldiers who fought under Somerled were more than just fighters; they were bound to him by ties of allegiance, reinforced by events like these, whereby their commander proved his value not only in battle but also in leadership and kinship.

This was a site of diplomacy and government as well. Legal issues were discussed in front of both noblemen and common warriors; alliances were made over shared meals and drinking oaths; conflicts were resolved before the assembled crowd. A ruler's power came from his capacity to inspire allegiance through words and deeds in addition to his sword.

The Household as a Microcosm of the Isles

Although these halls were set aside for nobility and reigning chieftains, they were not secluded places. Rather, they served as little replicas of the bigger world Somerled ruled. The fusion of Norse and Gaelic craftsmanship, architecture, and creative traditions shaped the Isles' entire culture and was not limited to aristocratic homes.

The hierarchical system, the storytelling customs, and the complex knotwork patterns carved into beams and brooches were fashioned by Gaelic inspirations.

- Shipbuilding methods, longhouse design, and the strong animal motifs found in jewellery and weapons clearly reflected Norse influences.
- Timber, stone, iron, and textiles – the resources used – were obtained both locally and via commerce, connecting Somerled's realm with the larger networks of the North Atlantic.

Somerled's kingdom's material culture was dynamic, always changing as fresh influences from Scotland, Ireland, and the Norse realm came to affect it. The tools, weapons, domestic items, and historical artwork all point to society at a crossroads where two once-separate worlds had combined to create something new.

Still, the high-status items of the ruling class merely scratch the surface. If one is really to grasp the material reality of Somerled's realm, one must also turn outside these great halls to the daily lives of the farmers, traders, fishermen, and craftsmen who constructed, sustained, and fought for the Isles. The tools, ceramics, basic fabrics, and common household goods they left behind reveal a society strongly linked to the land, the sea, and the rhythms of everyday survival.

The narrative of Somerled's period is about the people who lived under his authority as much as it is about leaders and fighters. Though long past, their world, which was fashioned of iron and wood, stone and wool, leather and bone, remains in the fragments of the artifacts they left behind.

Art and Craftsmanship in Somerled's Time

Art and workmanship in Somerled's day went beyond ornamentation. These were declarations of legacy, authority, and identity. Everything from the curvature of a ship's prow to the designs etched into a warrior's broach revealed the mix of Gaelic and Norse traditions. These combined into something that mirrored the reality of the Isles, a country where Gaelic chieftains and Norse immigrants had coexisted for years, hence forming a shared material culture rather than different artistic styles fighting against one another.

Seen in their stone carvings, metalwork, and manuscripts, the artistic traditions of the Gaels have long been based on knotwork, patterns, and spiritual meaning.

Reflecting their warrior culture and marine way of life, the Norse preferred strong lines, geometric shapes, and stylised animal motifs.

These two traditions merged rather than replaced one another when they came together. Their distinctive Norse-Gaelic artistic approach was visually arresting and profoundly significant.

This union was most evident in the goods created for soldiers, nobility, and religious leaders – things that were not only useful but also symbols of status, lineage, and workmanship.

Jewellery, Metalwork, and Stone Carving

Personal ornamentation – the brooches, rings, and pendants people wore to indicate their status and allegiance – was one of the most obvious kinds of artwork in Somerled's day. Often made in gold, bronze, or silver, these objects include complex engravings combining Norse animal themes with Gaelic knotwork.

Brooches, a mainstay of apparel, were used to fasten cloaks or tunics. A noble's brooch served more than only a fastening pin. Often with Celtic motifs or stylised Viking animals chewing their own tails, it was a show of riches and identity.

Soldiers and chieftains wore arm rings and torcs, often awarded as rewards for allegiance. While the Gaels utilised more delicate filigree motifs, the Norse preferred strong, twisted metal bands; these styles started to mix in Somerled's day.

Sometimes appearing together in surprising ways, an ornate cross can have vestiges of Norse mythology in its engravings, reflecting both pagan and Christian ideas and revealing how belief systems have intertwined just as much as their artistic traditions.

Metalwork covered more ground than jewellery. Belt fittings, drinking cups, and weapon hilts all had etched designs highlighting the local artist's talent. A high-status warrior's sword might have a Gaelic cross carved into its pommel while the handle was wrapped in leather using a Norse-style pattern. The specifics of an object mattered; they revealed the owner, where they had been, and the world they belonged to.

Another field where Somerled's time left a lasting impression was stone cutting. Celtic high crosses, carved with religious images and knotwork, have long been a feature of the Western Isles; yet some of these monuments acquired unmistakeably Norse features both during and following Somerled's lifetime.

With their images framed by Gaelic spirals and Norse serpentine motifs, several of the tomb slabs and memorial stones cut in the Highlands and Isles show long, thin warriors clutching swords and shields.

Many of these memorial stones honoured the deeds of the dead by featuring battle scenes with warriors on horses or ships headed into combat. Some stones even have runic inscriptions next to Gaelic engravings, an uncommon but important indication of cultural fusion.

Long after Somerled, these artistic traditions would still be influencing the West Highland tombstones of subsequent years, still showing remnants of the workmanship and artistic ideas that evolved during his lifetime.

Weapons and Military Craftsmanship

If jewellery and stone carvings stood for prestige and legacy, weapons were the most direct emblems of power. An extension of a warrior's identity, his sword, axe, or spear defined his reputation and served more than only a weapon of war.

Swords of this age periodically displayed both Norse and Gaelic inspiration. Whereas the Norse built smaller, well-balanced swords meant for quick attacks, the Gaels preferred broad-bladed swords with decorative hilts.

A hybrid style combining Gaelic adornment with Norse practicality developed during Somerled's lifetime, producing swords both lethal and attractive.

Particularly in the Western Isles, axes were also extensively used. While the Gaels had long depended on lighter, faster weapons for battle in difficult terrain, the Norse were renowned for their broad, single-bladed axes. Different axe designs resulting from the trade of methods were specifically fit for the fighting in the area.

Spears stayed mostly as weapons of battle, and their designs changed as well. While Gaelic spears were broader and usually ornamented with etched motifs, Norse spears often had longer, tapering points. Spearmen in Somerled's day probably carried weapons combining the qualities of both civilisations.

Shields also showed varied skills in workmanship. While the Gaels favoured smaller targes, often reinforced in the centre, the Norse custom used circular wooden shields. Decorated wooden shields with Celtic knotwork and Norse geometric patterns proliferated over time, demonstrating that artistic expression remained vital even on the battlefield.

The Meaning Behind the Craftsmanship

Somerled's time's artistic and technical mastery expressed power, identity, and legacy rather than only serving a practical need.

- A brooch marked status more than it did just decoration.
- A carved stone cross honoured the melding of two civilisations rather than only a religious emblem.
- A birlinn was not only a ship but a tool of conquest, a statement of naval supremacy, and a link between the Gaelic and Norse worlds.

These things lasted since they had a purpose. Echoes of Somerled's world still abound today in the carvings left on old stone slabs, in the creative patterns still defining Highland workmanship, and in the stories that have endured across centuries.

Although nobility and fighters left behind the most ornate objects, it is the things utilised by common people that really define a civilisation.

Everyday Objects and Daily Life in Somerled's Kingdom

The high-status items of Somerled's era – ornate brooches, finely made swords, and stone sculptures depicting kings – painted a picture of power and distinction. Beyond the boundaries of great halls and military armaments, though, was another world: the daily life of the people who laboured the land, fished the oceans, and laid the groundwork for the country Somerled ruled.

While kings and warriors left behind marks of status and power, ordinary people left behind daily artifacts that exposed the rhythms of life in the Western Isles.

Though they seem less spectacular than a warrior's sword or a carved stone cross, these artifacts – tools, pottery, textiles, and trade goods – tell just as much about the world in which Somerled lived.

Tools, Pottery, Textiles, and Clothing

For the common individual living in Somerled's realm, survival came from farming, fishing, herding, and workmanship. Designed from wood, iron, and bone, their basic but indispensable tools were simple but vital.

- While sickle-shaped blades helped them gather grain, farmers worked the ground with iron ploughs and wooden digging tools.
- Fishermen brought food from the sea using nets, bone fishhooks, and wooden boats.
- Iron chisels, hammers, and saws were employed by blacksmiths and woodworkers to create daily goods, build dwellings, and forge weapons.

Another common daily item used for cooking, storing grain, and transporting commodities was pottery. Although high-status homes might have owned exquisitely created metal or wooden drinking cups, most people used basic clay containers, hand-made or on a slow wheel, then baked in a pit kiln.

While some displayed minor designs or marks reflecting local workmanship, these containers were practical rather than ornamental.

Somerled's time saw mostly wool on straight looms and dyed with natural plant-based dyes in clothing. Farmers and workers often wore coarse, undyed tunics and cloaks; wealthier people might acquire delicately coloured clothing in hues of blue, green, or red.

Textiles also clearly displayed a mix of Norse and Gaelic inspiration. Although the Isles' traditional apparel was Gaelic cloaks and long tunics, brooches and Norse-style belts were often employed to tie clothing.

Often attached at the shoulder with a basic ringed brooch, woollen cloaks drew on both civilisations. Using fur linings, sheepskin boots, and thick woollen hoods expressed the pragmatic need for warmth in a country where the wind and water may turn hostile at any moment.

Trade and Commerce – Goods Imported into the Isles

With the Isles serving as a crossroads between Gaelic Scotland, Norse kingdoms, Ireland, and even more extensive European trade networks, trade was very crucial in Somerled's environment. Although many commonplace items were created locally, some materials and luxury goods had to be imported.

- Salt, wine, and fine cloth came from Ireland and England.
- From Scandinavia and the British mainland, metal items like fine iron and silver were imported.
- Rare but often found in the Isles via Irish or Norse trade routes were exotic goods such as silk and spices. Timber from Norway and Scotland was a valuable commodity, especially for shipbuilding.

The Isles were a significant component of the commercial routes spanning the North Atlantic, with coastal towns and island harbours humming with traders, fishermen, and craftsmen exchanging commodities.

As Norse and Gaelic artists absorbed skills from one another, honing their respective crafts throughout time, the trade of resources also resulted in a mixing of artistic and technological influences.

How Material Culture Reflected Social Status and Daily Routines

The daily items individuals used in Somerled's period also revealed their social level and occupation, much as a well-made sword or a nicely carved stone cross represented the riches and reputation of lords. Material culture was a visual depiction of status, identity, and the responsibilities individuals performed within their societies.

A high-status warrior, someone serving a chieftain or nobleman, might carry a superbly made Norse-style sword, its hilt wrapped in leather and its blade fashioned with the best iron available. Such a weapon was evidence of warrior class rank, competence, and allegiance.

An ordinary soldier or a lesser-ranked clansman, on the other hand, would carry a basic iron spear or a short sword, weapons that were practical but lacked the artistic flourishes and superb workmanship reserved for people of higher status. The quality of a weapon typically reflected the social order of its owner, therefore underlining the fact that battle was not only about ability but also about status.

One could observe a similar difference in domestic objects. Emphasising riches and hospitality, an aristocratic house would use silver goblets and finely carved drinking horns. Feasting was about showing might and kindness.

By contrast, farmers and craftspeople used hand-thrown earthenware and wooden cups – simple but robust objects fit for daily use. While chieftains and nobility could afford imported items like finely woven fabrics or ornamented metalware, people lower in the hierarchy depended on locally created tools and utensils, usually fashioned from clay, bone, or carved wood.

Clothing, too, reflected rank. A chieftain's cloak would be fastened with a big, intricate brooch made of silver or bronze with decorations that highlighted his affiliations or ancestry. Usually offered as a gift or a reward for loyalty, a brooch was a badge of identity rather than just a fastening. On the other hand, a farmer or a fisherman might tie his cloak with a basic wooden or iron pin, thus fulfilling the same functional need but without the majesty of a noble's decoration.

These differences in tools, home goods, and clothes reveal that every object carried meaning beyond its use. Whether it was a modest clay cup, a highly crafted brooch, or a decorated sword, every object revealed the status, wealth, trade, and location in Somerled's world of use.

Every everyday object held meaning as well. A wooden loom in the corner of a house indicated many cold evenings spent weaving wool into cloth. An iron knife was used for numerous meals, and its grip was smooth owing to years of use. Once part of someone's daily life, a cracked clay pot discovered in an abandoned hamlet reminds us that life in Somerled's time was about the people who kept the kingdom alive as much as about soldiers and rulers.

Though many of the great symbols of Somerled's time – castles, ships, and carved stones – are what we remember now, it was these little, daily items that really moulded life in the Isles. They were the markers of trade, the tools of survival, the goods that crowded houses and markets, farms, and feasting halls.

The civilisation of the Isles grew together with Somerled's realm. His authority made a lasting impression on the material culture of the area with the introduction of fresh products, the mixing of customs, and the improvement of workmanship. But how much of this shift was transient, and how much remained outside his lifetime? Examining how material culture changed during and following his rule will help us to fully appreciate his influence on the Isles for the next generations.

The Evolution of Material Culture Under Somerled

Somerled's rule influenced the Western Isles' material culture in ways that persisted long after his death, transcending mere political and military transformation. Under his direction, architecture evolved, trade networks grew stronger, and workmanship improved – all of which would impact the area for generations. While some of these developments were minor, others clearly and permanently altered the landscape and culture of the Isles.

Influence on Craftsmanship, Architecture, and Trade

Somerled's ability to unify Gaelic and Norse traditions was not only reflected in politics but also in the objects and structures created during his rule.

Weapons and Metalwork
The hybrid Gaelic-Norse style of swords, shields, and armour became increasingly distinct under Somerled. The craftsmanship of warrior brooches, rings, and ceremonial weapons continued to reflect both traditions, ensuring that his warriors carried the symbols of their heritage and their allegiance.

Shipbuilding
Developed under Somerled's direction, the birlinn remained the Western Isles' principal warship for generations. Its design combined the demands of Gaelic naval warfare with Norse longship building to enable quick movement and strategic superiority at sea. This change in marine technology confirmed the naval might of Somerled's descendants, particularly the Lords of the Isles.

Stone Carving and Religious Art
Reflecting a mix of Celtic and Norse artistic influences, the stone crosses and tomb slabs cut during this era became artistically distinctive. Appearing in later Highland tombstones and clan memorials, these designs would be carried on for decades.

Trade networks also grew stronger under Somerled's rule since his dominance over important areas allowed the Isles, Scotland, Ireland, and Norse colonies to engage more regularly economically.

Once uncommon items, including imported iron, wood, and exquisite textiles, became more readily available, thus enhancing the local material culture. Fortified towns and trade centres guaranteed that these interactions would continue long after his rule ended.

Lasting Cultural Imprints: What Endured in Later Centuries

Many aspects of the material culture from Somerled's time did not disappear with him. His legacy can be seen in:

- **The continued influence of the Birlinn**: The Gaelic lords who ruled after Somerled continued to use the Birlinn, refining its design over time. Until clan warfare collapsed in the seventeenth century, this ship remained a symbol of Highland and Island naval might.
- **West Highland grave slabs**: Originally developed in Somerled's time, the style of carved warrior tomb slabs changed and became a distinctive characteristic of Highland funerary art. A tribute to the ongoing impact of this age, many of these later carvings nevertheless exhibit the same Norse-Gaelic creative combination.
- **Clan symbols and heraldry**: Highland society still carried the concept of warrior identity represented in artifacts like brooches, rings, and adorned shields. Somerled's successors, particularly the MacDonalds, continued using these symbols, therefore strengthening their connection to his legacy.

The material culture that developed during Somerled's lifetime became firmly ingrained in the identity of the Highland and Isles even as successive kings tried to centralise control over them.

The Material Legacy of Somerled

Somerled's impact is evident in the objects and customs that survived him, even if many of his physical relics from that era have been lost to the elements. His dominion left a legacy not only in politics and history but also in the very fabric of daily existence, making sure the world he created endured long after he was gone.

Though the Isles have evolved, the echoes of Somerled's material culture – his ships, his weaponry, his art – remain markers of the age he defined.

Chapter 26

Somerled's Strategic Strongholds

Dunaverty Castle, perched high on a rocky cliff at Kintyre's southernmost point, represented power over the western shore. Ignoring the changing tides of the North Channel, it watched where the choppy waves between Scotland and Ireland naturally discouraged invaders. Dunaverty's height gave its defenders an unhindered view of the surrounding shore, enabling them to identify approaching ships long before they could ground.

On three sides, the windswept cliffs and rugged outcrops formed an almost impervious shield that left only a single approach by land – a limited, twisting passage that would be readily reinforced with barricades, guard towers, and armed patrols.

This was not a castle designed only for visual splendour but a fortification created for survival. Unlike the vast castles of later years, Dunaverty's fortifications were built with practical intent. Multiple layers of defence came from strong timber palisades, stone walls, and secret viewpoints. The ground itself served as an always alert defender, discouraging even the most tenacious enemies.

Dunaverty was a dangerous stronghold as fierce storms pummelled the coast and waves hammered against the rocks. It was also a haven. Any opponent trying a siege had to first negotiate the perilous path to get to it – a difficulty few could overcome without injury.

However, Dunaverty was not only a fortification but a key component of Somerled's more ambitious plan. Unlike earlier warlords who depended on isolated castles, he understood that actual power was derived from a linked system of defences. Dunaverty was not only an outpost; it was a major link in his growing chain of defences. Its position allowed him to supervise trade, military operations, political relationships, and trade between Scotland and Ireland, therefore controlling the crucial sea routes. Somerled saw that ruling the western coast meant controlling its waters – whoever managed the flow of ships, fighters, and supplies possessed the actual force.

Life Within the Walls

Inside Dunaverty's strong walls, politics and battle changed life. Along with seasoned guards and hardened fighters, the castle housed artists, couriers, traders, and noble families who all helped to maintain Somerled's territory under running order.

Fundamentally, Somerled and his closest advisers planned battles, formed alliances, and made choices that impacted the future of his kingdom from the vast hall, which was an active centre.

Burning at all hours, the blacksmith's forge created swords, axes, and armour needed for both assault and protection. Each person living in the fortress had a goal. Skilled craftsmen made sure weapons, armour, and fortifications stayed in perfect shape; hunters left the protection of the walls to bring fresh game; fishermen braved the choppy coastal waters to provide sustenance. Dunaverty was never still; it was always getting ready for the next unavoidable conflict even while no wars were raging. Still, life at Dunaverty was more than simply conflict. During peace, the fort acted as a central administrative centre, supervising the nearby territory and guaranteeing discipline. Within its hallways, nobles, envoys, and warriors convened where feasts celebrated successes, alliances were formed, and authority was claimed.

Thus, Dunaverty was a house, a haven, and a symbol of fortitude against the tides of uncertainty for those who lived inside its walls.

A Castle at the Crossroads of Conflict

Though scant records from Somerled's period remain, Dunaverty was clearly significant in the power wrangles that influenced the age. Its strategic position made it too valuable to be overlooked – a fortitude never likely to remain uncontested.

Eager to recover lost power, the Norse considered it a major fortress that helped them rule the western seaboard. Concurrently, Scottish kings apprehensive of Somerled's increasing strength would have aimed to undermine his control over the area and place it under their jurisdiction.

Constant clashes, changing alliances, and war preparation most certainly defined Dunaverty's history. Maintaining reserves of food, weaponry, and reinforcements, defenders would have guaranteed the garrison could withstand protracted sieges.

In terms of the balance of power, the castle acted as everything from a barrier against outside threats to a launching pad for Somerled's own military operations.

One thing is clear: Dunaverty was significantly more than just a stronghold, even if much of her precise contribution under Somerled is lost to time. It was a statement of Gaelic resilience, a proclamation of intent, and a symbol of marine might. It was a warning as well as an invitation, a message to anyone who dared question Somerled's authority, and a lighthouse for those who came together behind him.

Dunaverty, though, was only the start. Beyond its strengthened walls was a great network of castles, fortresses, and defences, each strategically placed to reach Somerled. Let's look beyond a single fortification to the web of fortifications, allowing him not only to survive but also to conquer, appreciating his military genius.

The Network of Fortifications in Somerled's Territories

Dunaverty Castle was only one pillar in the defensive network Somerled created over the western coast. He understood that no matter how strong a fortification was, actual security could never rely on one. Rather, the dominance of the area needed a sequence of strongholds, one supporting the next to guarantee that his influence was not limited but broad.

From the Kintyre Peninsula to the far-off isles of the Hebrides, his military, political, and naval plans rested on a well-positioned network of fortresses, administrative centres, and power bases. These strongholds let him regulate trade, control movement, and quickly organise soldiers.

Fortresses arranged this way meant that no one attack could overthrow his rule. Should one site come under attack, others might send soldiers, supplies, and reinforcements to support it. Somerled ensured he could always command land and sea by holding these strategic sites, thus preserving a presence that was difficult to displace.

Whether Scottish kings or Norsemen, his enemies would discover that his defensive web stayed intact even if they hit one target.

The Many Faces of Somerled's Strongholds

Though each stronghold served a specific function in maintaining Somerled's power, his fortifications were not consistent in construction or goal. While some were erected solely for military defence, meant to resist sieges and repel invaders, others served as centres of government where laws were enforced, alliances were formed, and important decisions were rendered.

This strategic diversity let Somerled dominate not just with force but also with a well-organised network, maintaining his territory's security and powerful influence.

A Network of Strongholds with Distinct Purposes

- **Coastal strongholds**: Rising on steep cliffs with a view of the sea, castles such as Dunaverty acted as watchtowers and initial lines of protection against naval attacks. Their positions provided Somerled authority over important sea lanes, which let him monitor enemy movements and respond quickly to approaching fleets. These strongholds were almost formidable to assault from the sea, given their commanding vistas and natural barriers.
- **Island fortresses**: Sites like Aros Castle on Mull and Finlaggan on Islay capitalised on natural island defences, which makes an attack quite challenging. Any enemy trying to seize these locations requires major naval resources as well as the capacity to maintain an extended siege on hostile ground. By separating these strongholds, Somerled was able to keep control over the Isles even if the mainland was in danger, as these fortifications stayed safe.
- **Hillforts and earthworks**: Under Somerled's direction, many historic Gaelic hillforts and earthworks were strengthened and used rather than abandoned. Found in Argyll and the Inner Hebrides, these high-ground defences gave fighters somewhere solid inside where they might gather and launch

counterattacks. They also provided fallback sites; even if a coastal fortification was lost, the defenders could withdraw to these strongholds, ensuring that Somerled's army was never totally vanquished.

- **Administrative centres:** Not all of Somerled's fortifications were focused on battle. Finlaggan on Islay was one of his most important sites, not as a military fortress but as a political heartland. Leaders convened here, decisions were taken, and government was undertaken. Such sites were vital in preserving order over Somerled's growing domain, guaranteeing that his authority was not only one of conquest but of organised control.

This expertly constructed system of defences guaranteed Somerled's strength went much beyond the boundaries of any one fortress. He built a strategic network that allowed him to precisely and dynamically command the western seaboard, avoiding depending on force. Whether in defence of important sites, protection of trade lines, or application of justice, his fortifications cooperated in establishing his authority and resisting ongoing military challenges.

The Influence of Norse and Gaelic Traditions

Although Somerled's identity was strongly anchored in Gaelic culture, his attitude to fortifications was far from entirely Celtic. Centuries of Norse influence in the Hebrides and western Scotland shaped his world of cultural fusion. Rather than rejecting this Viking inheritance, he embraced and reworked it, combining Gaelic defensive tactics with Norse military engineering.

This blending of customs allowed him to design a hybrid fortification system specifically fit for the difficulties of the Western seaboard rule.

- **Emphasising Norse strongholds:** Many of the strongholds under Somerled's authority were first constructed or occupied by Norsemen. Rather than demolishing these buildings, he turned them around and strengthened already-existing defences, therefore personalising them. Already in strategic places, these outposts gave his growing military network a strong basis.
- **Integrating ancient Gaelic defences:** Somerled also made use of ancient Celtic and Pictish defensive systems, such as duns and brochs, constructed centuries before. These fortified hilltop enclosures and circular stone towers were not abandoned relics – they were modified and supported into his broader defensive system.
- **Function over monumentality:** Unlike the great stone castles that would subsequently define mediaeval Scotland, Somerled's fortifications were constructed with practicality in mind. Using a combination of timber, earth, and stone, he favoured buildings that were fast to repair, flexible, and fit for swift military reactions. His objective was not to create grand castles

but rather to create sturdy fortifications that would change with the needs of battle.

This mixing of building methods and cultures produced a defensive network specifically fit for the erratic character of power in the Isles. Unlike the strongly constructed castles of the Scottish mainland, Somerled's strongholds were meant to change with the tides of war, readily reinforced, enlarged, or modified as needed.

Somerled's perspective was shaped by the area he governed, a realm where power was always in motion, where conflicts were waged as much at sea as on land, and where adaptation was the key to survival rather than replicating the great fortifications of European feudal rulers.

A Fortress is More Than Walls

To Somerled, a fortress was a declaration of control; it stood for rule over the nearby territory and population. Having a castle meant underlining political influence, law enforcement, and commerce control. His fortifications were about fighting as much as they were about symbolism.

By carefully arranging his defences, Somerled made sure his presence could be felt over the western seaboard, even in his absence. One of his castles, perched high on a cliff or tucked within the protective embrace of an island, served as a reminder of his power – a statement to both friends and foes that he governed this land and that his control would not be readily broken.

This network of fortifications was not a result of an accident in history but a deliberately created system of power and defence. Somerled developed a territory that could withstand not just conflicts but also the test of time by controlling important maritime, coastal, and inland sites. His fortifications made sure his dominance endured beyond his own lifetime by allowing him to hold his place against Scottish kings, Norse rivals, and renegade clans.

Somerled's rule had strength outside one castle, one island, or one battlefield. It lay in the connections between his strongholds, the web of fortifications that made him unshakeable.

But Somerled's mastery of defence did not rely solely on walls and warriors – he understood the greatest advantage of all: the land itself. His use of geography in warfare and defence was unparalleled, turning mountains, inlets, and islands into weapons.

Somerled's Use of Geography in Defence

More than just the fortifications Somerled commanded, his strategic genius was about how he employed the territory itself as a weapon. He understood that geography dictated actual defence, not only of walls, battlements, or tall watchtowers. The western seaboard's rocky beaches, deep inlets, tall mountains, and strewn-about islands were his greatest aids in battle, not barriers. While others saw obstacles, he saw chances to mould the battlefield to his benefit, therefore transforming nature itself into an extension of his dominion.

The Power of the Coastline

For Somerled, rule over the seashore equated to rule over the whole area. The seas of the Hebridean Sea and the North Channel were not only barriers; they were roads permitting the quick flow of troops, supplies, and fleets between his scattered holdings.

Unlike landbound rulers who depended on marching armies, Somerled headed an empire that existed as much on water as on land. His domination of the sea paths connecting Kintyre, Argyll, and the Hebrides guaranteed that his soldiers could be sent rapidly to bolster any threatened position.

Some fortresses, including Aros Castle and Dunaverty, were placed especially near strategic marine chokepoints. These fortifications governed the waterways before them, not alone watched over the ground behind them. Any fleet trying to travel through these strategic points would have to deal with Somerled's men, therefore giving him the advantage in trade as well as in battle.

But mastery of the oceans meant more than simply military supremacy – it also provided a means of sustaining power. For trade, the western shore was a vital artery carrying riches and resources into his domain. Supplies were ferried by merchant ships between strongholds, guaranteeing that his troops stayed well-stocked even during times of war. This fluid, mobile approach to power allowed him to react swiftly to changing hazards, strengthening his control in a way that land-based governments could never equal.

Islands as Natural Bastions

The islands of the Inner Hebrides were defences. Somerled did not need to build massive fortifications on every island because nature had already provided formidable barriers. Direct assaults were challenging, with steep cliffs, rough coastlines, and dangerous waterways forcing attackers to face both the weather and Somerled's troops.

- Surrounding lochs and marshlands naturally protected Islay, home of the great seat of Finlaggan. A direct land assault would bog down in difficult terrain, giving defenders the upper hand.
- With its deep glens and soaring mountain slopes, Jura provided not only defence but also a calculated backup area. Should the lowlands be assaulted, Somerled's troops could withdraw into the highlands, encouraging invaders to pursue them across hostile, foreign terrain where ambushes were certain.

- Mull and the other islands established a defensive network whereby watchtowers and lookouts could warn against approaching dangers, preventing any invasion from surprising them.

These island strongholds were part of a living, breathing system of defence. Each one served a role, from housing warriors and supplies to acting as an early-warning station that kept Somerled one step ahead of his enemies.

The Landscape as a Tactical Advantage

Although his coastline and island defences created the first line of defence, Somerled's knowledge of Scotland's internal topography provided him with another advantage in combat. His forces flourished in difficult, erratic terrain, unlike those of regular armies fighting in open fields.

- **Mountains and highlands**: Somerled could withdraw into the highlands, where steep hills and deep valleys turned the ground into a natural fortress when confronting bigger, better-equipped foes. Unfamiliar with the difficult terrain, enemy forces would battle with limited mobility, limited supplies, and continuous ambushes from hidden fighters.
- **Narrow inlets and sea lochs**: Using Scotland's various inlets and lochs as covert routes, Somerled's fleets could move supplies and fighters undetected. Because his ships were designed to be swift and agile, he was able to launch surprise attacks and vanish before his adversaries could respond.
- **Dense forests and marshlands**: Instead of depending just on fortifications, he turned the ground itself into a maze, guiding attackers into hostile, tough terrain where they could be weakened before a major fight.

These natural advantages meant that unless Somerled chose to fight, he was never compelled into open conflict. He set the parameters of combat, striking where he wanted, then disappearing into the sea or mountains before his adversaries could respond.

Repurposing the Past for the Future

Somerled's use of geography extended beyond the battlefield – it planned the very foundations of his strongholds. He appreciated what previously existed, and instead of wasting money on pointless buildings, he strengthened and modified historic fortifications, revitalising old defences.

- **Norse longphorts**: Temporary Norse fortifications, originally built as raiding bases, were transformed into permanent bastions of power. What had once been a tool of Viking plunder was now a weapon in Somerled's arsenal.

- **Gaelic hillforts**: Many of the centuries-old castles were strengthened with timber palisades, stone walls, and contemporary defences. Long abandoned by lesser warlords, these sites became vital hubs in his defensive network.
- **Natural caves and coastal coves**: Somerled's army made use of secret enclaves along the coast for cover, supply storage, and surprise attacks in addition to castles, therefore avoiding depending just on them. These locations allowed for rapid regrouping and unexpected strikes against invading forces.

This effective method of fortifications allowed Somerled to increase his authority quickly without draining his means. His capacity for adaptation, repurposing, and reinforcement made sure his defensive system was always changing – never fixed, never predictable.

The Legacy of a Landscape Warrior

Somerled projected his force not from great stone strongholds or tall citadels. His power came from his capacity to shape Scotland's terrain, therefore extending his control from its mountains, rivers, islands, and beaches.

His defence strategy was one of the limited alternatives, movement control, and making sure no opponent could ever occupy his territory without struggle. Each of the seaboards, the highlands, the lochs, and the islands was a tool, a bit of a bigger puzzle only he could use.

Though his foes might have been stronger on paper, they were always struggled with his terms, in his universe, against a man who knew how to bend the country to his will.

Somerled's rule was evidence not only of castles and warfare but also of the power of knowledge of geography. He did not just hold the western seaboard – he made it his greatest weapon.

The Lasting Impact of Somerled's Fortifications

Somerled was not only a warrior or a king but a visionary strategist whose approach to fortifications rewrote the balance of power in the western seaboard for decades to come. His network of strongholds, defensive ideas, and knowledge of geography did not disappear with his death; rather, it set the groundwork for those who followed, shaping the way power was consolidated and defended in Scotland's changing political scene.

Later, leaders seeking to subjugate the Western Highlands and the Hebrides turned to his ideas of mobility, adaptability, and marine domination as their model. Though the political tides would change, his impact persisted, especially in the ascent of the Lords of the Isles, who expanded on the very network of fortifications and strategic strongholds he had created.

A Legacy Carried by the Lords of the Isles

Clan Donald passed on Somerled's tradition. The MacDonalds, who would later be the Lords of the Isles, realised that controlling the sea was just as important as keeping land in preserving their great island reign.

Many of the castles he built or converted became essential power bases for the Lords of the Isles, enabling them to claim authority over the western seaboard much as Somerled had done.

Finlaggan on the Isle of Islay, which grew to be the administrative centre of the Lordship of the Isles, was among the most enduring emblems of this continuity of authority. It was no accident that Somerled's place of solidified dominance, Finlaggan, remained a centre of power decades after his death.

Expanding upon these key sites, the Lords of the Isles modified them to fit mediaeval developments by building more advanced defences, stone towers, curtain walls, and strengthening fortifications. Still, the basic strategic rationale of Somerled's fortified network stayed the same even as they embraced more modern architectural forms.

Somerled's Fortifications vs. Later Mediaeval Castles

The fortifications from Somerled's time were very different from the enormous castles of later Scottish leaders. Even if later mediaeval Scotland saw the construction of gigantic stone castles with towering battlements, deep moats, and well-guarded gatehouses, Somerled's fortifications were constructed with a different idea in mind.

- **Tactical positioning over monumental construction**: Somerled gave naturally defended sites a top priority. Protection not matched by any stone wall came from steep cliffs, passageways, and secret sea inlets.
- **A blend of cultures**: His fortifications used aspects from Gaelic and Norse traditions, therefore fusing them. They were specifically suited to the Hebrides, not the soaring towers of Norman lords nor the timber dwellings of Viking chieftains.
- **Adaptability over permanence**: Many of Somerled's castles were designed to be useful rather than spectacular, were partly timber, and could be readily rebuilt. This adaptability made quick repairs and changes possible, enabling his defences to change with the moods of battle.

Somerled's style indicated a transitional period in Scottish fortification, whereas following Scottish monarchs and noble houses would migrate toward more centralised, well-fortified stone castles. His structures bridged the gap between earlier Norse and Gaelic traditions and the larger, more complex castles that would come to dominate the Scottish landscape in later centuries.

Ruins That Still Speak of Somerled's Rule

Many of the sites Somerled formerly commanded now remain silent reminders of his impact, even after centuries have passed. The remains of Dunaverty Castle still hang on its majestic platform, their position evidence of the defensive planning that made the castle so robust.

Though now only crumbling walls, Aros Castle on Mull still shows traces of its strategic importance in safeguarding the Inner Hebrides. Finlaggan on Islay is a constant reminder of the political and military systems Somerled created; archaeological finds there still provide insights into the culture he formed.

And even if time has destroyed the wooden palisades, watchtowers, and clay defences that once stood in these sites, Somerled's tactical skill is shown in the very position of their deployment. These were not haphazard locations; rather, they were carefully picked to be relevant for centuries, even as political environments and combat changed.

A Defensive System, Not Just a Collection of Castles

Somerled's legacy was more than just a question of brick and mortar; it was evidence of his grasp of how to run a territory under the control of its natural and constructed defences. His fortifications were part of a greater defensive system, where every site reinforced the next to form a linked web of power rather than separate fortresses.

His goal was not to erect one perfect castle but to create a network of fortified sites that would let him move, strike, defend, and rule effectively. Long beyond his lifetime, his successors carried on this wise approach.

Even outside the Lords of the Isles, Somerled's method of fortifications affected the western shore of Scotland's military operations for centuries. For Scottish clans battling for control of the Highlands and Islands, their basic approach remained reliant on coastal castles, island fortresses, and natural topography.

- Later, the Highland clans adopted his methods, using tactical positioning, natural barriers, and quick-moving naval forces to secure their lands.
- Following that, Scottish monarchs, like Robert the Bruce, would rely on some of the same ideas of mobile defence and geographic advantage Somerled had invented.
- The strategic sites of his fortresses remained important even as warfare changed; several were still in use long into the Middle Ages, changed and strengthened by later kings.

Understanding mobility, terrain, and fortifications – which guaranteed that Somerled's legacy went much beyond his own lifetime and affected generations of leaders who followed him – was part of his defensive plans.

Although many of his castles are now ruins, his impact has never really diminished. The sites he promoted remain monuments to his vision; his name is still revered in the Western Highlands and Isles. Unlike other kings of his day, he understood geography as a weapon, could combine Norse and Gaelic defensive traditions, and built a fortified maritime network.

Somerled was one leader who knew how to run a whole territory as his extension of authority. His strongholds served as representations of his fortitude, tenacity, and strategic vision. Beyond the boundaries of his strongholds, he saw that real power was found in the capacity to move, adjust, and use the terrain as a shield and a sword.

Even now, centuries have passed, and his impact is still felt in the western seaboard of Scotland. Though his fortifications might be ruins, their strategic value never fades; they are evidence of a ruler who dominated the area rather than merely ruled it.

Chapter 27

Somerled in Popular Culture

The name Somerled has endured through the ages, appearing in historical records as well as in Scotland's and other countries' cultural imaginations. Historians, writers, and artists have often returned to him because of his legacy of defiance, firmness, and tactical genius. Despite the complexity of his real life, which was marked by alliances, disputes, and political scheming, his image has changed over time, occasionally reaching almost legendary status.

Even though many mediaeval individuals have become obscure, Somerled is still fascinating. His narrative has been told and rewritten not only for poets, writers, and modern media producers who aim to capture his spirit but also for historians who are researching his political and military accomplishments. While others view him as a national hero who opposed foreign domination, some consider him an astute tactician who adeptly handled the power conflicts of his era. He is now more than just a historical figure from all angles. He represents the tenacity and uniqueness of Scotland.

These different representations illustrate the ways in which Somerled's own legacy has been shaped by successive generations, sometimes with historical accuracy and sometimes through romanticised embellishment. His enduring influence is a testament to the persistence of interest in his life, both as a historic ruler and as an individual who continues to fascinate audiences and narrators.

Earliest Historical Accounts: The Foundations of His Legend

Like many mediaeval figures, Somerled's story was influenced by writers who lived long after his time. Mediaeval chronicles were frequently impacted by political motivations, oral traditions, and the prejudices of the persons who recorded them, in contrast to contemporary biographies which strive for factual truth.

Chronicles of the Kings of Mann and the Isles

The *Chronicles of the Kings of Mann and the Isles*, a mediaeval Latin text written by monks at Rushen Abbey on the Isle of Man, contains one of the most significant early mentions of Somerled. The chronicle, which spans the eleventh to thirteenth centuries, contains some of the earliest references to Somerled's ascension to power. It is an inexact account, though. Because of the impact of the Norse Kings of the Isles at the time of composition, Somerled is described as negative, and the narrative serves to advance the objectives of the kings.

Somerled appears as a doughty and defiant warrior in resisting the Norwegian rule of the Hebrides in the *Chronicles of the Kings of Mann and the Isles*, which describes how he fought battles with the Norse rulers of the Isles, with Godred Olafsson, King of Man and the Isles.

Somerled is, in the chronicle, a proficient military leader who can mobilise men, create strategy, and execute operations against his foes. There is, of course, a patent bias in the terms used to portray him, and these, often, tend to portray him as a usurper rather than as a sovereign. Somerled is reported to have been viewed as a threat rather than a hero by the utterly dominant Norse rulers of the Hebrides.

Mediaeval Gaelic Sources: A Different Perspective

Somerled is presented differently in mediaeval Gaelic texts compared to the Norse-influenced *Chronicles of the Kings of Mann and the Isles*. He was considered a more heroic figure in the Gaelic traditions, which were passed on orally prior to being recorded. In some of the stories, he was a deliverer who resisted foreign domination and defended the rights of the Gaelic people.

Thus, Somerled is referred to casually and often in a vague way in the Irish *Annals of Ulster* and the *Annals of Tigernach*. In the absence of the severe prejudice found in the Norse chronicles, they attest to his military skills and portray him as a significant player in the battles fought on the western coast of Scotland. In Gaelic poetry and subsequent storytelling traditions, he was presented as a kingly character who resisted oppression and struggled to recover the land for his people.

Somerled's background is said to be half Norse and half Gaelic in one of the most enduring Gaelic myths. It marks the blending of the cultures during mediaeval Scotland. Due to his double role, he was a bridge and a battleground between the realms of the Norse kings of the Isles and the Gaelic clans.

Warrior, King, or Rebel

Somerled can be interpreted as a rebel, a monarch, or a warrior. In Norse-influenced narratives, he is portrayed as a disruptive force who opposed the status quo. In Gaelic texts, he is frequently depicted as a legitimate monarch who is fighting for the independence of his people. These deviating interpretations demonstrate how the authors of history influence it.

This raises an important question: Was Somerled really a rebel, or was he merely a leader trying to hold on through an era of constant strife? The reality is most likely somewhere in between. Like many other mediaeval monarchs, he fought for survival in a world where strength was achieved through strategy, marriage, and war. Whether one considers him an opportunist or a freedom fighter, his actions left a lasting mark on Scottish history.

Bias and the Historical Context

The discrepancies in these early stories serve as a reminder that history is rarely written objectively. Mediaeval chroniclers frequently shaped their narratives to suit political goals and wrote with certain audiences in mind. While Gaelic sources, particularly later ones, hailed Somerled as a hero, Norse chroniclers viewed him as a challenger to their authority.

The limits of mediaeval record-keeping must also be considered. Before being recorded in writing, many of Somerled's life events were transmitted orally for many generations. This implies that some facts might have been omitted or changed over time to accommodate rulers' and storytellers' demands.

Reading between the lines and considering what was written and why it was written in a specific way are essential to comprehending Somerled's early depictions. By doing so, we can begin to learn more about the man who created the legend – a leader whose tale has been rewritten over the course of centuries.

Somerled in Mediaeval and Early Modern Scottish Literature

The people who recounted Somerled's tale in early modern Scottish literature and mediaeval chronicles helped create his image throughout time. Later narratives started to emphasise his symbolic status as a leader and figure of resistance, in contrast to the early historical stories, which were frequently shaped by Norse and Gaelic political objectives. During this time, his story spread beyond historical documents into poetry, folklore, and nationalist literature, guaranteeing his name's continued existence in Scotland's cultural memory.

Mediaeval Chronicles: Reinforcing the Warrior's Image

Scottish and Gaelic historians continued to record Somerled for decades after he died, balancing myth and reality. Perhaps the most prominent of these sources are the *Books of Clanranald*, two seventeenth-century Gaelic manuscripts with very much earlier oral tradition on which they relied. In this literature, Somerled is described not only as a war leader but also as the founder of a dynasty that ruled as the ancestor of the MacDonalds.

The *Books of Clanranald* portray Somerled as a rightful king fighting to recapture his family's land, as compared to the *Chronicles of the Kings of Mann and the Isles*, which painted him as a figure of rebellion overthrowing Norse domination.

The document reinforces his Gaelic heritage and portrays him as a hero who resisted foreign domination. Rather than merely recording Somerled's behaviour in history, these stories significantly altered his reputation and brought him closer to Scottish patriotism.

The fourteenth-century John of Fordun's *Chronica Gentis Scotorum* (*Chronicle of the Scottish People*) is another major source of the era. Fordun's is one of the first attempts at an overall history of Scotland and does little justice to Somerled but places him in the conflict between Scottish and Norse tradition.

The nationalistic tone of the chronicle predicts the way in which later writers would recount Somerled's history, suggesting his disobedience had been part of Scotland's continuing struggle for dominion.

Scottish Nationalism and Gaelic Traditions

Somerled's reputation became increasingly intertwined with Gaelic cultural identity and Scottish nationalism in the early modern period (sixteenth–eighteenth centuries). In this period of great turmoil, Scotland was frequently dithering between English control and its own independence. Somerled was hailed as a protector of Scottish identity against foreign influence, and writers and poets looking to respect Scottish heritage turned to him as an icon of resistance.

His legend was kept alive in large part through Gaelic oral tradition. There have been generations of Highland bards and poets who have spun stories about Somerled. These stories often emphasised his bravery, wisdom, and leadership qualities, so he became a virtual legend.

Evolving Narratives: From Rebel to National Hero

Literary and historical accounts of Somerled's legacy reflect more general transformations in Scottish identity. He was commonly seen as a warrior or a local chieftain who fought in the affairs of his day during the Middle Ages. But by the early modern period, he was something different: an ancestor for numerous Highland clans, a champion of Scottish independence, and a monument to Gaelic resistance.

It was the political needs of future generations that did this. Men like Somerled were reinterpreted to fit the narratives of patriotism and resistance. In legend and literature, Somerled was described as a legendary hero whose legacy can still be found in Scottish culture today, although the real Somerled was pragmatically interested in acquiring power for himself and his heirs.

Somerled in Modern Fiction and Historical Novels

Because of the enduring historical interest in Somerled, contemporary writers have persisted in using historical fiction to retell his tale. Modern authors have attempted to examine his personal hardships, goals, and the society he lived in, whereas older chronicles and mediaeval literature concentrated on his political and military responsibilities.

By using fictionalised versions of his life to fill in the gaps left by history, these novels frequently aim to achieve a balance between historical authenticity and imaginative storytelling.

Somerled in Historical Fiction: A Warrior Reimagined

By allowing readers to see the mediaeval world through Somerled's eyes, historical fiction offers a distinctive method to relive his story. Novelists have employed creative licence to paint a more complete image of the man behind the legend despite the paucity of historical documentation regarding his early years, relationships, and innermost thoughts. While some highlight his intelligence and vision for Scotland's Gaelic peoples, others present him as a ruthless warrior intent on establishing his own empire.

The incomplete nature of the historical record is one of the main obstacles faced by novelists who write about Somerled. Writers must choose how to reconcile contradictory stories because a large portion of what we know about him comes from texts that were published long after his death and frequently from skewed viewpoints.

Was his primary motivation selfish power, or did he genuinely consider himself a liberator of the Gaelic lands? Was Alexander only responding to the unstable political climate of his era, or did he aspire to bringing the western regions of Scotland under a single authority?

Despite all doubts, Somerled is frequently represented in contemporary fiction as a strong, resilient character. He is portrayed as a character who personifies the Gaelic people's fight against alien domination. He is a compelling protagonist for historical fiction because his life fits with the themes of leadership, resistance, and the price of ambition.

Major Novels Featuring Somerled

Several historical novels have attempted to bring Somerled's story to life. Each offers a unique interpretation of his character, such as:

- **Nigel Tranter's *Lord of the Isles*** (1983): This well-known Scottish historical fiction presents Somerled as a perceptive and aspirational leader who emerges from obscurity to oppose the Norse rulers of the Isles. His portrayal of Somerled is closely linked to his Gaelic heritage, and the book delves into his political connections, military expeditions, and the establishment of his dynasty. Despite being fictional, the book is still largely based on real occurrences, which helps readers visualise mediaeval Scotland.
- **Kathleen Givens's *On a Highland Shore*** (2006): This novel is set in the thirteenth century and refers to Somerled's legacy, but it is not solely focused on him. Givens's narrative emphasises the enduring effects of Somerled's reign and the continuous struggle between the Gaels and the Norse. The book demonstrates how Somerled's impact on Scottish culture persisted long after his passing by fusing romance and history.
- **J. R. Tomlin's *Somerled: Hammer of the Norse*** (2021): This book is a contemporary fictional representation that mostly concentrates on Somerled's early hardships and ascent to prominence. It adopts a more action-oriented approach by showing Somerled as a warrior with a distinct concept of resistance against Norse dominion. It also highlights his tactical skill and persistence while focusing on the heroic elements of his reputation.

These books support the position of Somerled as a significant character in Scottish history despite having different depictions. They skilfully combine historical details with imaginative storytelling to produce gripping tales.

Balancing Historical Accuracy and Creative Storytelling

The issue of writing historical fiction about Somerled is deciding how much creative freedom one should allow oneself. Authors must rely on a combination of historical study and creative reconstruction because many aspects of his life are still unclear. This frequently results in different views of his personality. For instance, he is portrayed as a practical warlord who recognised and took advantage of opportunities, while other depictions highlight his position as a freedom fighter protecting Gaelic identity.

Some historical events may be changed or reconstructed for dramatic effect, and the political difficulties of twelfth-century Scotland are frequently simplified to make the story more interesting for contemporary readers.

Despite such artistic licence, the finest historical fiction about Somerled is grounded in the realities of his era, including his fight against Norse influence, the unstable political climate of mediaeval Scotland, and the significance of clan affiliations. In addition to presenting a story that appeals to modern audiences, authors work hard to give their characters a sense of authenticity.

Somerled's Lasting Appeal in Literature

The strife, ambition, resilience, and legacy that characterise historical fiction are all present in Somerled's personal narrative. He is a perfect topic for narrative since his ascent from near insignificance to become a strong ruler reflects the traditional hero's journey.

Whether portrayed as a brave warrior or a cunning negotiator, he never fails to captivate the interest of both authors and readers. He is still relevant in Scottish historical fiction and popular culture because his story speaks to contemporary concerns of identity, leadership, and the fight for independence.

Somerled's name will probably live on as new writers continue to delve into his legacy, not just as a historical figure but also as a literary symbol that embodies the essence of mediaeval Scotland.

Somerled in Film, Television, and Popular Media

Somerled's character has yet to appear in a prominent film or television programme, although he was important to Scottish history. Compared to other historical figures, he is still heavily underrepresented in visual media.

There are several reasons why Somerled has not yet been the subject of a big-screen or TV series. Unlike William Wallace or Robert the Bruce, he is not well known beyond Scottish history. Although historians and enthusiasts enjoy his achievements, his tale does not have the general knowledge that tends to appeal to filmmakers. Furthermore, since records pertaining to him in history are scarce and occasionally contradictory, making an accurate and compelling account would involve substantial interpretive imagination.

Another issue is the difficulty of the time during which Somerled existed. The twelfth century was a period prior to Scotland's wars of independence and is, therefore, less well-known to audiences. It was a world of Norse-Gaelic warfare, sea battles, and fluid political allegiances. Although these things are dramatic, they need to be handled with strong historical context so that they can be presented in a manner that is accurate yet still understood by the audience.

Somerled's narrative is similarly bereft of a villain, on which many historical dramas rely. As with Wallace, who rebelled against King Edward I of England, or Bruce, who fought English armies, Somerled's principal enemies were the Norse leaders of the Isles. While this struggle is compelling, it is less familiar to broad audiences and, thus, a tougher sell for filmmakers seeking tales involving widely recognised stakes.

Despite all these problems, Somerled's life is full of the sort of drama, ambition, and strife that would be worthy of a blockbuster historical epic. With the resurgence of interest in mediaeval and Viking-age narratives, his story may yet have a place in cinemas.

The popularity of historical dramas such as *Vikings* and *The Last Kingdom* proves that people are more interested in mediaeval tales beyond the popular English-Scottish wars. These series have brought lesser-known eras to the forefront, demonstrating that, with proper storytelling, even characters outside mainstream history can gain worldwide attention. Somerled's tale, which is full of rebellion, family heritage, and war, has all the ingredients to be a part of this genre – if presented the right way.

Although not explicitly depicted on screen, numerous historical and fictional personages bear a resemblance to Somerled. Perhaps the most similar is Ragnar Lothbrok of *Vikings*. Ragnar, too, is a half-legendary warrior whose historical existence is tied together by myth. His elevation from low-ranking nobility to dominant sovereignty mirrors Somerled's own.

We can also draw parallels with Robert the Bruce in *Outlaw King*. Although Bruce battled the English instead of the Norse, his style of leadership – blending strategy and daring military action – is very much like what we have learned of Somerled's battles. Rob Roy MacGregor of *Rob Roy* is another apt parallel. A Highland warrior who defied foreign rule, his life has themes of resistance and survival that would work well for a characterisation of Somerled.

With how well-received these characters have been in TV and movie roles, it's not difficult to imagine that a tale about Somerled might be a hit. Well-crafted, a film or television series featuring his wars with the Norsemen and his quest to establish a long-lasting Gaelic kingdom would put his reputation on the radar for a lot more people.

Somerled's Influence on Folklore, Music, and Art

Somerled might not have a role in mass-market films or television, but his legend continues to thrive in Scottish society, especially in the forms of folklore, song, and painting. His life has been retold generation by generation, not only as a piece of history but as a hero whose legacy is an integral part of Scotland's identity.

Oral traditions in Gaelic have maintained Somerled's memory for centuries. In Highland folklore, he is not only a warrior but nearly mythical. In some stories, he was said to be favoured by the gods and that he could vanquish foes even when they outnumbered him. In others, he was said to possess a profound, almost mystical relationship with the earth and sea, all of which indicated that he was meant to be a leader. Even as written history grapples to reconstruct the complete facts of his life, these myths have seen to it that his name has never been forgotten.

Somerled's legacy also continues in Scottish music. Folk ballads and songs have ensured his name and his tale continue to live, especially in the Western Isles, where his wars were fought. An example is 'Sons of Somerled' by Steve McDonald, a song that celebrates him as a unifying symbol for Scottish and Gaelic identity.

Ancient Gaelic ballads, handed down through centuries, also allude to Somerled's time and battles as well as to notable figures of the era, though not always his own name. The rebellious, strong, and loyal nature that epitomised his life still echoes through Scottish music traditions, ensuring his presence remains alive in the songs' melodies and lyrics commemorating the nation's history.

Art and Visual Representations

Somerled has also been depicted in different forms of art, such as in paintings of the past, statues, and clan symbols.

Most of their symbols, such as the galley or birlinn, are directly associated with Somerled's sea power and leadership. These emblems remind us of his control of the western seaboard and his reputation as a powerful ruler of the Isles. Though Somerled lacks towering statues like Bruce and Wallace, his name has not been forgotten. There are numerous historical plaques and memorials throughout Scotland, especially in the Western Highlands and Isles, that honour his efforts. These locations commemorate sites important to his life and conflicts, keeping his tale a part of Scotland's history.

Could Somerled Gain More Recognition in Popular Media?

With the increased popularity of Scottish- and Viking-period history in contemporary media, there is huge scope for Somerled to be brought back before the masses. A quality film, television show, or documentary can do him justice, and his tale could be brought alive by emphasising his themes of identity, leadership, and struggle for independence.

Following the popularity of shows such as *Vikings*, *The Last Kingdom*, and *Outlaw King*, it is not far-fetched to picture a production based on Somerled – Lord of the Isles – potentially taking his legacy to an international audience. His life, full of politics, warfare, and individual aspiration, contains everything a good historical drama should have.

Until then, his legacy lives on in Scottish heritage, preserved in folklore, clan customs, and works of art.

The Enduring Appeal of Somerled

Somerled remains a fascinating presence in Scottish history. His life is still holding fast the interests of historians, writers, and listeners alike, compelling attention from all those drawn to mediaeval dynastic conflicts, Gaelic cultural identity, and the struggle against foreign rule. What, then, is there in Somerled that he remains such an abiding theme for research and interest? His appeal lies in a mix of historical importance, nationalist feeling, romanticism, and mythology – all of which have sustained his legacy and kept it changing over the centuries.

Somerled's tale has not been lost to the ages as so many have been for other mediaeval kings. Even now, he is a compelling character of interest to historians, writers, and taletellers alike. One of the reasons for his appeal is that he did not inherit grand power – he achieved it through conquest.

Somerled's ascension from a lower noble to the lord of Scotland's western coast makes him an underdog, a man who forged his own path. His capacity to defy both Norse and Scottish leaders is a testament to his intelligence, determination, and ambition, qualities that continue to appeal to people today.

His struggles against the Norse leaders of the Isles also reflect a much greater theme in Scottish history – the struggle for independence. Scotland has battled for centuries to preserve its identity and stand up to foreign occupation. Somerled's struggle is a precursor to these later battles, making his tale very relevant in discussions of nationalism and self-rule. His determination and defiance represent the will of a people to govern themselves, something that still resonates with many.

One of the reasons Somerled remains so interesting is his history, which shows that he was a man of two worlds – half Norse and half Gaelic. He knew both, living between them as much a statesman as a warrior. He was a fighter more than anything, a statesman, and a visionary for uniting people. This double heritage complicates him and makes him a more intriguing character that will engage modern audiences obsessed with stories of cultural identity and belonging.

Maybe what sustains Somerled's memory the most is his mystery. His life is fragmentarily documented historically, and the accounts of him vary from source to source. For this reason, historians, authors, and artists have had their imaginations play freely around him, alternating between projecting him as a warrior-king, a freedom fighter, and something in between. This adaptability has enabled his legend to change through the years so that he can continue to remain relevant even centuries after his passing.

The Role of Nationalism, Romanticism, and Mythology

Somerled's history has largely been influenced by greater ideological forces, most notably nationalism and romanticism.

In the nineteenth and early twentieth centuries, during a period of increased interest in Scottish identity and history, Somerled emerged as a figure of Gaelic pride. The increased interest in the Gaelic language, literature, and culture further ensured his status as a heroic figure of Scotland's Western Highlands.

Somerled emerged as a source of pride for Highland clans in general and particularly for the MacDonalds, to whom they lay claim as their ancestor.

This nationalist explanation of Somerled still holds sway today, particularly in arguments regarding Scottish independence. His story has been read as an early template of Scotland's own resistance to foreign rule, with similarities drawn between his defiance of Norse rule and later struggles against English rule.

The Mythological Somerled

Over time, elements of myth have been woven into Somerled's story. Some Gaelic oral traditions depict him as having supernatural qualities or divine favour. For instance, certain tales claim he was guided by omens or possessed extraordinary strength, further elevating him to near-legendary status.

As interest in Scottish history and mediaeval storytelling continues to grow, Somerled's story is poised for further exploration in books, film, and television.

With the success of historical dramas, there is an increasing appetite for narratives about mediaeval power struggles and warrior-leaders.

In the coming years, we may see:

- **A major film or TV adaptation**: Somerled's story could provide rich material for a historical drama if filmmakers look beyond the known figures. Somerled's life provides the elements of a great cinematic story, including battles, family rivalries, political conspiracy, and personal ambition.
- **New historical novels**: Authors might continue to explore the life of Somerled in new and innovative ways because historical fiction remains a popular genre. They can focus on his personal motivations, achievements, relationships, and complexities of his era.
- **Documentary exploration**: Many historians have written about Somerled, but a well-produced documentary or series could bring his story to a wider audience. They could blend archaeological findings, dramatic renovations, and historical analysis to create a documentary.
- **Increased role in popular culture**: We may see more references to Somerled in music, folklore, and artistic representations because people continue to have an interest in Scottish and Norse history and culture.

Somerled's story serves as a demonstration of the power, strength, and identity of the ruler. He maintained his legacy, which inspires those who are interested in Scottish history and culture. He was not only a conqueror but a leader who weathered a chaotic world and left a lasting impact on the Western Highlands.

Somerled's legend will necessarily change, reflecting the vision and values of the tellers as each new generation finds his story. Whether in history, literature, or popular imagination, his name will continue to be part of Scotland's past, guaranteeing that his memory will last for generations to come.

Somerled's legacy continues as a testament to resilience, leadership, and the intricate dance of history and myth. From the earliest chronicles through contemporary fiction, his tale has been conditioned by changing narratives – at times, a rebel, a warrior, or a national hero. His Gaelic and Norse roots placed him at the juncture of two cultures and, thus, his ascension to power all the more so.

Though he is less well-known in popular media, his legacy continues to be felt in historical studies, literature, folklore, and clan lore. As interest in mediaeval Scotland continues to expand, there is immense potential for his life to be reimagined on screen, television, and page, making his name more widely known. Whether as a shrewd leader or an idealised hero, Somerled's story remains compelling, showing that history's forgotten heroes still have tales worth telling.

Chapter 28

The Genetics of Somerled's Legacy

For years, people have tried to understand and piece together the story of Somerled. His family had a long legacy, and history now clearly shows his effect.

Like many historical tales, our knowledge of Somerled derives from family histories, folklore handed down over the years, old papers, and records. Although these materials enable us to better understand the past, they are not always perfect, and occasionally, real events mingle with mythology. This makes it difficult to discern precisely what is true and what time has modified.

For historical people like Somerled, whose descendants are thought to have dispersed widely, genetic research has shown itself to be a powerful tool for tracing back ancestry. The goal of these investigations is simple: to determine whether he left behind a genetic imprint and the extent to which his offspring have carried it forward.

When historical records are lacking, scientists can use DNA analysis to confirm long-held beliefs, dispel falsehoods, and, in some cases, fill in the gaps.

How DNA Can Help Trace Somerled's Lineage

Researchers focus on different types of DNA when studying ancestry through genetics. So, in the case of Somerled, the most important one is Y-DNA. This is a specific type of DNA that is found in the Y chromosome and passed down from father to son. This DNA contains very little change over generations, as this DNA is useful for tracing direct male–line descent. This makes it an ideal tool for studying the legacy of Somerled.

So, if Somerled had made descendants who continued his ancestry, their Y-DNA should share common markers, forming a genetic signature that connects them together.

Over the years, genealogists and scientists have conducted various studies to identify the genetic signature of Somerled. They collected DNA samples from men who claim descent from Scottish clans traditionally associated with Somerled. Among them, most notably, are MacDougalls, MacDonalds, and MacAlisters.

These studies have helped link Somerled to a particular Y-DNA haplogroup (a genetic classification that shows deep ancestry). This discovery is groundbreaking because it provides scientific evidence of his genetic legacy and allows us to track how his lineage spread over time.

Significance of Genetic Studies on Somerled's Descendants

According to gene data, Somerled's male ancestors were not only very numerous but also quite effective at controlling succeeding generations. This is in line with historical accounts that portray his successors as significant individuals who influenced the course of Scottish history.

Additionally, genetic studies bring yet another dimension of accuracy to tracing heritage. Genealogy, as written in documents, is either partial, lost, or biased. Yet DNA is unbiased and can't be impacted by historical perception. Because of this, it is a very useful tool for verifying historical claims and offering a more lucid view of ancestry.

Although genetics is powerful, it improves history rather than replaces it. DNA does not reveal the complete story of how and why things happened the way they did, but it can tell us who was linked. We still need historical research to determine that combined historical and genetic research allows us to see Somerled's impact in a more complete and accurate way.

Why Somerled's Lineage Is of Particular Interest

In contrast to most mediaeval monarchs whose lineage disappeared with time, Somerled's descendants live on today through thousands of individuals. Through genetic research, it is revealed that a substantial percentage of Scottish men, and especially those in some clans, have a direct paternal connection with him. The extensive genetic presence is unusual and indicates just how powerful his heritage was.

In addition, his descendants did not stay in Scotland only. Over the centuries, through expansion, war, and migration, Somerled's Y-DNA has extended outside Scotland, occurring in places like Ireland, North America, and even Scandinavia. This not only makes his genetic history a Scottish story but an international one, illustrating how the past endures in today's populations.

The DNA Evidence and Somerled's Lineage

With the groundwork of genetic research laid, we now proceed to the actual results – what DNA has told us about Somerled's ancestry and how far his genetic heritage has reached. Scientists researching mediaeval lineage tend to use Y-DNA analysis, and in Somerled's instance, this technique has yielded interesting results.

The Y-DNA Haplogroup Associated with Somerled

Through deep DNA sampling, scientists have found that there is a specific Y-DNA haplogroup connected with Somerled's male-line heirs: R1a-L165 (alternatively referred to as R1a1a1b1a3a1 in other classifications).[1]

1. G. Matharu Lall, M. H. D. Larmuseau, J. H. Wetton, C. Batini, P. Hallast, T. I. Huszar, D. Zadik, S. Aase, T. Baker, P. Balaresque, W. Bodmer, M. A. Jobling, T. E. King, & E. J. Parkin. (2021). Subdividing Y-chromosome haplogroup R1a1 reveals Norse Viking dispersal lineages in Britain. *European Journal of Human Genetics*, 29(3), 512–23.

The haplotype is important since it is rare in Scotland compared to other haplogroups that are mostly derived from Gaelic backgrounds. Rather, it has close associations with Norse roots, which coheres with a recorded history that implies Somerled was of Norse-Gaelic mixed descent.

The fact that R1a-L165 has been found in contemporary men tracing back to Somerled's descendants is strong evidence that this haplogroup was inherited through his direct male line. Because Y-DNA does not change much from father to son, the fact that so many men today share the same marker is strong genetic proof of a common ancestor – likely Somerled himself.

How Common Is This Genetic Marker Today?

One of the most astonishing discoveries from this DNA research is how many men today bear Somerled's Y-DNA signature. Three stand out from the Scottish clans traditionally associated with Somerled:

- **Clan MacDonald** – originating straight from Donald, Somerled's grandson, one of the largest and most strong Highland clans.
- **Clan MacDougall** – having descended from Somerled's son, Dougall, his line running over the Lords of Lorn.
- **Clan MacAlister** – having begun from Somerled's great-grandson, Alasdair.

DNA research has verified that a large percentage of men from both clans possess the R1a-L165 haplogroup, which gives them a direct ancestral connection to Somerled. Some indications are that one in every five MacDonalds carries his Y-DNA.[2] This is an incredibly strong genetic trace, one that indicates how far-reaching and long-lived Somerled's lineage has become.

What These Findings Mean

The finding of a shared Y-DNA marker among thousands of men strongly suggests that Somerled had many male descendants who successfully maintained his line. This is consistent with historical accounts that describe his family as dominant and heavily involved in Scottish politics for centuries.

In contrast to some mediaeval leaders whose lineages went extinct over time, Somerled's legacy has been genetically preserved, extending far beyond his own time.

In addition, this information indicates that his descendants did not only rule but prospered, branching out to various parts of the region and establishing themselves. Through conquests, alliances, or mere natural growth in numbers, Somerled's

2. L. McDonald. (2 Jul. 2024). 'Origins'. Clan Donald Heritage. https://clandonald-heritage.com/origins/

descendants kept on growing, and his genetic trace today is a biological connection between past and present.

Scientific Challenges in Tracing Direct Descent

While scientists have provided invaluable insights into Somerled's genetic heritage, their findings are still being challenged. The tracing of direct paternal descent through the centuries carries scientific constraints, and scientists must painstakingly review various factors to provide accurate results.

One of the most significant is mutation rates and genetic diversity. Y-DNA experiences minor mutations over time, so even individuals with a shared ancestor may exhibit minute genetic distinctions.

Although such mutations can assist researchers in tracking when and how various branches of a family tree split, they make it hard to establish precise relationships unless comparing several samples of DNA. Due to this, a single DNA test is insufficient – investigators require numerous samples to affirm patterns and links.

Another significant limitation is sample availability. Historical characters such as Somerled left no direct DNA samples for researchers to analyse, unlike modern-day individuals. This implies that all genetic inferences are made from the DNA of his putative descendants instead of Somerled himself.

Also, not everybody undergoes DNA testing, and therefore, there could be unknown descendants whose DNA might offer even greater insight. As the testing is optional, the data provided is merely a fraction of the true population that possesses Somerled's Y-DNA.

There are also issues of adoptions and non-paternity incidents. Over generations, instances of adoption, change of name, or situations where the biological father is not the father listed can confuse direct lineage tracking. Although these occurrences are not as common, they complicate gene research and render it more difficult to believe that all members of a particular clan are biological descendants of Somerled.

Despite all this, the general consistency of DNA results from many studies ensures that Somerled's Y-DNA lineage was properly identified and is still being transmitted today.[3]

The Spread of Somerled's Genetic Legacy

Somerled's influence did not end with his reign over the Isles. His descendants carried his legacy forward, not just in political power but also in their genetic imprint, which spread far beyond the western coast of Scotland. DNA evidence has given us a clearer picture of how his lineage expanded, helping historians understand the movement of people, the role of intermarriage, and how mediaeval Scottish society was shaped by this powerful bloodline.

3. Project updates. (11 Mar. 2025,). MacDougall DNA Research Project. https://macdougalldna.org/project-updates/

How Somerled's Descendants Spread Across Scotland, Ireland, and Beyond

From what we know of history, Somerled's family established dominant ruling houses in Scotland, most notably through his sons and grandsons. The MacDonalds, MacDougalls, and MacAlisters became rising strong clans that kept extending their authority throughout time. However, according to genetic studies, Somerled's progeny was not limited to the Western Highlands and Isles; his genetic heritage extended considerably deeper.

Scotland

His ancestors kept a stronghold in areas long under Somerled's control, the Hebrides, Argyll, and the western coastlines of Scotland. For years, these areas stayed essential to his family; the MacDonald and MacDougall clans became major players in the area. However, as time passed, many of his descendants moved further inland, expanding their influence beyond the western coast.

Members of the MacDonald and MacDougall clans mixed into Highland and Lowland villages over generations, creating new alliances and claiming territory all around Scotland. While some became landowners, others had important roles in local administration such that Somerled's family stayed linked to the changing political scene of the nation.

Apart from their residence in clan territory, numerous Somerled's ancestors became well-known in military and noble spheres. Men from these bloodlines fought, advised, and even acted as lords as Scotland's power systems changed, therefore carrying on the tradition of leadership their ancestors had created. Somerled's family's legacy goes beyond mere numbers to include the ongoing impact his successors had on forming Scottish history.

Ireland

Driven by trade, war, and changing political alignments, Scottish migration to Ireland was a well-established trend during the mediaeval and early modern periods. Among those who crossed the Irish Sea were Somerled's descendants who took his heritage outside of Scotland. They discovered fresh possibilities in Ireland, building castles that would last for decades, much as many other Scottish clans would have done.

Among Somerled's most prominent branches in Ireland were the MacDonnells of Antrim, an Irish offshoot of the MacDonald clan. Rising as a major power in Ulster during the sixteenth and seventeenth centuries, they changed the political and military scene of the area. Their impact was felt not just in Ireland but also in Scotland since they maintained close relationships with their relatives over the sea.

Modern DNA testing has provided scientific evidence to support this historical migration. Research has revealed that many men in Northern Ireland and areas of western Ireland have the same Y-DNA haplogroup linked with Somerled's family. This supports the theory that his descendants maintained their genealogical ties to Scotland while firmly settling in Ireland and integrating with the local people.

Beyond Scotland and Ireland

As waves of migration brought Somerled's ancestors to other countries, the Scottish diaspora spread his legacy much beyond the boundaries of Scotland and Ireland. Many Scots were pushed to search for possibilities overseas by periods of conflict, financial difficulty, and colonialism, which resulted in notable population shifts over the years. Whether driven by need or desire, Somerled's descendants joined the worldwide Scottish diaspora and dispersed his genetic legacy over many countries.

Scottish Highlanders travelled to North America, Australia, and New Zealand, bringing their family histories and cultural customs. Among these emigrants were descendants of Somerled, who passed his Y-DNA to generations living far away. Scottish colonies kept close ties to their heritage, passing on the legacy of their forefathers across time when they settled in different areas.

Modern genetic research has verified that groups with Scottish ancestry throughout Canada, the United States, and even some of Scandinavia carry Somerled's Y-DNA markers. Scandinavia is especially remarkable for his genetic signature, which probably results from his Norse background and ties to Viking history. This broad genetic legacy emphasises exactly how far Somerled's family has gone, securing his position among Scotland's most iconic ancestral characters.

This broad genetic dispersion implies that Somerled's bloodline was effective in surviving and growing over centuries. Although many mediaeval leaders left political legacies, few have left such a broad genetic legacy.

How Many Living Men Today Carry Somerled's Y-DNA?

Just how many males currently carry Somerled's Y-DNA is among the most amazing revelations in genetic study. Scientists believe that tens of thousands, maybe even more, are directly descended from him through the male line. Somerled lived in the twelfth century; hence, this is an amazing legacy that has been passed on for almost 900 years.

A sizeable fraction of MacDonalds, MacDougalls, and MacAlisters that underwent DNA testing fit the R1a-L165 haplogroup, which has been connected to Somerled. This helps many of the males in these clans today to corroborate what historical records have long indicated by tracing their direct paternal heritage back to him. Still, his genetic footprint has a reach that goes beyond that.

According to some geneticists, Somerled descended through the male line could be the source of 500,000 men globally.[4] Based on the spread of his Y-DNA haplogroup, this figure represents what is probably even truer given that just a portion of the population has had DNA testing.

Future studies may show an even greater dispersion of his bloodline as more people are interested in genetic ancestry and testing becomes more easily available.

4. 'DNA shows Celtic hero Somerled's Viking roots'. *The Scotsman*. 18 Sep 2005.

The Role of Viking and Gaelic Intermarriage in Somerled's Genetic Legacy

With Norse and Gaelic roots mixed, Somerled's ancestry was a tie that greatly affected his identity and what remained of his legacy. R1a-L165, his paternal Y-DNA haplogroup, is most strongly associated with Scandinavian origin, suggesting that his father most likely sprang from Norse Viking ancestors. This fits historical records of Viking presence in the Hebrides and western Scotland, where Norse immigrants had been maintaining a fort for ages.

Though his paternal line came from Scandinavia, Somerled's mother and cultural background were Gaelic; therefore, his upbringing, customs, and identity were firmly anchored in the Celtic realm. His dual origin produced a product of two strong traditions: the clan-based, landholding Gaelic people and the warrior-driven, seafaring Norsemen. His successors thus absorbed both influences, hence determining the course of the clans bearing his name.

In the Hebrides and western Scotland, where Viking immigrants had intermarried with native Gaelic people for centuries, this form of Norse-Gaelic mixing was typical. These people created a distinctive hybrid culture over time, combining Norse military might with Gaelic clan systems. Somerled himself became a symbol of this mix, and his successors carried on that legacy, making sure that both Norse and Gaelic genes kept influencing Scotland's history.

Descendants of Somerled carried on this legacy by marrying into both Gaelic and Norse lineages as they grew. This clarifies the reason his genetic signature has been discovered in populations of Norse background as well as Scottish Highland clans. Scotland's identity was permanently changed, and the mediaeval Kingdom of the Isles was largely shaped by the interweaving of these two cultural groups.

Using Genetic Research to Map Migration Patterns

Tracking how a lineage has migrated and expanded throughout time is one of the most fascinating features of genetic study. Scientists have been able to reconstruct the likely migration paths of Somerled's ancestors by examining where his Y-DNA is most found today, therefore providing a fresh understanding of how his ancestry extended outside of Scotland.

DNA research reveals that, especially in areas traditionally connected to the MacDonald, MacDougall, and MacAlister clans, Somerled's genetic signature stayed strongest in western Scotland. But his descendants did not remain limited to these areas. Following well-documented migration patterns between Ireland and parts of England, his Y-DNA eventually dispersed over both nations. Beyond the natural expansion of his family, who sought new horizons, this movement was also moulded by conflict and shifts in the political landscape.

Fascinatingly, researchers have also discovered evidence of Somerled's Y-DNA among Scandinavian communities, therefore bolstering the hypothesis that some of his ancestors stayed close to their Norse background. Somerled himself was of mixed Norse-Gaelic origin; hence, it is likely that certain branches of his family kept interacting with Viking-influenced areas through alliances, trade, or direct migration.[5]

Scottish Highlanders left in great numbers in the following ages, hence extending Somerled's genetic heritage. Following noted Scottish migration patterns, his Y-DNA has been found in North America, Australia, and New Zealand. Economic difficulty, political turmoil, and opportunities outside drove many Highlanders from Scotland, assuring that Somerled's line descended into the worldwide Scottish diaspora.

Along with verifying historical migrations, this DNA mapping offers a fresh understanding of mediaeval Scottish society. It supports what was long suspected by historians: that successful ruling families, such as Somerled's, dispersed their bloodline far beyond their initial territory and that power and influence in mediaeval Scotland were intimately linked to family lineage.

Now that DNA data has established that Somerled's genetic imprint was widespread, we must determine what this means for mediaeval Scottish society.

What Genetic Findings Reveal About Mediaeval Scottish Society

Finding Somerled's genetic trace scattered across thousands of males living now provides more than just evidence of his ancestry. It provides valuable insight into how mediaeval Scottish society functioned.

DNA evidence doesn't just trace ancestry. It also helps historians better understand kinship structures, leadership inheritance, and the social dynamics of the time. Examining the genetic impact of the ruling families of Somerled can help us get a clearer picture of how power was maintained and how clans were structured.

Kinship and Clan Structures in Mediaeval Scotland

Mediaeval Scottish society was based on kinship and familial relationships; practically every element of your existence was dictated by your birth circumstances. In mediaeval Scotland, power was nearly entirely inherited, unlike today, where leadership is sometimes based on elections or merit. The strongest and most powerful families carried their legacy from generation to generation, ensuring that power continued in their DNA.

The Y-DNA of Somerled is a very evident reflection of this system. The fact that so many men today bear his genetic mark implies that ruling families maintained control over their male progeny, therefore confirming their domination over time. Family history was thus the basis of leadership and power, not only a question of legacy.

---

5. A. Helgason, S. Sigurðardóttir, J. Nicholson, B. Sykes, E. W. Hill, D. G. Bradley, V. Bosnes, J. R. Gulcher, R. Ward, & K. Stefánsson. (2000). 'Estimating Scandinavian and Gaelic ancestry in the male settlers of Iceland'. *The American Journal of Human Genetics*, *67*(3), 697–717.

Scottish clans were more than just political entities; they were frequently extended kin networks. Therefore, many members were really linked by blood. Since leaders in clans were family patriarchs as well as monarchs, this system fostered great allegiance within them. DNA studies have confirmed that several Highland clans – including those descended from Somerled – were biologically linked rather than merely vaguely connected.

Somerled's descendants, particularly the MacDonalds, MacDougalls, and MacAlisters, kept their dominance not just by military might and strategic alliances but also by their heritage.

These families guaranteed their power for centuries by keeping leadership within the same gene pool. Their hold on Scottish history was not political – it was genetic, a permanent reminder of how clan and kinship structures dominated mediaeval Scotland.

The Connection Between Power, Status, and Genetics

The fact that Somerled's DNA remains so prevalent today indicates that his descendants were especially successful at hanging on to their supremacy. But why do some gene lines survive for centuries, only to vanish from the record, while others keep going? The reason lies in the way in which mediaeval Scottish society worked, where status, power, and genetics were highly interdependent.

Leadership in Somerled's time was inherited and transferred nearly solely to the direct male line. Rulers' sons were to continue their father's family business, keeping it within the family. This made a robust male heir crucial – without one, a ruler's power might dissipate rapidly, and another family could seize it. This pattern of male-line succession is partly why Somerled's genetic line continued so overwhelmingly throughout the centuries.

Marriage was another important factor. In mediaeval Scotland, marriages were political weapons meant to forge alliances and increase family influence, not only about love.

His lineage also survived because governing families had higher survival rates than the common population. Those born into power had access to better resources, protection, and opportunities since leadership was inherited, raising their chances of having more offspring who might carry on the family name. This let Somerled's Y-DNA proliferate across generations, leaving a genetic legacy in Scotland and beyond.

What historians have long suspected – elite families having a significant impact on the genetic makeup of the population – is confirmed by a DNA study. Tens of thousands of men now still carry the Y-DNA of one mediaeval king, demonstrating exactly how firmly rooted these dominant bloodlines grew. Somerled was not only a strong man in his own lifetime; his genetic heritage has shaped the ancestry of his successors for almost 900 years.

How Genetics Supports the Role of Elite Ruling Families

Somerled is not the only historical person whose genetic legacy has been discovered. Studies conducted worldwide have revealed that aristocratic ruling families generally left an excessive genetic legacy relative to the general population.

For example:

- Genghis Khan's lineage is said to be carried by millions of males throughout Asia, demonstrating the great genetic influence of strong leaders.
- The O'Neills in Ireland, one of the strongest Gaelic families, also had a clear Y-DNA marker originating from their mediaeval forebears.

Somerled's instance shows a similar trend: his achievement as a king guaranteed that his line not only descended but also thrived. His genetic signature became more widely distributed as his descendants carried on wielding power for generations following his death.

The fact that we can find his Y-DNA in individuals living today emphasises how hereditary leadership was in mediaeval Scotland, with reigning families controlling for decades. The distribution of Somerled's DNA indicates that his bloodline was especially successful in acquiring influence, territory, and resources.

The Implications for Broader Mediaeval Scottish History

The genetic evidence surrounding Somerled's lineage does more than confirm his widespread descendants. It also helps historians rethink how mediaeval Scottish society functioned.

Clan Structure and Identity
Clans were not only political allies; they were sometimes actually extended families. Many of the individuals were biologically linked, supporting the theory that clan loyalty sprang from kinship. This explains why clans fiercely protected their leaders.

Succession and Leadership
In mediaeval Scotland, power was usually inherited through male lineage. DNA evidence confirms that leadership rarely passed outside established ruling families. People didn't just take power – they were born into it.

Social Mobility
Although power was mostly hereditary, some people could rise through marriage, military service, or land ownership. However, dominant genetic lineages suggest that true upward mobility was rare. Ruling families held control for generations.

Ultimately, genetic studies reinforce what historians have long understood about mediaeval Scotland: power was tied to blood, and those who controlled the bloodlines controlled the land and people. Somerled's genetic legacy is a perfect example of how a single ruler could leave an imprint not just on history but on the very DNA of future generations.

The Impact of Genetic Research on the Study of Somerled

DNA-based Somerled's ancestry research has given our already existing knowledge about his life and legacy a remarkable depth. For centuries, archaeologists, oral histories, and written records have helped historians to put Scotland's past together.

Genetic research now provides us with fresh means of verifying, questioning, or polishing those historical accounts. This scientific approach has not only confirmed Somerled's widespread lineage but has also sparked fresh discussions in both historical and genealogical circles.

How Modern Genetic Findings Enhance or Challenge Traditional Narratives

Before genetic research, most of what we knew about Somerled came from historical records written long after his time. The Chronicle of Mann and the Isles and various clan histories describe his leadership, battles, and descendants. However, these sources often contain biases, gaps, or exaggerations. DNA research has helped separate fact from legend in several ways.

Confirmation of Widespread Male-line Descendants

Historical records suggested that Somerled's bloodline continued through generations of Scottish nobility, especially in the MacDonald and MacDougall clans. Genetic testing has confirmed this, as many men in these clans carry Somerled-linked Y-DNA.

Some Revealing Norse Ancestry

While others suggested Norse roots, sources said Somerled was Gaelic in origin. According to a DNA study, his Y-DNA haplogroup (R1a-L165) is quite closely associated with Norse Viking background. This proves that he was of mixed Norse-Gaelic background, as his paternal line was Scandinavian.[6]

Clarifying Clan Structures and Migration

DNA studies have mapped how Somerled's lineage spread, aligning with historical migration patterns between Scotland, Ireland, and beyond. They also reinforce the

6. G. Matharu Lall, M. H. D. Larmuseau, J. H. Wetton, C. Batini, P. Hallast, T. I. Huszar, D. Zadik, S. Aase, T. Baker, P. Balaresque, W. Bodmer, M. A. Jobling, T. E. King, & E. J. Parkin. (2021). Subdividing Y-chromosome haplogroup R1a1 reveals Norse Viking dispersal lineages in Britain. *European Journal of Human Genetics*, 29(3), 512–23.

idea that clans were not just political groups, but real extended families connected by blood.

These results challenge some conventional wisdom even if they confirm most of what history points to. Not every man whose last name is MacDonald, MacDougall, or MacAlister carries Somerled's Y-DNA. This challenges the conventional wisdom that all clan members shared a straight lineage since not every clan member was physiologically derived from him.

Rather than erasing history, genes are adding fresh layers to it. By blending traditional records with modern science, we gain a clearer and more accurate picture of Somerled's true legacy.

How These Findings Have Reshaped Genealogical Research

Finding Somerled's genetic legacy has generated a lot of curiosity among Scottish people about DNA testing. Many people with surnames connected to Somerled's lineage – MacDonald, MacDougall, MacAlister, and others – have looked for DNA testing to find whether they contain the R1a-L165 haplogroup, therefore verifying their direct paternal connection to him.

Particularly in cases where written records are lacking, many genealogists today use Y-DNA testing to confirm conventional family trees. Clans have set up DNA programs to assist members in deciding whether they really are derived from their ancient forebears.

Genealogy used to depend largely on oral traditions and surname-based research, which can be erroneous depending on historical errors, name changes, or adoptions. These days, genetics provides a scientific means of tracking lineage, hence increasing the degree of certainty of family origin.

Unbelievably strong genetic links between people living in Scotland, Ireland, Scandinavia, North America, and North America have been found by DNA investigations, therefore highlighting the extent of Somerled's ancestry. For those with a Scottish background, this has enabled the discovery of far-off relatives they never knew existed.

The study of Somerled is only one instance of how DNA testing is changing how individuals view their lineage; the function of genetics in genealogy is fast becoming increasingly important.

Though the genetic study on Somerled is fascinating, opinions on how to understand the results vary. Scientists and historians have brought some quite significant issues and questions forward.

Is the Y-DNA Haplogroup Really Somerled?

Researchers depend on Somerled's presumed descendants, as we do not have his actual DNA from his remains. Some critics argue that we can't be one hundred percent sure the R1a-L165 haplogroup belonged to him, even though the evidence strongly suggests it.

Some experts believe that focusing too much on Y-DNA oversimplifies how Scottish clans worked. Many mediaeval clans included non-biological members, such as adopted warriors or political allies. This means that not all historical MacDonalds or MacDougalls were direct blood relatives, even if they shared the same clan name.

There are concerns that emphasising DNA too much in genealogy could exclude people who identify with a clan culturally but do not share its Y-DNA. Others worry about privacy issues and the influence of commercial DNA testing companies on historical research.

These discussions remind us that DNA is only one element of the jigsaw, even if it is a useful tool. Understanding the past still depends much on history, archaeology, and written records. A balanced approach is needed to respect both scientific discoveries and cultural traditions.

Genetics as a Tool for Understanding Somerled's Legacy

Genetic research has opened a new chapter in our understanding of Somerled's legacy. For centuries, history has painted him as a warrior, a ruler, and the founder of powerful Scottish clans. But DNA evidence has now confirmed that his influence was not just political or cultural – it was biological.

Somerled's Y-DNA, passed down through generations, has been found in thousands of men today. This proves that his bloodline endured through centuries of change, conflict, and migration.

Through genetics, we have been able to trace his lineage across Scotland, Ireland, and beyond, verifying and, in some cases, challenging traditional narratives. His descendants did not just carry on his name; they spread his genetic imprint across the world, forming one of the most enduring bloodlines in Scottish history.

Although genes alone cannot fully explain the picture, historical studies paired with them help produce a far more accurate and clearer image.

For centuries, conventional sources such as clan histories and chronicles have detailed Somerled's successors, influencing our view of his legacy. Still, these stories were frequently penned long after his time and included exaggerations, prejudices, or mythologies. Many of these historical assertions have been scientifically confirmed by DNA testing, which also offers a fresh layer of data to either support or refute earlier knowledge.

The proof of Somerled's Norse background is among the most important revelations. Although some traditions claimed he was entirely of Gaelic background, genetic studies show his paternal line was Scandinavian. This result supports his mixed Norse-Gaelic background, which clarifies his leadership approach and the friendships he developed.

Genetics has also helped us to better grasp mediaeval kinship by illustrating how power was carefully preserved within dominant lineages and how leadership was passed on through generations.

Beyond confirming historical narratives, DNA studies have established a physical link between the past and the present. Many contemporary ancestors may now explicitly link themselves to Somerled, one of the most powerful figures in mediaeval Scotland.

Combining genetic data with historical records lets one provide a more accurate and whole picture of Somerled's legacy. Rather than supplacing conventional history, genes improve it by enabling the distinction between myth and reality and preserving Scotland's rich cultural legacy.

The Future of Genetic Research in Mediaeval Scottish Ancestry

With advances in genetic technology, the study of mediaeval ancestry is only just beginning. Somerled's instance demonstrates how DNA might improve our knowledge of history, so genetic study could offer even more revelations about Scotland's past in the future.

Finding additional mediaeval Scottish leaders using genetic markers presents one of the most fascinating opportunities. More accurate mapping of old bloodlines will enable researchers to confirm long-standing genealogical claims and follow the history of important historical figures.

Rather than depending just on studies of historical characters' putative descendants, DNA research might offer direct evidence of their genetic markers should ancient remains be found and tested.

Showing how mediaeval Scots migrated, settled, and mixed with other people across time, genetics could also help us better grasp migration patterns. This might help to paint a clearer picture of how cultures merged and how lineage shaped mediaeval Scottish society.

Our capacity to investigate mediaeval ancestry will only get more robust as more people engage in genetic investigations and new technologies develop. Combining DNA research with historical records will help us to reveal closer links between Scotland's past and present, therefore animating history in hitherto unthinkable ways.

A Final Thought: Connecting the Past to the Present

What this trip signifies for people now may be the most interesting aspect of it. The research of Somerled's DNA has linked modern people to their mediaeval background, transcending the confirmation of historical beliefs. Finding that one carries Somerled's Y-DNA is for many more than just a scientific discovery; it's a personal revelation, a physical link to history formerly believed to be unreachable.

Ultimately, genes teach us that history resides inside every one of us and is not only something we learn about in books. Somerled's narrative goes beyond the twelfth century; it carries his legacy forward in ways he would never have dreamed of in the DNA of thousands of people today.

Chapter 29
Somerled and His Contemporaries

Somerled was more than just a warlord or local leader. He emerged during a phase of shifting power balance in Scotland and the Isles. Somerled crossed paths – directly or indirectly – with some of the most significant personalities of his period, including Fergus of Galloway, King David I of Scotland, and the Norse kings of the Kingdom of the Isles. As he ascended to power, his decisions, aspirations, and eventually the legacy he left behind were shaped in great part by these relationships.

The twelfth century saw a period of transformation. Under feudalism, a more ordered system replaced the old methods of government, whereby local chieftains and monarchs oversaw their domains separately. In Scotland, this was particularly true under David I.

At the same time, Norse influence in the western seaboard remained strong, making the region a melting pot of Gaelic, Norse, and emerging Anglo-Norman cultures.

Somerled found himself at the centre of these competing forces, and his actions would determine whether the western seaboard would lean toward Scottish kingship, Norse rule, or retain its independence.

Somerled was important because he stood against the rising power of kings who wanted full control, especially King David I.

David ruled with the help of the Norman system. He relied on powerful lords and a strict hierarchy. But Somerled took a different path. Following the earlier Gaelic and Norse customs, when family and allegiance took precedence over any form of territory or title, he

His style of governance was very different from the changes occurring on the Scottish mainland, where feudalism was gathering traction and reorganising power systems.

Knowing the leaders of his day – especially David I – helps one to see Somerled's reign in perspective. He was a leader battling to preserve a different way of life in a world fast changing, not just a warrior seeking personal dominance.

Somerled also belonged to a larger European narrative. Rulers were centralising authority, building stronger governments, and extending their influence over the continent through diplomacy and violence. Under David I, Scotland was headed in that direction; England was firmly ruled by the Angevins. Though still significant, the Norse dominance in the Isles was starting to fade as local leaders like Somerled acquired territory.

In many ways, Somerled's struggle was part of a much bigger pattern. His efforts can be seen across Europe, where smaller rulers resisted the power of central authorities. Somerled fought for control of his own lands. His conflicts were mostly for independence and self-rule. Looking at Somerled alongside other leaders of his time helps us see what made him stand out.

Somerled vs. David I: Two Models of Kingship

Despite ruling in the same era, Somerled and David had different visions of leadership. David was deeply influenced by the English Crown, and he ruled to reform Scotland with the help of feudalism, Norman institutions, and centralised rule. He relied on a powerful lords' system to strengthen royal control.

On the other hand, Somerled's leadership was different. His was more of Gaelic and Norse traditions, where power was more localised. So, instead of feudal hierarchies, he relied on family ties, personal loyalty, and naval strength to maintain his authority.

These opposite approaches of Somerled and David showed a struggle between the new tradition. The two men were not direct enemies in a traditional sense, but they had two competing visions for Scotland's future.

To fully understand Somerled's role in history, it is important to compare his leadership style to that of David.

Governance and Administrative Style: Feudalism vs. Kinship Rule

By implementing feudalism – a system whereby land was given by the king to devoted lords in return for military service – David I changed the political scene in Scotland. This paradigm centralised power in the kingdom and let David replace customary Gaelic chiefs with Norman knights, many of whom had already served under either Henry I of England or Alexander I, his brother. Under David, the land turned from something handed down through generations inside a tribe or kin group into a commodity under the authority of the monarch.

Somerled chose the Gaelic-Norse system over installing a feudal regime over his domains. By his leadership, he won acceptance and command of naval might.

Unlike a cohesive monarchy, his rule was more erratic and dispersed, with power distributed among relatives and important followers rather than centralised. This approach gave him flexibility in his governance. Instead of constructing large, centralised administrative centres, he secured island strongholds and established a network of loyal clans to maintain control over his territories.

Territorial Control and Expansion: Land vs. Sea

David I wanted to expand his control over land. He used military campaigns and political marriages to secure borders. He focused on Lothian and Cumbria, bringing them under Scottish rule. He also encouraged Norman settlers to move into Scotland, giving them land and titles in exchange for loyalty.

In contrast, Somerled ruled a maritime kingdom. His authority derived from the western seaboard, where land was less crucial than maritime control. Long under Norse domination, Somerled aimed to fight their dominance rather than acquire territory from the Scottish kings.

Somerled first took Argyll, then extended his control to the Hebrides. He even tried to conquer the Isle of Man. Unlike David, who expanded through legal claims and feudal grants, Somerled used naval raids, strategic marriages, and military conquests.

Military and Naval Strategies: Knights vs. Seafarers

David used military strategy, which was highly influenced by Norman warfare. He built stone castles to secure his rule. He also relied on armoured knights to impose his authority. His forces were trained in Europe, where cavalry charges and disciplined formations were a major component of battle.

David fought in a structured manner in fights such as the Battle of the Standard, using the same techniques as his Norman and Anglo-Saxon counterparts.

Somerled's approach to warfare was completely different. His strength lay in his naval power and the mobility it provided. His warriors, drawn from the Gaelic-Norse warrior tradition, were not trained for large land battles but for quick, decisive strikes along the coast. He launched raids, set footholds, and quickly answered threats using his fleet. By allowing him to travel quickly between the Isles and the mainland, his longships gave him a strategic advantage over land-based kings.

David I relied on fortifications and standing armies to defend his territory. Somerled used his fleet and the ability to strike quickly before his enemies could react. His style of fighting was more like Viking warfare than the feudal battles of the Scottish mainland.

Religious Policies and Patronage: Church as a Tool of Power

Deeply pious, David I considered the Church to be an essential component of his rule. He erected many churches and abbeys, welcomed religious orders such as the Cistercians and Augustinians into Scotland, and backed monastic changes. He exploited the vast tracts of territory he donated to monks to bolster his rule and disseminate Norman influence.

For David, the Church served purposes beyond only spiritual ones. It also served to underline his power. On the other hand, Somerled interacted with the Church in a more complex manner. Although he helped religious establishments, he did not employ them as David did to augment his authority. His backing was more local and personal, favouring some abbeys above general reform.

There is proof that Somerled helped the church at Iona, a prominent holy site in the Gaelic realm. Somerled's relationship with religion was more about preserving local legitimacy, though, unlike David, who utilised the Church to centralise power.

Their attitude to Rome was another important distinction. David brought Scotland into line with the papacy and linked it to the larger European Church. But Somerled governed in an area where Norse and Gaelic customs persisted, and the pope had less of an impact on his power.

David I and Somerled stood for two quite distinct routes Scotland's future might follow. While Somerled maintained a more independent, maritime-oriented rule anchored in Gaelic and Norse traditions, David fought for a centralised, feudal monarchy closely matched to European standards. Their disparities were military, cultural, and political. While Somerled governed from the sea, depending on family and naval might, David erected castles and applied feudalism to dominate territory.

Ultimately, David's concept of government helped define Scotland for generations. But the legacy of Somerled did not vanish. His successors, the Lords of the Isles, kept his vision of Gaelic-Norse freedom alive by persistently opposing centralised Scottish authority for decades.

Somerled's Relations with Key Figures

Somerled's impact in the twelfth century transcended the western seaboard of Scotland. His rule was greatly shaped by his contacts with other influential people of his period, both allies and rivals.

Beyond his well-documented conflict with David I, Somerled engaged with some of the most significant kings of the era, including ecclesiastical leaders, Henry II of England, and the Norsemen of the Isles. Power conflicts, changing alliances, and the more general political shifts taking place in Britain and elsewhere defined these interactions.

The Norse Rulers of the Isles: A Complicated Relationship

Somerled's administration was notable for its ongoing war with the Norsemen of the Kingdom of the Isles. For centuries, the Scottish western seaboard had been under Norse influence. Scandinavian leaders who had close ties to Norway oversaw the Kingdom of the Isles, which comprised the Hebrides, the Isle of Man, and areas of the Irish Sea.

Godred Olafsson, who had inherited rule over the Isles in the middle of the twelfth century, was the reigning Norse monarch by the time Somerled ascended to power. Maintaining control over the western seaboard via a mix of military might and vassalage, Godred followed the conventional Norse paradigm of kingship.

Among many of the native Gaelic chieftains, who were bitter of Norse rule, his authority was unpopular. Not only for his personal benefit but also to claim more Gaelic autonomy in the area, Somerled saw a chance to question this rule.

When Somerled started a determined naval war against the Norse king in 1156, tensions between Somerled and Godred peaked. The conflict produced a compromise: Godred kept the northern Isles while Somerled came to rule the southern Hebrides. This was a turning point since it seriously undermined Norse rule and prepared Somerled's eventual aspirations.

Two years later, Somerled drove Godred from the Isles after decisively defeating him in battle, therefore seizing complete rule of the Kingdom of the Isles. This triumph was more than just a military triumph; it was a clear indication that Norse control of the West was no longer unopposed.

Henry II of England: A Distant but Powerful Influence

Although Somerled's immediate worries were of Scotland and the Isles, the ascent of Henry II of England had indirect but major repercussions for his rule. Rising to be king of England in 1154, Henry II was among the strongest rulers in all of Europe.

Establishing the large Angevin empire from England to Normandy, Anjou, and Aquitaine, he became a major player in British and European politics.

Henry aimed to increase his power over Scotland; hence, his aspirations were also included there. Henry had little desire to preserve Scotland's autonomy, even though David I of Scotland had been an ally of his predecessor, King Stephen. Rather, he aimed to subjugate Scottish leaders under his power, therefore undermining leaders like Somerled, who prized autonomy.

Although there is no clear evidence of fighting between Somerled and Henry II, the larger Angevin spread would have been an issue. Henry's increasing power in Scotland most certainly put pressure on Somerled to confirm his own dominance in the Isles and oppose further southern feudal incursions.

Henry's actions might also have affected the 1164 campaign, in which Somerled started an invasion of mainland Scotland. Some historians believe that growing Anglo-Norman pressure in the area contributed in some measure to this invasion. Whether Somerled tried to diminish Henry's influence or just aimed to increase his own power, the growing dominance of the Angevins helped define the political environment that determined his choices.

Henry II's expansionist ambitions indirectly affected Somerled's behaviour since the spread of Angevin power most certainly helped him oppose centralised rule.

The Papacy and Church Leaders: Seeking Legitimacy or Avoiding Influence?

Somerled's connection with the Church was multifarious. Somerled kept a more conventional and localised approach to ecclesiastical patronage than David I, who deliberately exploited religious organisations to support his power. That does not mean, however, that religion disappeared from his rule.

Scotland was hardly an exception, as the twelfth century saw growing papal authority all throughout Europe. With reforms meant to fit the Scottish Church into the larger European ecclesiastical system, it was progressively coming under the direct jurisdiction of Rome.

David I had welcomed this transformation, establishing monasteries and allowing monastic groups like the Cistercians to call Scotland home.

Somerled, on the other hand, worked in an area where more ancient customs still predominated. Iona, the ancient centre of Gaelic Christianity, had long shaped the Church on the western seaboard. Iona had formerly been the main religious force in Scotland, but as Roman practices acquired traction, her impact declined. Somerled's backing of Iona points to his alignment with the more centralised, Rome-aligned Church preferred by David I and Henry II rather than the traditional Gaelic Christian traditions.

Somerled is thought to have visited religious locations, including the Hebrides and monasteries in the western Highland. He did not, however, pursue extensive reform or use religious establishments to unite authority in the manner David I did. His attitude to religion was probably pragmatic: he supported religious establishments where it enhanced local allegiance but forbade the Church from dictating his policies.

Another crucial element of Somerled's religious approach is whether he asked for papal approval of his rule. Unlike succeeding leaders who aggressively sought Rome's favour, there is less indication that Somerled engaged in a formal connection with the pope. This would suggest that he favoured ruling free from outside influence and preserving religious freedom in much the same manner he opposed feudal domination. Somerled maintained traditional Gaelic religious establishments like Iona but did not include his rule in the rising Roman Catholic hierarchy in the manner David I did.

Somerled's interactions with important people of his day expose the convoluted political terrain he negotiated. His disputes with the Norse kings changed the balance of power in the Isles, his indirect rivalry with Henry II reflected larger tensions between local leaders and the growing Angevin empire, and his careful approach to the Church highlighted his inclination for regional autonomy over centralised control.

Somerled deliberately shaped his own road, not only responding to these numbers. He was a strategic leader who saw the tides of power changing, not only a warrior or a rebel. Whether via diplomacy or confrontation, his capacity to balance these ties helped him create a legacy in a period of tremendous transformation.

Somerled in the Broader European Mediaeval Context

Somerled's rule was part of a far more extensive mediaeval change altering power systems throughout Europe, not a single chapter in Scottish or Norse history.

His time was one of changing political environments where local leaders collided with newly centralised kingdoms, and maritime power was essential in military strategy and trade and conquest of mixed cultures.

Somerled's narrative fits cleanly into these more general patterns; hence, he is not only a Scot or Norseman but a leader whose hardships reflected more general changes occurring across mediaeval Europe.

The Changing Power of Local Kings vs. Centralised Monarchies

One of the defining characteristics of his era was the growing dominance of centralised monarchy. Rulers were striving to unite their power all throughout Europe.

The emergence of feudal states and organised government endangered the autonomy of regional leaders who had customarily retained power through kinship and local alliances.

Through military campaigns and legislative changes, Henry II increased royal authority in England, diminishing the power of individual barons.

The Capetian rulers of France were progressively centralising more of their land. David I implemented feudalism even in Scotland, giving Norman lords land and reorganising the administration to diminish the power of Gaelic chieftains. But Somerled stood for another kind of leadership, one that bucked this centralising trend. Maintaining a Gaelic-Norse system of governance where power was based on kinship, personal allegiance, and marine strength rather than land grants and legal contracts, he refused to follow a feudal hierarchy.

His government approach resembled an ancient society in which kings relied more on their capacity to command warriors than on charters produced by a king far away.

One might relate his opposition to concentrated power with that of other European politicians who fought the predominance of monarchy:

- The Welsh princes who resisted Anglo-Norman expansion in Wales and fought to maintain their own independent rule.
- The Irish kings who struggled against the growing influence of the English crown and the Norman settlers arriving in Ireland.
- The Scandinavian jarls who attempted to maintain their autonomy against the increasing authority of the Norwegian kings.

Eventually, Somerled battled to uphold a separate concept of government while leaders such as David I and Henry II were determining the course of centralised kingdoms. His leadership had as its primary goals local autonomy, kinship, and marine mobility. His battle was not only personal but also a part of a greater European struggle between newly established state-based kingdoms and old local rulers.

The Role of Maritime Power

Somerled's authority was defined in great part by his naval might. He mainly depended on the water, whereas many mediaeval leaders concentrated on land-based fortifications, cavalry, and castle-building. This put him among other outstanding nautical leaders of the mediaeval world, like the Byzantines, the kings of Mediterranean city-states, and the Norsemen.

Somerled's fleet constituted his military's backbone rather than only a method of mobility. Inspired by Viking longships, his ships offered numerous major benefits. Somerled's army could travel quickly down the coast, unlike land troops who travelled slowly, depending on roads and supply lines. This let him attack unexpectedly and withdraw before the enemy could react.

Slaying the sea also meant slaying trade. Domesticated over the western seaboard, Somerled could control trade, pay tribute, and upset his rivals' economies. This bestowed on him not only military might but also financial clout.

One might relate Somerled's use of naval might to other notable maritime leaders of the day. By means of their ships, the Norse monarchs of Denmark and Norway dominated the North Sea. With strong ships, Venice's leaders extended their influence over the Mediterranean. The Byzantine Empire maintained supremacy in the Eastern Mediterranean through its fleet.

His style of warfare aligned with a larger pattern in mediaeval Europe, where supremacy or loss largely rested on sea control. Unlike feudal lords who relied on castles and knights, Somerled's power lay in his ability to command the waves.

Cultural Exchange and Hybrid Identities

During Somerled's lifetime, the western coast was a singular site of cultural convergence. For ages, the Gaelic, Norse, and growing Norman civilisations had been interacting – sometimes through trade and marriage and other times through resistance and conquest. Somerled himself was a product of the hybrid world that was produced by this mixing of customs.

Interactions with Norman Influence

Somerled was not completely isolated from the Norman feudal model despite his opposition to it. Norman culture had started to permeate Scotland by the middle of the twelfth century, impacting disciplines including administration, architecture, and war. From Somerled's military activities against David, it seems he understood the changing balance of power and acted to halt Norman expansion inside his own country.

Some historians speculate that Somerled might have strengthened his control by implementing some Norman tactics. For instance, he may have adopted aspects of organised government, such as the Norman administrative system, to designate local leaders, even though he did not entirely adopt feudalism.

The rule of Somerled was a special blending of civilisations. He was a king who negotiated all three, producing a unique hybrid identity on the western seaboard, not really Norse, not just Gaelic, and not quite hostile to Norman encroachment.

More than merely a Scottish or Norse warlord, Somerled was a leader whose narrative captures more general European mediaeval patterns. His struggle against centralised monarchy mirrored the conflicts of local rulers across the continent. His reliance on naval power placed him among the great maritime rulers of the time. His cultural identity embodied the fusion of traditions that were shaping mediaeval Scotland and beyond.

His influence persisted even if his opposition to feudalism finally did not stop the development of the centralised monarchy. His descendants, the Lords of the Isles, carried on his semi-independent government, therefore preserving the Gaelic-Norse identity for years. The language, history, and customs of the places he governed still bear his imprint.

Apart from conquest, Somerled's narrative also explores adaptability, survival, and the fight to protect a unique way of life in the middle of a major transformation.

Somerled's Unique Contributions

Somerled's story is often told through the lens of his battles – his conflicts with the Norse rulers of the Isles, his opposition to David I's feudal reforms, and his strategic use of naval power. Beyond these specifics, though, his legacy permeates politics, military strategy, and society, therefore influencing events much beyond his own lifetime.

Political Legacy: A Vision That Outlived His Reign

Though Somerled's death ended his personal rule, the political system he struggled against did not vanish overnight. Maintaining a local, kinship-based type of government that stayed powerful on the western shore long after he was gone, he opposed the feudal system engulfing Scotland.

The most evident continuation of his power was his descendants, the Lords of the Isles. By upholding his concept of semi-independent rule, his family – the Clan MacDougall and eventually the Clan Donald – established themselves as powerful players in Scottish politics over decades.

The Lords of the Isles kept a Gaelic-Norse identity and ruled much as Somerled had – by juggling alliances, regulating marine trade, and opposing Scottish kings trying to concentrate authority.

Though the Lords of the Isles were finally incorporated into the Scottish monarchy in the late fifteenth century, their reign proved that Somerled's style of leadership was enduring. Generation after generation, the concept of a semi-autonomous kingdom inside Scotland – a territory neither entirely Norse nor entirely Scottish – survived.

Still, it is also true that Somerled's political impact stayed essentially regional. Unlike David I, whose feudal changes covered the whole kingdom of Scotland, Somerled's rule was confined to the western seaboard. Indirectly, his influence on the larger framework of Scottish control was evident in the resistance movements active in the Highlands and Isles long after his death.

Through the Lords of the Isles, Somerled's political model persisted and shaped the Western Highlands and Isles government for centuries. However, his impact did not reach the larger Scottish kingdom, where feudalism was proliferating.

Military Legacy: A Blueprint for Resistance

Somerled's military achievements went beyond his prowess in combat. Later, Scottish leaders would borrow the tactics he employed to fight centralisation in their own conflicts.

Somerled fought from the sea, unlike many mediaeval kings who depended on castles and land-based armies. Later wars in the Isles modelled his fast-moving ships, surprise attacks, and island strongholds strategy to combat. Long into the late Middle Ages, his descendants – especially the Lords of the Isles – kept using maritime force to oppose Scottish kings.

Scottish nobles and Highland clans would often object to Edinburgh's centralising of authority in the following centuries. Highland soldiers in the Jacobite risings, for example, supported kinship-based authority above centralised monarchy, much as Somerled did.

Although Somerled himself was not a Jacobite leader, his attitude to challenging authority set a standard for the following disputes between Highland chiefs and the Scottish monarchy.

One recurring motif in Scottish history was its resistance to Anglo-Norman rule. Among the first to fiercely reject this development, Somerled later inspired Scottish leaders who sought to retain local autonomy in the face of feudal encroachment.

Somerled's ultimate loss in 1164 exposes the limits of his strategy, even with his major military victories. Unlike later Scottish kings like Robert the Bruce, who successfully combined guerrilla warfare with state-building, Somerled's approach stayed based on a localised, seaborne type of warfare, unable to totally counter the growing strength of centralised kingdoms.

Scottish officials embraced Somerled's military strategies – naval power, fast mobility, and local resistance – later in their own challenges against central authority. But his approach was essentially defensive, which limited its long-term potency against the growing might of feudal governments.

The Lasting Impact on Gaelic and Norse Identities

Among Somerled's greatest long-lasting accomplishments are the preservation and development of the Gaelic-Norse character of the western seaboard. During his rule, the mix of Norse and Gaelic influences began to shift, hence transforming Scotland's cultural heritage.

Though Norse cultural influence continued, Somerled's victory over Godred Olafsson signalled the end of Norse governmental dominance in the Isles. The Kingdom of the Isles maintained some degree of autonomy for some time, but it was no longer governed by Norse people.

Norse control in Scotland vanished during the next centuries, and Gaelic chiefs – including descendants of Somerled – became the main force in the area.

The Survival of the Gaelic Language and Traditions

Somerled governed in a fashion that maintained Gaelic culture, unlike the feudal lords of mainland Scotland. His court probably spoke Gaelic, and his government's approach stressed kinship ties and traditional practices over Norman legal systems. This helped ensure that Gaelic customs survived in the Isles even while Anglo-Norman influences proliferated elsewhere in Scotland.

Somerled's Place in History

The narrative of Somerled tells of a man at a historical crossroads. His rule mixed several customs, and his conflicts were political as well as cultural. This is the reason his legacy went well beyond his own life.

Although he finally failed to stop a centralised monarchy from emerging in Scotland, his opposition stopped its spread in the Western Isles and guaranteed that another form of government – one based on kinship, maritime might, and Gaelic traditions – survived for generations. His descendants continued his battle, and even after his passing, the Lords of the Isles stayed a potent force.

Above all, Somerled stayed strong and embodied the dependability of his identity throughout the height of centralisation. Clearly, his legacy teaches us that monarchs and empires do not create history alone; those who battle to preserve their own way of life in an era of significant change are important in history.

Though he left behind something just as strong – a legacy of defiance, cultural survival, and the continuing spirit of the western seaboard – Somerled may not have left behind a kingdom in the manner David I or Henry II did.

30: The Enduring Mystery of Somerled

After all the stories, battles, alliances, and turning points we've walked through together, we now arrive at the end of Somerled's journey – or at least, as much of it as we can see. We've traced his rise, examined his choices, and tried to understand the world he lived in. And yet, with every step forward, we've also come face to face with what we still don't know.

Some figures from the past leave behind a trail that is almost too clear, shaped by chroniclers eager to praise or condemn. Somerled, on the other hand, is different. His presence is strong throughout the records but always just slightly out of reach.

There are parts of his life that feel vivid, almost close enough to touch. But then there are long shadows, places where the light doesn't quite reach.

And maybe that's part of what keeps the interest in him alive. Somerled's story feels unfinished – not in the sense that it lacks a proper ending, but in the sense that it invites us to keep asking and keep wondering. Historians have uncovered much, but the full picture still escapes us. What kind of man was he, really? What did he hope for? What did he believe?

As we open this final chapter, one thing is clear: even after centuries of study, Somerled remains wrapped in mystery. And perhaps that's exactly how he's meant to be remembered. There's something about unanswered questions that keeps a story alive, and Somerled's life has more than a few. The deeper you dig, the more you realise how much is still uncertain. For a man who changed the course of history in the west of Scotland, it's surprising how many parts of his life remain unclear.

One of the biggest questions is about his ancestry. While some accounts say he had Norse ancestry, others gravitate more toward a Gaelic background. Did he originate from a dynasty of Norse-Gaelic warlords or derive from the ancient monarchs of Dál Riata? Though the documents don't say enough to resolve it, the reality might lie somewhere between. This question isn't just about names on a family tree – it matters because it shapes how we understand his identity, his alliances, and even his claim to power.

Then there's the question of his motivations. Was Somerled motivated by loyalty to his people, ambition, or something else entirely? Did he consider himself a new type of leader influenced by both Norse and Celtic traditions, or as a revival of ancient Gaelic ways? The way he moved between cultures, navigated politics, and built his following suggests a man with a vision. But what that vision exactly was, we can only guess.

And finally, the circumstances of his death are still debated. Most accounts agree he died in 1164 during his final campaign near Renfrew, but the details are murky. Some say he was betrayed. Others suggest a collapse in battle. There's no clear record of how it ended. Just like parts of his life, his death feels incomplete – like a final chapter with the last page missing.

These gaps – his roots, his reasons, his end – don't weaken his story. If anything, they add to it. They leave space for curiosity. They keep historians digging, and they let each generation find something new in him. It's this sense of mystery, the parts we'll probably never fully know, that gives Somerled's story a kind of quiet power. He remains open to interpretation, which makes him feel alive in a way few historical figures do.

Legends in the Gaps

Where records fall silent, stories tend to grow. That is very true for Somerled. The uncertainty around some aspects of his existence has given way over time to myths, oral stories, and folk tales – each adding something unique and each influencing his memory.

Somerled has long been more than a historical person in the Highlands and Islands. In other stories, he is a warrior gifted by the spirits of the country, under protection from old forces as he crosses the western seas. In others, he is a king able to read the wind like a map or converse with birds. Though these are not specifics found in official records, they have persisted in the spoken stories handed down over the years.

Somerled is sometimes supposed to have descended from the fabled Irish monarch Colla Uais from the fourth century. Linking him to a proud and ancient bloodline, this concept has helped confirm his proper Gaelic leadership. Many academics, however, have challenged the veracity of this assertion, implying that it most likely developed long after Somerled's lifetime, probably more as a means of legacy than as a factual correctness.

Even his name now serves as a symbol. Somhairle translates in Gaelic as 'summer traveller' or 'summer warrior' – a suitable picture for a man who travelled over countries and seas with such vigour and vision. Names, though, acquire a life of their own, just like tales do.

Fascinating is how these stories improve rather than merely distort the historical picture. They reveal his great degree of mental immersion among his people. Somerled was cherished, fantasised, even revered, not only remembered. And that speaks quite movingly about his influence.

Ultimately, the combination of fact and mythology is what gives his story such a timeless quality. Maybe this is the point as the legendary and historical Somerled are entwined in a difficult, separable manner. Maybe it's not about finding the exact line between truth and tale. Maybe it's about understanding why people needed to tell these stories in the first place.

Even when we set the legends aside and focus only on what's written in historical records, there's still plenty of room for debate. Scholars have spent years trying to piece together what Somerled really stood for, and while they've uncovered a great deal, some of the most important questions remain unsettled.

One of the biggest topics is Somerled's ambition. Was he trying to become a king in the full sense of the word – a ruler who could challenge the authority of the Scottish Crown? Or was he more focused on securing independence and stability for his own region without any grander designs?

Some historians see him as a monarch of a rebuilt Gaelic state, with regal aspirations that transcended the Isles, perhaps. Others contend he was more of a regional strongman – clever and shrewd, yes, but mostly focused on defending his territory rather than growing it into a kingdom.

Directly related to that is the issue of his political function definition. Was he a rebel against the growing influence of the Scottish monarchy? A unifier trying to bring together divided clans under one banner? Or perhaps a king-in-waiting, building something that would outlast him? The truth is likely a mix of all these things, depending on the moment in time. His actions don't fit neatly into one box, which is part of why historians continue to debate them.

Then, one considers his cultural identity. Norse and Gaelic customs helped define Somerled's life. Though he also supported Gaelic culture and religion, he was connected to the Viking legacy of the Isles. While some consider him someone who embraced a dual identity – using both sides to his advantage – others see him as a symbol of opposition against Norse control. Was he producing something fresh that combined the two cultures, or was he trying to revive something older and entirely Gaelic?

There is no obvious agreement on these issues, and perhaps there never will be. Every generation of historians raises fresh issues, viewpoints, and methods for examining the past. But no matter the angle, Somerled always seems to stand just slightly apart – a man whose actions invite interpretation but resist easy conclusions.

Still Speaking to the Present

For a man who lived almost nine centuries ago, Somerled has never really faded from view. In some areas of Scotland, his name still has weight not only as a historical person but also as a symbol of strength, independence, and cultural pride. His legacy has found a permanent home in the modern world, whether in folk memory or historical accounts.

Somerled is sometimes seen as a symbol of resistance in Scottish society today – someone who battled against outside powers to defend his people's way of life. That picture really speaks to me in discussions of national identity and autonomy. His narrative is occasionally brought up as an example of early self-rule, long before Scotland joined the United Kingdom, during periods of political unrest, or as a historical review of Scotland.

His presence is also felt in Clan Donald's pride since their ancestors directly backed up to him. For many clan members, Somerled is the basis of their identity rather than only an ancestor. Gatherings, songs, and family histories honour his memory and help preserve the link over the decades.

There are also echoes of Somerled evident in music and literature. Inspired by his story, writers and poets have frequently highlighted the combination of myth and history in which he lives. His name has been mentioned in traditional Gaelic ballads; more recently, artists have returned to his legacy in works combining modern techniques with folk customs, demonstrating how his story changes alongside the society that remembers him.

Somerled is intriguing because he does not fit only one interpretation of history. Though he was a warrior and a leader, he was also a man moulded by two civilisations, Norse and Gaelic. That dichotomy is particularly relevant now when issues of identity, legacy, and belonging are still very much alive, that complexity, resilience, and the belief that some legacies are strong enough to withstand ambiguity and time.

Historians return to him often, and stories about him are still told because they are relevant. Somerled may be a man of the past, but the impact he left is very much part of the present.

What We've Yet to Find

For all that has been written about Somerled, there's still so much left to discover. His story is far from complete, and the future may hold new pieces of the puzzle – waiting quietly in the ground, in old texts, or even in modern technologies we're only beginning to apply to the past.

The Western Highlands and islands contain mostly undiscovered archaeological sites. Some are believed to be connected to Somerled's time, maybe locations his adherents lived, traded, or worshipped. Using modern technologies and fresh eyes to excavate these sites will enable us to learn more about the way his people lived, what they created, and how they traversed the terrain they previously controlled.

Additionally, there is the written record, which is fragile, scattered, and occasionally disregarded. Many mediaeval charters and chronicles, particularly those in Latin or Old Norse, survive only partially translated or examined. Hints buried in the margins of these records could be names, dates, or links to help close the gaps around Somerled's life and the network he belonged to. Even quick references in foreign archives – Irish, Norse, or Manx – may provide novel perspectives.

One then has the possibility of multidisciplinary research. For historians, advances in disciplines, including digital mapping, landscape archaeology, and genetic genealogy, offer fresh paths. DNA research, for example, might elucidate Somerled's ancestral roots or assist in tracking his descendants. Landscape studies could expose areas of impact, travel paths, or settlement patterns that fit the narrative handed down orally. Comparing data from other fields helps us approach the reality he lived in, not only the one recounted in myth or chronicle.

There are restrictions, of course. Much has been erased by time. Frequently, what remains is partial or skewed. Occasionally, the remaining hints are so elusive that they pose more questions than they do answers. However, acknowledging what is lacking while remaining receptive to the opportunities that may arise is a necessary component of the task.

The hunt for Somerled is essentially just beginning in many respects. Though the past does not always readily reveal its secrets, even a tiny revelation might shed fresh light on a narrative we have carried for ages.

Piecing Together the Past

When we consider Somerled's story, it is abundantly evident how much of what we believe we know is moulded not only by what is present but also by what is absent. Often, historians deal with fragments – scattered records, second-hand tales, and suggestions buried in language or terrain. Attempting to create a whole picture from it is like trying to assemble a puzzle with half the pieces gone via time.

For Somerled, the difficulties are rather obvious. Often by persons far from his life, the accounts we have were penned long after his death – monks in far-off abbeys, reporters with personal loyalties and agendas. Although their stories are insightful, they are not objective. They interpret, exaggerate, and sometimes omit entirely. So, the Somerled we meet in the historical record isn't just the man himself – it's also a reflection of how others saw him or wanted him to be seen.

And then there's us – the historians, the writers, the readers. We bring our own questions, our own hopes, and interests to the story. Whether we see Somerled as a freedom fighter, a political strategist, or a symbol of cultural fusion depends, in part, on where we're standing. Interpretation fills in the blanks, but it also shapes the image we hold.

That does not devalue the task or make it any less important. It reminds us, if anything, that history is about perception as much as facts. It's about meticulously examining, challenging gently, and realising that the past does not always provide obvious solutions. It occasionally allows us the leisure to ponder, dream, and wonder.

And maybe that's one of the greatest ways to approach a person like Somerled – not as a whole narrative but as a story still being written.

The Legacy That Endures

As we back off and consider Somerled's life – what is known, what is surmised, and what is imagined – it is evident that his significance transcends his lifetime events. He was not only a regional leader or a warrior. He changed Scotland's western seaboard, questioned the rising authority of kings, and left a legacy that rang throughout centuries.

Militarily, he demonstrated that naval might and local leadership could equal even the toughest of adversaries. His campaigns disrupted both Norse and Scottish ambitions, forcing larger kingdoms to take him seriously.

Politically, he carved out a form of rule that was neither fully Norse nor fully Gaelic but something in between – something new. His leadership laid the groundwork for the Lordship of the Isles, which would dominate western Scotland for generations after his death.

Culturally, his impact is just as deep. He stands at the crossroads of two traditions, and in doing so, he reminds us that identity is not always fixed – it can be a meeting place or a bridge. The fact that he is remembered both as a historical figure and a legend only adds to that richness. His story has become a part of the cultural memory of Scotland, carried in names, songs, and stories passed down through time.

And yet, his legacy stretches even beyond Scotland. In a wider world history, Somerled represents the kind of leader who defies easy categorisation. He was shaped by different influences, challenged dominant powers, and left behind a story that still sparks curiosity centuries later. That kind of presence – one that blurs the lines between history and myth – is rare.

In the end, perhaps Somerled's greatest legacy is the mystery itself. The gaps, the questions, the legends – they're not just obstacles to knowing him. They're part of what keeps his memory alive. They invite us to keep asking, to keep searching, to keep imagining.

And maybe that's how he would have wanted it.

He left behind no crown, no throne – but in the silence between what is known and what is guessed, Somerled still walks the edge of land and sea, half seen, never forgotten.

Appendix

The Newly Discovered Castle at Finlaggan

In September 2025, new research brought fresh attention to Finlaggan, long regarded as the ceremonial and political heart of the Lords of the Isles. Archaeologists announced the discovery of previously unknown remains at the site, believed to be part of a substantial stone-built castle dating from the twelfth and thirteenth centuries.

The findings were widely reported in the press, including by the BBC, and generated considerable excitement because they add another layer to the history of Islay and to the story of the Lordship itself. For decades, Finlaggan has been recognised as the power base of Somerled's descendants, the MacDonald Lords of the Isles, but the evidence of a large rectangular stone tower and associated buildings points to an even earlier phase of high-status occupation.

The discovery suggests that Finlaggan was already a site of considerable importance during the age of Somerled and his immediate heirs. The rectangular tower is comparable to keeps built by Anglo-Norman rulers elsewhere in Britain and Ireland, raising the possibility that the rulers of the Isles were adopting architectural forms that demonstrated both wealth and authority.

According to archaeologists, this earlier castle may have been abandoned or destroyed before the later palace and ceremonial complex of the MacDonalds was constructed. Nevertheless, it highlights the continuous significance of Finlaggan across the centuries and reinforces the idea that Islay was not only central to the Gaelic and Norse-Gaelic world, but also engaged with wider European traditions of lordship and power.

For a book devoted to Somerled, this discovery is particularly resonant. Finlaggan was the symbolic heart of the Isles and the stage on which his descendants asserted their independence and authority. The recent findings confirm that the story of Somerled and the Lordship remains a living subject of historical and archaeological research, capable of producing new insights even today.

Index